AROUND THE WORLD

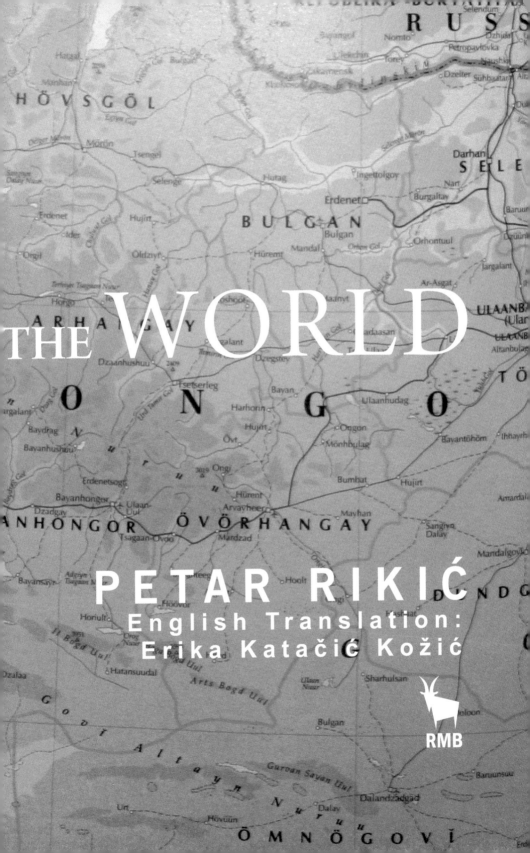

THE WORLD

PETAR RIKIĆ
English Translation:
Erika Katačić Kožić

RMB

Rocky Mountain Books
www.rmbooks.com

LIBRARY AND ARCHIVES CANADA CATALOGUING IN PUBLICATION
Rikic, Petar
[Oko svijeta '09. English]
Around the world / Peter Rikic.

Translation of: Oko svijeta '09 / Petar Rikic. — Koprivnica :
Petar Rikic : Baltazar, 2011.
Translated by Erika Katacic Kozic.
Issued in print and electronic formats.
ISBN 978-1-927330-67-8

1. Rikic, Petar—Travel. 2. Voyages around the world.
3. Motorcycle touring. 4. Motorcyclists—Croatia—Biography.
I. Title. II. Title: Oko svijeta '09. English.

GV1060.2.R54A3 2014   910.4'1   C2013-908255-7

PRINTED IN CANADA

Rocky Mountain Books acknowledges the financial support for its publishing program
from the Government of Canada through the Canada Book Fund (CBF) and
the Canada Council for the Arts, and from the province of British Columbia
through the British Columbia Arts Council and the Book Publishing Tax Credit.

This book was produced using FSC®-certified, acid-free paper,
processed chlorine free and printed with vegetable-based inks.

With gratitude, this book is dedicated to everyone, and especially to those who support and follow the project

Expedition - AROUND THE WORLD '09 – 40 000 km

1. Vukovar	12. Toronto	23. Regina	34. Prince George
2. Zagreb	13. Ottawa	24. Saskatoon	35. Vancouver
3. Ljubljana	14. Montreal	25. Edmonton	36. Tokyo
4. Milan	15. Quebec	26. Calgary	37. Seoul
5. Lucerne	16. Oromocto	27. Banff	38. Sokcho
6. Lyon	17. Halifax	28. Jasper	39. Zarubino
7. Nimes	18. Sydney	29. Fort Nelson	40. Vladivostok
8. Toulouse	19. Sudbury	30. Whitehorse	41. Khabarovsk
9. Madrid	20. Sault Ste. Marie	31. Dawson City	42. Chita
10. Lisbon	21. Thunder Bay	32. Inuvik	43. Ulan-Ude
11. London	22. Winnipeg	33. Stewart	44. Lake Baikal

45. Ulaanbaatar	57. Aktobe	
46. Kharkhorin (Karakorum)	58. Atyrau	
47. Arvaikheer	59. Astrakhan	
48. Bayankhongor	60. Volgograd	
49. Altai	61. Rostov-on-Don	
50. Hovd	62. Mariopul	
51. Olgiy	63. Yalta	
52. Barnaul	64. Odessa	
53. Semipalatinsk	65. Uman	
54. Almaty	66. Lviv	
55. Shymkent	67. Debrecen	
56. Aralsk		

Journey to NORDKAPP 2008 - 10 000 km

1. Zagreb	7. Husqvarna
2. Vienna	8. Stockholm
3. Prague	9. Umeå
4. Bielefeld	10. Kiruna
5. Copenhagen	11. Nordkapp
6. Malmö	12. Narvik

CONTENTS

At Croatia's border crossing with Slovenia, to the policeman's question: "Where are you going?" I answered: "Home, to Croatia. But first I've got to go around the world."

IDEA

For a long time the idea of motorcycle journeys to faraway places had been spinning in my head. I sold the scooter that I had been riding for two seasons so I could buy something bigger and stronger. Since I intended to travel without being limited by the roads, or especially by the terrain, my choice was very simple: Enduro. I turned all the dealerships inside out, yet the model that I was looking for could not be found in Croatia. I phoned other dealers in Europe, but with no luck. Unbelievable. By then the thought crossed my mind to just fly to Japan and ride across Asia on the way home to Croatia. That way, I could get the motorcycle I wanted while having an adventure.

However, by early July, the news came that there was an Enduro in Austria, in Wiener Neustadt, and it was just the colour I liked. Yes! Great, it had probably been waiting for me. With the money I had received from selling my old scooter, plus some more of my own, and some borrowed from friends, I went to get it.

Hit the saddle and hit the road! The first journey was Wiener Neustadt, Austria–Primošten, Croatia: 700 km. A whole bunch of complications awaited me at customs, but that didn't matter. What mattered was that Tenere was coming home.

TO NORDKAPP (16/9/2008) 10 000 km

By the end of the summer job season, with a craving for a ride, and without any special preparation or adequate equipment, I sped off to Europe's northernmost point, Nordkapp. The conditions under which this trip was realized were pretty demanding. Because of a cold front that was passing through central Europe, I only came across a few motorcyclists, and in Scandinavia I didn't see any at all. Rain, wet roads, and the cold kept me company especially in Northern Sweden and Norway. North of the Arctic Circle, while riding with summer gloves on, my fingers were freezing. I stopped often to dry my gloves and warm my fingers in the exhaust pipe's smoke. The wind was blowing my motorcycle down, my ordinary army pants were letting the cold seep through, and the raindrops hurt like needles. Despite all of that, I was happy, because I was doing what I wanted to do.

Even on my way home I began planning my next journey. The Western Sahara seemed interesting; a dry and warm southern climate instead of this harsh northern one. And a motorcycle named Tenere was longing for the desert, also.

After returning from Nordkapp, convinced that prospective sponsors would be thrilled with the idea of supporting me, I tried to get in touch with them. But I learned quickly. Their courteous, "We'll get back to you," just meant forget it.

. . .

In mid-December, while hiking in the mountains of Velebit with my disobedient dog Medo, I thought about ways to raise money for the rest of this journey. I figured it would be easier if I had something greater and more important to offer, so I put into action an idea that I had been working on earlier about circling the world. Of course! Why wait?

After returning from Velebit, I announced the news to my family. My father was happy. "Way to go! I was expecting something like that." I wasn't surprised. I knew he trusted me a lot, but my mom did get a bit worried.

So I said, "I've got a plan. I'll collect as much money as I can by myself, but I am counting on my share of the profit from this summer's seasonal work."

You see, my family runs a seasonal business, and everything we earn during the summer, we spend during the rest of the year. "If I don't collect enough, I'll just hit the road and manage somehow."

Those interested in just a travelogue can skip the next chapter.

WHY I (BE)CAME THE WAY I AM

I grew up in an atypical family that values something along the lines of, "Don't just dream, live your dream." Without any support or inheritance, we started out as nomads, and managed in many ways. We moved a lot: within the city, out of the city, from city to city, from the city to the countryside, and we still move at least twice a year because of the nature of our small family business, based in tourism. Part of the year we spend inland, and the other part, at the coast. Growing up, I was purposely "deprived" of most pleasures on television that my peers enjoyed: video games, a great deal of Hollywood's productions, sports games. Anyway, my family and I just weren't in the habit of watching television. We hadn't owned a TV in a long time. Besides that, I was subjected to many forms of "torture": swimming, rowing, rafting, martial arts, horseback riding, archery, working out in the gym, mountain climbing. Numerous times, I would spend an entire summer in a tent, partly because of our job, and partly by choice. When I was between the ages of about twelve and thirteen, around the mountains Bjelolasica, Bijele Stijene (White Rocks), and Samarske Stijene (Samarske Rocks), we hunted for bears with our cameras and did some training in orienteering. In our house, it's always easier to trip over an atlas or a pile of maps on the floor than to avoid them.

During winter break of my freshman year of high school, in 2005, instead of going to the soccer match at a local stadium, my father and I bought tickets on credit and flew to India. It was not advisable to travel to Nepal, where we had wanted to go in the first place, because of the civil war. Of course, after our journey through India we ended up in Nepal and the Himalayas anyway. In one way, this was "interesting":

we were met by bombs exploding, crossings at separation lines, police curfews. In another way, it was so much more: Kathmandu, Pokhara with Phewa Lake reflecting the Himalayan peaks, and trekking around Annapurna and Dhaulagiri. What can I say? Unforgettable! I was quite late for the start of the second semester, but because of our different approach towards traditional schooling, this did not worry me. All that I had seen and experienced had left a great impression on me, while also teaching me so much. And that's how my idea about the study of life *was* born.

Back to the travelogue.

19/12/2008–14/1/2009

So, with bad timing, in other words, during what's known as an economic crisis, I began planning my project. I chose my route, did the paperwork, made a more detailed budget, and, most importantly, I made a list of potential donors. And that was it. In general, I don't like to work out too many details in advance, and enjoy my travels more when I don't know what's awaiting me. So even when preparing for this journey, I relied more on my gut feeling and not on strict planning. As for for when to start the journey, I determined when the climate in Siberia was the best for road travel: July.

15/1–19/3/2009

Since the most important factor was funding, I mainly focused on that. I prepared a portfolio and letter of introduction with the logo AROUND THE WORLD to make a better impression with contacts and potential sponsors.

If I had had the amount of money necessary for the trip, who knows, maybe a dilemma would have ensued? As it turned out, I had much less. And because I had less, it was easier to decide what to spend it on. Sometimes, too much money isn't such a good thing.

From the loads of information and unexpected administrative non-sense, my head was filled with confusion! To be more efficient, I made a plan, set priorities and due dates. I approached prospective sponsors

To Nordkapp, October, 2008.

LEFT: While preparing in Velebit, Croatia, mid-December, 2009.
BELOW: Packing for the trip, April, 2009.

and donors, respecting their specific needs, and adjusting my approach to individual profiles. I even tried to set meetings in the afternoons, after lunch, when people were more relaxed. But what never worked to my benefit was my age. Most of the people I had contacted were expecting a team of "mature" men, not one young man. Obviously I didn't appear very convincing. No matter how much I prepared myself in all possible ways, everything seemed to be going well except for the funding. That wasn't progressing at all!

The first rustle of joy came from my hometown, Koprivnica. After that, only one businessman chipped in, also from Koprivnica. It would be easier to list whom I hadn't contacted, rather than whom I had. Anyways, the top-notch skills in rejection displayed by those who turned down my requests amazed me. I had even sent a request to my country's president, more as a joke, just to see what he would say! He replied with congratulations, but without support. I was planning on describing all of that, and had even prepared a text about my manoeuvres in financial acrobatics, but believe me, the list was so long, it would have made printing this book too expensive.

Nevertheless, the few that did believe in me did make this trip easier to accomplish. Without any funding, it would have turned out differently. Who knows, maybe the book would have then been more interesting. Obviously, that was all just a fun mental exercise.

While searching for sponsors, I was also getting visas. I had already contacted Tatjana, from the Russian agency, and since she already knew me, she took over preparation of all the documents so that I would only have to pick everything up at the consulate.

Not expecting any complications, I applied for a visa to the United States. I paid the required fee of $260 and went to the embassy. Then, whoa! Like, I was slapped in the face!

They said, "You're unemployed, young, and you want to stay illegally in the United States." I showed them the route I was planning to travel, the receipt from the Russian agency, the letter of invitation from Mongolia, and proof from the bank that I had money in my account, but I headed home in disbelief. Whatever, what the hey, I'll prepare even better and return in a week or two, and explain my plans once more.

I gathered a pile of certificates and documents and returned to the US embassy. As soon as I reached the counter, the clerk began writing a rejection! I remember his words exactly: "You can try again, but you won't get a visa." Unbelievable! So I could forget about the United States. They took my $260, though. I was bewildered. But not for long!

In order to go completely around the globe, and since the United States was no longer an option, I was going to have to go across Canada, and I needed a visa for that country, too, which I had heard was even harder to get than for the United States. At least, that's what I thought: If I couldn't get a visa for Canada, then I couldn't cross North America at all. Latin America, because of its many countries and visas, seemed even more complicated, and what about the many different languages spoken? I definitely needed to get a visa for Canada.

Despite all the obstacles, I wasn't thrown off balance, and felt that within the year my plan would be put into action.

19/3–30/4/2009

On the motorcycle and travel forum, Motori.hr, I opened my own topic and announced my plans. A while back when I was writing about Nordkapp, most of the biker population liked my writing style. I liked creating situations where I could study human behaviour and enjoyed reading the reactions of the motorcyclists, most of whom were surprised, confused, but also positive. Some thought I was joking or exaggerating because I was going by myself at 19 years of age. Whole teams usually gather and prepare for these kinds of things! And what's more, I wasn't rambling about problems, doubts, fears, and I wasn't looking for advice. That was totally unusual and baffling.

FINAL PHASE OF PREPARATION

> When you really want something,
> everything falls into place….
>
> —P.R.

You just have to make an effort.

—P.R.

I found out that visas for Canada were no longer required. Yes, that's just the news I needed to hear! Other than the lack of funding, I didn't have any more serious obstacles to starting my journey. I moved my route further north, in order to accommodate crossing Canada, got my Russian visa, and put off getting my Ukrainian one—I'd request it while in Moscow on my way back. For the Mongolian visa, I went to Budapest and got it the same day.

I tried to organize my travel accommodation as much as possible online. I used Couchsurfing International, especially in Canada, where accommodation was really expensive. Couchsurfing works like this: you register, fill out your profile, and find people with similar interests who offer each other accommodation. It turned out to be effective, even though I was sometimes a few days late.

I decided to start my journey on May 3, the day of the city of Vukovar, by joining the great biker gathering that was organized as part of the many events honouring this day.[1] This traditional biker gathering, which also marks the opening of the biker season, is actually a caravan of motorcyclists that starts in Dubrovnik, a city in Croatia's south, then crosses the entire country and ends in the eastern city of Vukovar. I contacted members of the motorcycle club, MK Vukovar. They were a

---

1 The day of the city of Vukovar is a historic date that this city celebrates. It's the day Vukovar was declared a free royal city, back in 1231. Before the Croatian War of Independence (1991–1995), Vukovar was a prosperous multicultural and multi-ethnic city. In 1991, the Yugoslav National Army (JNA) attacked Vukovar. The city was completely destroyed during this eighty-seven-day siege. After the atrocities of the war ended, Vukovar was a symbol of suffering and pain. Today, although the scars have not healed fully, Vukovar is proclaimed a town of peace and tolerance, with the *Vučedolska Golubica* (Vučedol Dove), its most famous symbol. This dove, found in an archeological site near Vukovar in 1938, is a bird-shaped ritual vessel made from baked clay that dates to sometime between 2800 and 2500 BC. To date, it is the oldest dove figure found in Europe.

bit astonished, but invited me to join them anyway. There we could go over some details.

And now, mainly about mechanics (for motorcyclists!)

Time was flying, and the motorcycle was being prepped according to plan at my friend Anton's service centre in Trogir, along with additional preparation in Varaždin at a Yamaha service centre called Lovac. Both teams patiently taught me how to service my motorcycle; that is, they taught me the mechanics, and nothing more, since I was a beginner. I carefully paid attention and tried out what they had taught me. Before the trip, the motorcycle's mileage had already reached 23 000 km, so we changed its oil and filters, and gave it a new chain, sprockets and rear disc plate. We "tightened" the valves, adjusted the suspension, and checked and lubricated all its parts so that in the end it was like new. Even better than new! The parts we had ordered came: case guards and racks for the luggage. Since the firm that promised to donate panniers (cases for holding luggage) backed out, a friend improvised and made some for me in a hurry. What was important was to get by as cheaply as possible. I wrapped alpine rope around the handles to protect them, my own personal trademark. Later on this turned out to be a big hit in Canada because some guys who saw it did the same. Uvex sponsored me by supplying me with complete motorcycle gear: a helmet, jacket and pants. However, none of the sponsors had Enduro boots in size 48 (European size), and I wasn't about to buy any. Just before I left, my friend Dominic got me a pair of almost-new boots, so I took them to the shoe repair shop, where they were adjusted as much as possible to fit my feet. The tire centre, Gumi Pađen, gladly gave me two pairs of Metzeler tires, which was cool.

Once again, for everyone!

At Iglu Sport, our most complete outdoor store with affordable prices, I got some clothes and the rest of what I needed for camping: a tent, sleeping bag, pants, sneakers, socks and rope. My effort to get myself a video camera to mark interesting moments didn't get past being an effort, as well as my attempt to get a satellite telephone.

I was managing OK with everything, except for the funding. Most people used the recession as their top excuse. Twenty days before the start date, I had HRK 5,000[1] in my bank account (about $900) and some promises that I just needed to trust, but as I said, when you really want something . . .

Shortly before the departure date, HRK 10,000 was deposited to my account by a lady from Zagreb who wished to remain anonymous. I couldn't believe it, after everything. The big day was all the more near, my friends and relatives all the more worried, and I was all the more content and happy.

---

1   HRK stands for Croatian Kunas.

FROM EUROPE TO THE ATLANTIC
(2/5/2009–12/5/2009)
4 100 km

VUKOVAR–BERN

On May 2, with my friends Miško and Mario from the motorcycle and travel forum, Motori.hr, I rode 250 km to the city of Vukovar, where the great biker gathering was taking place. Upon arrival, Mario had to head back home to Koprivnica take care of some business, so Miško and I continued on to where a welcome party was organized for the motorcyclists coming from Dubrovnik. My motorcycle, ready for the big trip, was parked right next to the tent. We hung out and I talked with those interested in my trip. The caravan arrived from Dubrovnik, and soon after, a band named Atomsko Sklonište (Atomic Shelter) started playing. After midnight and after the concert, I was invited onstage to announce the start of my journey. I talked about my plans and when I expected to return home, then with loud support from the audience, I left the stage and headed towards my motorcycle. I was tired since I had spent the last several days rushing around to finish up financial preparations.

I rode my motorcycle to the hall where we were all to sleep. (No one knew my true financial situation, which was really interesting. My financial situation was "interesting" in the sense that I had no money.) Not even the loudest snoring, which was piercing the sound barrier a mere dozen metres away, could bother me. In the morning, after waking and talking with members of the MK Vukovar team in their quarters, I slowly left with Miško back towards Koprivnica. On the way out of the city, I stopped at a bus stop to take a picture of the mileage at the starting point. At that moment, my motorcycle had covered exactly 23 689 km. My adventure across Europe was now slowly beginning. We reached Koprivnica, said our goodbyes to friends, and then I went home to get some sleep because I'd be rising early the next morning.

When I reached Zagreb, I stopped at a store called Navigo-Sistem to get a map of North America, which would really come in handy, especially when passing through big cities. Immediately after that, I headed for Switzerland. It was already noon, and I had 900 km to go to get to Lucerne.

• • •

After crossing the border with Slovenia, while still near Croatia, I stopped at a gas station to check if there were any missed phone calls on my cellphone. There were only a few text messages from friends wishing me the best. More motivation for the journey. I soon reached Italy. I rode along the lowlands of Padua westward towards Milan, and then headed north towards Switzerland. Along the way, I was washed and dried several times, thanks to nature's moody weather. But I didn't pay much attention to that since I was just getting started. As I neared Switzerland, the landscape became all the more interesting, both for my motorcycle and for me. The mountains have always attracted me, and there I was riding across the Alps for the first time.

At the border between Italy and Switzerland, I accidentally changed lanes into the one designated for vehicles with permits. I knew I needed one to ride in this lane, but I didn't feel like getting off my motorcycle, and I tend not to pay if it's not really necessary. I stopped for a minute at a gas station and called the guys from MK Sokol (Hawks Motorcycle Club), who were waiting for me in Lucerne, to say that everything was going according to plan. I shifted into first gear and continued towards Lucerne. Night was falling, and a strong side wind reminded me to ride more carefully, so I kept to the speed limit, and even drove slower at times. It was good to see the sign for a tunnel ahead. I slowed down and warmed up a bit inside, then went out into the cold once again.

Soon, I saw a sign for Lucerne. I stopped under a bridge near the entrance to the city, took my cellphone out, and called the guys who were expecting me. After about ten minutes, a powerful motorcycle bearing the logo, MK Sokol, and the characteristic Croatian checkerboard coat of arms arrived. The biker, a man in his fifties, made a U-turn on the street, and then came to a halt by my Yamaha.

"You arrived?" he asked.

"I did. It took me a while longer, but here I am." I said.

"All right, we're waiting for you, get on your bike and follow me."

"Let's go." I answered.

We rode towards the downtown and reached a shopping centre with a restaurant, where the Hawks of all Hawks—the members of MK Sokol, had gathered. I got off my motorcycle and set it on the kickstand. It really was well loaded. I took my tank bag and went up the steps to the restaurant. When I opened the door, I could see the shopping centre was closed and several large tables were set together in the middle of the hallway. The Hawks were waiting to meet me and the atmosphere was great. I hadn't expected such a welcome; these guys were the greatest. All the food came from a restaurant owned by one of the bikers. We talked about my ride to Lisbon and about the route for the next few days. They gave me some money, which, of course, I didn't want to take, but they insisted, so I accepted.

Fatigue had almost gotten the better of me several times that day, and now, once again it was reminding me to recharge my "battery." I retreated to an apartment with some of the guys. We parked the motorcycle in the parking lot by the building. I took what I needed, including the laptop that I had been carrying with me the whole time. I couldn't take the GPS off its bearing, not even with the help of a knife that I had, so I wrapped a bag over it and left it on the motorcycle. As soon as I entered the apartment, I jumped in the shower.

Afterwards, I took out my laptop to say "hi" to the people on Motori. hr, who were waiting to read about the first leg of the trip. I couldn't catch a signal for the wireless, so I went outside. I walked around the building and headed for the roof in search of a signal, and while at it, to check the weather forecast. Tomorrow would be a sunny day. My plan for the next day was to visit Switzerland's capital, Bern.

I awoke the next morning with the thought that I should get up as soon as possible and get going. A few moments later the doorbell rang. The Hawks had come. They took me on a tour of the city, and we stopped along the way at a biker shop where I bought some waterproof boot covers. Though they had been on my list of stuff to take on the trip, I hadn't packed them. We got in the car and went to the restaurant where we had eaten dinner the day before. Mealtime, once again. I was satisfied to eat another warm meal. Soon after, we went back to our motorcycles. Packing, picture-taking and some goodbyes, with some "see ya laters." Thanks to the Hawks for everything!

I left for Bern, which is about one hundred kilometres from Lucerne. The sunny weather and the thought that I would be visiting my friends, Anita and Bojan, whom I hadn't seen in a long time, got me thinking about them and enjoying the ride. I had already entered the address in my GPS and so let it lead the way to their apartment building. I parked the motorcycle by the place reserved for guests and walked to the entrance with complete biker gear still on, which made surprised passersby stare. Actually, I wasn't sure if they were staring because of the gear or because of my parking job.

After I pressed the button on the intercom, I heard a familiar voice:

"Who's there?"

"It's me," I answered.

"Oh, Petar. You got here!"

"Yeah, I did. C'mon open the door!"

"There."

Since I don't live in an apartment building, I'm almost always too slow to open the main entrance door after being buzzed in. I rang the intercom again.

"Alo?" Anita said.

"I didn't open the door in time, press again," I said.

"There you go."

This time I got in—probably because I pushed on the door as if I was playing rugby. I entered the building, dragging loads of equipment that I had taken off of the motorcycle. Lucky for me, the apartment was on the uppermost floor. I entered through the opened door and said "hi" to Anita. I took my stuff to the room where I was to sleep. Bojan came home soon after, so while the sun was still shining, we went to do some sightseeing in town. When we got back, I decided to stay in Bern for two nights instead of one for two reasons: first, because there was a great road for a motorcycle ride through the Alps, which Bojan had recommended, and second, how could I leave when they're the way they are?

Wanting to enjoy the ride and landscape, I took everything off the motorcycle except the tank bag. Soon, I came to where there's a great view of the mountains. A lot of snow was still lingering along the mountain

ABOVE: **Before departure.**
RIGHT: **In Lucerne with friends.**
BELOW: **The Alps.**

saddle. I stopped often to enjoy the sights, and to take pictures. However, I got carried away, lost track of time, and because of that, I didn't finish the planned route. But despite that, I was happy with what I had seen. The rest I'd see some other time.

BERN–TOULOUSE

The next stop was Toulouse, in France, about 800 km from Bern. I got on the freeway, settled myself comfortably astride the motorcycle saddle, and raced out of the Alps towards Lyon. After Lyon, I went down the Rhone Valley, travelling southward to Nimes, and then followed the sun westward. I enjoyed the landscape in France and waited for the time and the kilometres to pass. The only time I stopped was to refuel. And once I had stopped, I took advantage of the opportunity to grab a bite to eat before getting back on the road. At the gas station, I realized that my toll ticket was missing. While riding, I thought about how much my sloppiness was going to cost me. I got off at the exit for Toulouse and stopped at the toll house, where I told the official I didn't have my ticket. She was an elderly lady, and she looked at me and my motorcycle with confusion. Then she bent down to pick up a folder. A few sheets of paper fell out of it. She picked those up and then showed me a price list.

I ended up paying half as much as I would have had I had my ticket. Obviously, the attendant had made a mistake and charged me less. All right! There was still some change jingling in my pocket.

I reached Toulouse at about eight o'clock and texted the guy I had found through Couchsurfing to let him know that I had arrived. After getting acquainted with Gomez, I parked my motorcycle in his garage and then went with him on a tour of Toulouse, known as the Pink City, because of the colour of its brick architecture. Since it's full of students, the city is alive all through the night. But in order to be able to get going the next morning, I hit the sack early.

TOULOUSE–MADRID

I started the engine in the morning, and with the rain lashing down on me, I moved on. While leaving the city, I stopped in a parking lot because I felt as if I had forgotten something. Yeah, my cellphone was still in Gomez's apartment. I had left it under the table during breakfast. Returning to the Pink City took longer than it had yesterday because of the traffic in both directions.

Next stop, Madrid. I rode somewhat faster than usual, which must have been obvious to the police cameras. Luckily the border was near so I did not end up with a speeding ticket.

Rolling hills slowly replaced the valley. A serpentine road under a blanket of fog marked my reaching the Pyrenees. And mountains, being mountains, usually have mood swings. When I saw them from a distance, the sky above them was clear, but apparently I was destined to watch the road rather than enjoy the scenery. I adjusted my driving to the wet conditions and often wiped the visor, which kept fogging up. As I watched the road, my thoughts were on the next stages of the trip. A screech of tires and a bang woke me from my thoughts!

Thanks to the distance between me and other vehicles I had kept while driving, I avoided hitting the two cars that had crashed right in front of me. The crash was nothing serious, just some material damage done, so I continued pushing my way through the thick fog. My helmet's visor was constantly fogging up and I was continuously wiping it with my glove. Just a kilometre further down, another minor accident occurred. A long queue of cars formed because of the wet conditions. There was one car in front of me, and about a dozen behind me, all bumper to bumper. In order to escape the queue, I tried to take advantage of the fact that I was on a motorcycle—not in a car—and overtake the car that was in front of me. I stepped on the gas in order to pass a sharp curve through the thick fog, and crossed the solid line, but this only gave me a temporary escape from the queue. I thought I had finally gotten away from the line of cars when another queue formed in front of me. What the heck, I'd ride behind them while negotiating the many curves of the serpentine road, and then go at my own speed. Then I'd ride as fast as I wanted to. And that's how it was.

The weather improved as I went further inland into Spain, until finally the sky completely cleared up. There was about an hour of sunlight remaining, and I had over two more hours to go to get to Madrid. I kept to the same speed, mainly riding 120 kmph. The sun set quickly, and since my low beam had just burned out, all I could do was use the high beam. My motorcycle was pretty overloaded with equipment, so the rear end of the bike dragged lower, which made the high beam shine on the treetops instead of on the road ahead. As I rode down the highway, the cars approaching me from the other direction often flashed their blinkers as warnings to me.

I had arranged accommodation in Madrid through Couchsurfing, but I received a text message at the last minute notifying me that it was cancelled. So I found a cheap hotel and got ready for the next day. I went to sleep early, and by dawn was already heading for Portugal. Why did I want to reach Lisbon a day ahead of schedule? Since I usually do most things by myself, I hadn't really looked for advice or instructions. Though I had already arranged cargo transport for my motorcycle with a cargo company in Lisbon, I wanted to get there a day earlier just to make sure everything went according to plan.

MADRID–LISBON

Morning, and what else to do? Saddle up. I set the GPS to get me out of the city so I could get on the road that would take me to Lisbon. The GPS confused me a bit and led me to an exit that wasn't in use yet. There weren't any signs or directions anywhere. I headed towards a circular intersection, but that part of the road was still under construction. I turned the GPS off and played it by ear. Since I was riding an Enduro motorcycle, I didn't hesitate to pass the No Passage sign, and took a shortcut to the asphalt in hopes that I would see a sign for Portugal.

I was racing and fleeing gloomy clouds that were coming from the east. As much as I could, I was enjoying the view of the landscapes of Castile and Estremadura. Only a few kilometres separated me from the border with Portugal, when I encountered a swarm of bugs that made me stop at a gas station.

It was time to clean the visor on my helmet. I hadn't had to clean it before because, until then, I'd been lucky enough to have the rain do that job for me. While at the gas station, I took advantage of the opportunity to eat some noodles in a hurry in the restaurant behind it. The weather was hot and humid. Although I had been hoping to stay dry that day, I was glad to meet rain, which cooled me, as soon as I crossed over to Portugal.

The traffic was sparse from Badajoz to Portugal; only a few cars passed me. I rode without stopping to Lisbon. There I came upon a queue that seemed endless, but I drove properly without squeezing between the cars or splitting lanes. I turned the GPS on to see my location. A bridge was ahead that could be the reason for the queue, and as I approached it, the space between vehicles became smaller and smaller. The motorcycle began overheating, to its maximum limit. I travelled a bit further and came to a bridge where a toll booth was set for crossing. Here I am, now it's my turn! I dropped the coin in, lowered my helmet visor, and got ready for the side winds along the bridge. Crossing the bridge reminded me of the time I had crossed the bridge that connects Sweden with Denmark. There I had mastered riding with side winds blowing.

In Lisbon I hadn't managed to find free accommodation, so I typed up the address of the hostel I was going to stay in. The hostel was just a few kilometres away, as the crow flies. Just as I had entered a tunnel, however, the GPS stopped cooperating. Its light shut off, which took me by surprise. Maybe the cable that was plugged into the battery had disconnected, I thought. I emerged from the tunnel. I couldn't find a place to stop and check out what was going on. Across the street, a Mercedes pulled out of a parking spot. I glanced over my shoulder, all was clear. So I crossed to the other side, stopped, and parked the motorcycle. Pressing on the GPS's button didn't help, so I took out my tool set and looked for my hex keys. With the smallest hex key, I removed the batteries. When I put the GPS back on the bearing, it began working again. I put the tools back in the transport bag, and cruised towards the hostel.

The hostel that stood before me was situated within a complex of old buildings. The price was good, but the question remaining was where to leave the motorcycle overnight? When the owner of the hostel found out where I was headed, she let me put it in the hallway. "Great," I said.

I arranged my stuff in the room and turned the laptop on. I played some music and located the cargo agency on Google Maps. After that I drove to the airport, where I found it easily. However, I couldn't enter the agency because my plane reservation wasn't for that day. That was OK, though, because up until now, this had been a bit of a question for me. Now at least I knew where they were. The next day, I would take my motorcycle there, and that would be that, as far as Europe was concerned. I returned to the hostel and began packing my equipment in the panniers and cases. The most important stuff, which I would need while waiting for my motorcycle to reach Canada, I packed in my tank bag.

In the morning I headed for the airport wearing only a shirt and jeans. Almost all of my equipment was to be sent to Canada by way of the cargo agency I had visited yesterday. All I had in my tank bag were: a camera, laptop, toothbrush, shirt, notebook, and sunglasses. I rang the doorbell and the gate to the parking lot opened. I rode my motorcycle into the parking lot, and there was Anselmo waiting for me. He was the one I had arranged the transport with, through email.

"You got to Portugal, welcome!" Anselmo said.

"Yeah, thanks. I can't wait to get to Canada," I answered, while trying to remember my English.

"Yes, in Canada it'll sure be interesting, and kudos to you for your bravery."

"Thanks."

"Let's get up to the office to take care of the paperwork," Anselmo added.

"Sure."

The building, which seemed old and worn down on the outside, was amazingly orderly on the inside. A lot of theses agencies, I thought, have guards at the entrance, security cameras set to capture even the blind spots. It's really interesting for these people here, I thought. The office was on the second floor. We immediately got to work. Anselmo brought out a folder with one sheet of paper sticking out. The folder contained all the documents necessary for transport. The *Dangerous Goods* document had been prepared in advance, and was necessary since the motorcycle was considered a dangerous load in air-cargo terms. I signed the document and was handed some more papers that would be necessary in order to reclaim the motorcycle in Toronto. The crate in which the motorcycle was to be transported in had already been built according to the bike's dimensions. We drained out the fuel and put the motorcycle in the box; then we unplugged the battery and partially let the air out of the tires. I had already stuffed the panniers and transport bag beside and under the motorcycle. I secured the helmet to the seat with a luggage net so that it would arrive without being damaged. I took a few pictures to record how everything looked before the trip, just in case of damage during the flight. It was already late in the afternoon, so I took a taxi to the hostel and set my cellphone to wake me at nine o'clock. Then I hit the sack.

CROSSING THE ATLANTIC

A familiar sound woke me in the morning. Of course—my cellphone. I studied my plane ticket again, as I had often done before. This was the day I would fly British Airways via London to Toronto. I ate something in a hurry, took my bag, checked out and called a taxi.

The taxi driver drove as if on a racetrack. Each time he would reach a traffic light, or would be in any way hindered from driving at full speed, he would take a whistle from the ashtray and begin whistling while flailing his arms until the other cars would make way. With record speed we reached the airport. Since I didn't have any luggage, except for my tank bag, there was no need to go to the check-in counter. All I needed to do was type in the code on the machine that printed out plane tickets in front of the British Airways counter. The boarding and flight to London went perfectly well; otherwise this travelogue wouldn't be here.

• • •

I exited the plane and followed the signs for connecting flights. The London Underground at Heathrow took me from one terminal to the next, and I eventually reached the baggage carousel. As I had expected, unlike Lisbon, there were a lot more people and many more security checks. After I made it through security, I took my stuff. Satisfied with how things were going, I entered the waiting area for my next flight, to Toronto. About half an hour was left until departure time. I sat in a chair, crossed my legs, and then heard familiar words being spoken by an elderly couple sitting next to me. They were also flying to Toronto. After a short question-and-answer exchange, they were more than astonished. I heard the same reactions that I had heard back when I was preparing for the journey. Most people—including this couple—mainly asked: "Oh really, you're brave enough for something like that? How is it that your parents let you? But why are you going alone? Aren't you afraid?"

Few would say: "Of course, you're young and now is the time for adventures and journeys." I would prefer it if more people would perceive the world like this. By the way, here are answers to the aforementioned questions: "I am. It's simple, they don't have to let me go, I let myself go. Maybe I could travel with someone, but none of my friends have enough time or enthusiasm for something like this, like in many things in life, so I go by myself. I'm not lonely. No, I'm not scared."

While conversing with the couple, there was an announcement to prepare for boarding. I don't like crowds and pushing, so instead of getting up right away, I waited, and was the last one in line to have my boarding pass checked. An elderly man in a blue suit took my passport and plane ticket. He started to frown and express wonder. He called me aside, behind the counter.

"How is it that you travelled from Lisbon to London, and not from Croatia, where you are from?" Sherlock asked.

"Because I'm circling the globe by motorcycle, I rode to Lisbon, and now I need to get to the next continent." I answered, not seeing anything strange in it.

"Show me your credit cards!"

"Here they are, and they're in my name."

"Go get your luggage and come back so I can see . . ." He didn't finish his sentence, because I was already answering.

"What I'm holding is all I've got."

"That's it? How, where are your belongings?"

"All my stuff is in a crate with my motorcycle, and that's already on its way to Toronto." Then Sherlock's colleague came over and started asking stupid questions, based on a protocol they had to follow, I guess.

After repeating the entire procedure, they didn't find anything wrong, so although baffled, they let me board the plane.

"Oh man, hopefully I won't have to hassle with people like these again!" I mumbled under my breath while finding my seat on the plane. I rested during the flight. All right, I admit, I woke each time something was offered to eat or drink. We landed in Toronto on time. I had only taken one step off the plane, when a police officer stopped me.

"This is your first visit to Canada?" he asked after taking my passport.

"Yes, I'm here for the first time." I answered.

"Why did you come to Canada?"

"Tourism." I answered again.

"All right, enjoy!"

I then proceeded to a room with about twenty counters, of which only two were open. One was occupied, and behind the other there stood a clerk waving to me to approach. A police officer was standing behind her. Questions followed once again:

"This is your first time in Canada?" she asked, while resting her chin on her right hand.

"Yes. I'm here for the first time, as a tourist. I'm circling the world by motorcycle, now I'm in Canada . . ."

"You're not in Canada yet!" she interrupted.

"What do you mean, I'm not?" I asked, taken aback.

"You don't have a stamp on your passport, so you're not. And where's the rest of your luggage?"

"All my stuff is in a container with my motorcycle. I've only got my most necessary stuff with me until my bike gets here."

"Tell me, where do you plan to go by motorcycle? What's your route?"

"I plan on going east to Halifax, then . . ."

"Halifax? As in Halifax in Nova Scotia?" she asked me in awe.

"Yes, that Halifax. I don't know any other." I answered.

"But that's two thousand kilometres from Toronto!"

At that moment I realized a little white lie wouldn't hurt and would probably help, so I said that after going to Halifax, I planned on returning to Toronto and then flying from there back to Lisbon, together with my motorcycle. Although I wasn't going to do this, I did have a return ticket. Not logical, but it is often cheaper to buy a return ticket than a one-way ticket. This story seemed more acceptable than if I had said that I was planning on going to Halifax, and then Vancouver, then . . . and then . . . Still, I couldn't figure out why they were bugging me so much. Were they looking for something in the computer?

I was looking at the clerk and the police officer behind her and thinking to myself: "Why are they being so mistrustful? How would these officials feel if others showed so much lack of trust towards them if they went travelling?"

"Well, do I look like a terrorist?!" I asked, already exhausted.

By some miracle, the stamp appeared in my passport. Now I was officially in Canada!

CANADA
(12/5–16/7/2009)
17 400 km

In order to live free and happily
you must sacrifice boredom.
It is not always an easy sacrifice.

—Richard Bach

TORONTO

I rushed out of the airport and jumped into a taxi.

"Where to?" asked the taxi driver, whose turban was touching the roof of the car. Each turn of his head to the left or right demanded a special procedure.

"King Street West," I mustered, marveling that I was in Canada.

While riding in the taxi to the address where I had arranged accommodation through Couchsurfing, I thought about whether my motorcycle would arrive on time. Its route to its final destination was somewhat complicated. The cargo box embarked the same day as my flight, but first it flew to Porto, then to Paris, and then to Chicago before finally flying to Toronto. I was told it would take four days. However, it took nine. An additional two days were needed because the box was transported from Chicago by truck and not by plane, as had been agreed to. One more day was lost to a holiday, and the remaining additional days were due to time spent at Canadian Customs. According to a customs officer I had contacted by phone, the police needed to take a look at the bike upon its arrival.

However, when I finally took care of all the paperwork and went to the warehouse to see my motorcycle, I could tell the customs officials had only opened the box and taken a peek inside. That was it. Everything was in its place. I had still more paperwork to fill out, which I did with the help of my host in Toronto, whom I had located via Couchsurfing. Since I didn't understand some of the words on the form, I really appreciated his assistance. I got a copy of the papers that confirmed the motorcycle was legally in the country on a temporary basis, and a small green paper that said how many days I could ride it in

Canada. Exactly as many as I had asked for: 65 days. This left some leeway in case I stayed longer than planned. I went to the warehouse again and picked up the motorcycle. First, I mounted the licence plate, which I had removed prior to transport, then I got the luggage. After I filled the gas tank, I plugged the battery. It started at first try. There weren't any signs of trouble with starting the engine, which I had heard could happen. I was bursting with joy. Finally I could continue east to the Atlantic Ocean, and then west to the Pacific.

Time to saddle up and leave the warehouse. At the first intersection I needed to turn right, but the light was red, so I stopped and waited. The car behind me started tooting louder than the Vienna Philharmonic! I had no idea why. I turned around and waved my hand, not understanding what was going on. The light turned green, so I got going. The situation occurred again. At red lights, it seemed, cars were allowed to turn right, so I did too. Later on I realized what this was about: unlike in Croatia, right turns are allowed at a red light if there is no oncoming traffic from the left. That's a good thing.

While riding to the apartment where I was staying while in Toronto, I thought about the previous day, when I had wanted to rent a car to go to Niagara Falls. However, here, that is considered irresponsible behaviour for a 19-year-old. Whatever, now I had my own vehicle and could go wherever I wanted. Just then I came across a traffic jam. The sun was strong enough to make me break out in a sweat in my black outfit. To my right, a truck was driving the same speed as I was. I could tell he was speaking to me, and in a language that I have known longer and speak better than English.

"*Odakle si?* Where are you from?" the man shouted.

"From Croatia!"

"From where?"

"From Šibenik!" I answered, remembering that I had a licence plate with ŠI on it, which stands for the city of Šibenik. I'm actually from Koprivnica.

"How'd you get here?!" He pointed at the motorcycle.

"By plane!"

"Enjoy!"

"I will!" We're few but plenty, I laughed to myself.

I continued riding through town, toward the apartment where I was staying, and stopped at a gas station to refuel for the next day. My plan was to reach Niagara Falls, then return the same way to Toronto before heading for Kingston, where I had arranged accommodation.

THUNDERING WATER

I parked in front of the apartment building, packed everything and put it all in the garage, ready to grab when the time came to leave. My last day in Toronto, I thought. I was enjoying myself, walking around for several hours in the town whose name in Huron means "meeting place." This meaning suits it, for Toronto looks like a meeting place. Though British roots are evident in the city's centre, immigrants from all over the world shaped this interesting metropolis. But it's time to get going. My hosts in Toronto, probably out of fear of mega-popular stardom after I mention them in this book, have requested to remain anonymous. I am grateful to them for having let me be their guest, for having helped me with everything, and I'll see you again.

The next morning I started the motorcycle and headed for Niagara Falls, which I reached fairly quickly, since I took the highway. The city, as well as the falls, are located right at the border with the United States and are a popular tourist attraction. I could see that for myself when I arrived. Buses, cars, motorcycles and various other vehicles were jam-packed in the parking lot. From the parking lot I could hear the waterfalls thundering and could even feel the spray carried by the wind cooling my face. The huge waterfalls were pouring from the cliffs that were some fifty-five metres high. Truly impressive! At the height of the season, some thirty-five thousand people pass through here in a day. While watching the waterfalls, I could see another attraction travelling upstream from the distance—a tourist boat. It reached the waterfalls and everyone standing on the deck of the boat got soaking wet. Restaurants nearby were filled with tourists. It was almost impossible to find a place to sit, so I went back to my motorcycle, lay on the grass, took my biker boots off, opened a can of something, and enjoyed. In order to reach Kingston in time, I needed to hit the road as soon as I finished eating. I took the same route back to Toronto. A wind blew at the same spots where it had blown on my way to Niagara Falls, only this time from the opposite side. I took the freeway across Toronto, though I almost accidentally took an exit for the city's centre.

ALONG THE ST. LAWRENCE VALLEY

The road to Kingston got me there quickly. Some construction was underway at the entrance to the city, so once again I had to take advantage of what an Enduro motorcycle does best. Since I was too lazy to follow the detour signs, I entered the zone that was prohibited. The way the construction workers stared at me did not worry me.

A few blocks further and I reached the place I was to stay and had found on the Couchsurfing site. I only took what I needed most from the motorcycle. After taking a shower, I went to get acquainted with the city. However, when I reached the end of the street, I realized that after having driven almost 550 km, I was tired, so I put off getting acquainted with the city until next day.

The next morning I awoke full of energy. Melodie really went out of her way preparing breakfast. Though I was eager to get back on the road, to ride and enjoy the landscape, Melodie and her interesting friends convinced me to stay one more day.

Since I had used up all the lubricating spray for the chain, I drove without my luggage and gear to the Yamaha store, which was some 30 km from Kingston. The wide road and beautiful landscape made this ride a sheer pleasure. But then a police car appeared from behind a grove. I kept to the speed limit as I drove by, but after passing a hilltop and descending into a stretch of flat ground, from my rear-view mirror I could see the police car trailing behind. The officers approached me, but did not pass me. "All right, fine," I said, and pulled over onto the shoulder. A middle-aged policeman with a hat and sunglasses approached. He walked with an air of self-assurance, with his eyes focused on my licence plate.

Thundering water.

"Good afternoon," he said, while trying to take in the whole motorcycle with just one glance.

"Hello," I said.

"Where are you coming from?"

"Try to guess," I put myself in the position of an inquisitor.

"Hmm, I know the plate is from somewhere in Europe, hmm, but I don't know what country."

"I'm from Croatia."

"You got a registration card and driver's licence?"

"I do, I do, here, these are all my papers."

"All right, where are you going?"

"To the Yamaha store, I need new spray for my chain."

"Aha, just keep going, a few more kilometres down the road. The store is to the right, you'll see it."

"All right, thanks!"

I put the papers back in the tank bag and got going towards the store. A few kilometres further, I recognized the red Yamaha logo on a flag that was waving above a building that reminded me of a warehouse. A few motorcycles were parked outside. As soon as I entered the store I spotted the chain sprays and didn't take my eyes off them. That was what I needed. The chain was already starting to make strange sounds. I bought the spray right away and lubricated the chain while still in front of the store. The spray had an intense coconut scent that lingered everywhere I went. On the way back to Kingston, I waved at the patrol officers who had stopped me earlier. They didn't wave back, since they were busy. I returned to Kingston, packed my stuff in the pannier and prepared the motorcycle for the next day (in other words: I lubricated the chain once more). The evening was spent in the good company of Melodie and her friends. The next stop: Quebec City.

I entered the province of Quebec from the highway that runs northeast along the border with the United States. Most readers know that French is the official language here, but I'm writing this just in case someone (like my close friends—no offence, please), doesn't know. Soon I reached Montreal, which I was planning to visit on the way back. There I came across gridlock and the longest queue that I had ever seen. The queues in Zagreb are a joke compared to this one. For the next 30 km, I drove slowly, and was sweating. Soaking wet, I turned the motor off every now and then and pushed the motorcycle. Somehow, I managed to weave my way out of the traffic jam and speed up some. Only on the way out of the city did the traffic become less congested, and I was finally able to ride normally.

The roads in Canada are generally wider than the ones in Europe, making the ride more comfortable. However, the trucks drive at speeds of over 100 kmph, which I wasn't used to. Back home, even though they do exceed the speed limit, they don't usually drive so fast. Why am I writing this? Because that was approximately my touring speed, so oftentimes I would pass a truck while going uphill, but then downhill that same truck would pass me. And so on, several times.

I reached Quebec City by dark, and since my GPS brought me to the wrong address, I was forced to look for it myself. I stopped at a gas station, but couldn't find anyone who could speak and understand English. I moved on and approached another gas station. I could see a map of the city on the wall, so I stopped there, and luckily, the guy that worked there knew English. We looked for St-Pascal Street and found it in the upper right corner of the map. I memorized the route and reached the street. But then I had trouble figuring out which house was the one I was looking for because the houses lining the street differed only by the bushes in front of each. Everything else was almost completely identical. The next Couchsurfing group awaited me in one of these houses. I stopped, called the number, and heard the phone ring. A man answered with whom I had spoken earlier.

"Here I am, I got here!"

"OK, I'll open the door."

There were about six people in the house, not counting the dog, who spent the whole night next to the motorcycle. They let me sleep in the basement. A mattress was available and there was Internet access. Who needed more?

I stayed for two days in Quebec City, the capital of the province of

Quebec, and one of the oldest Canadian cities. A city with an undeniably French atmosphere, Quebec City has a famous old town and colourful neighbourhoods filled with restaurants and tourists. While walking around, before giving up, I had several comical attempts at communicating in French. Funny, and hard to describe.

NEW BRUNSWICK AND NOVA SCOTIA

I crossed the most populated and richest part of Canada, and followed the St. Lawrence River towards the Atlantic. I reached the province of New Brunswick, and, near the city of Fredericton, turned east into the town of Oromocto. There I had arranged accommodation at the home of an interesting couple, Alexandra and Edward. They had travelled almost the entire world. The bookshelf in their living room was filled with Lonely Planet guidebooks. Each book represented a country they had visited. Alexandra is Polish and at that moment, was finishing up college. By now she has probably graduated. Edward was a member of the Canadian Armed Forces, and was stationed near Oromocto. They were very kind to recommend me through the Couchsurfing network, which made it easier for me to find accommodation later on.

Since I had ridden 600 km that day and mainly through rainy weather, I fell asleep as soon as I lay down. Flashes of light in the night sky and explosions from all sorts of weapons awoke me. I wasn't expecting a war zone, but it turned out that there was a military base just a few kilometres away.

Later on, rested and refreshed, I got ready for my ride to Halifax. I grabbed my stuff and left the room where I had slept. I headed for my motorcycle with the intent to retreat; that is, to pack up and move it. I opened the front door of the house, and when I stepped out I could hear the shooting and see the flashes of light coming from the nearby military base even more clearly.

I left earlier than I had the day before, since I was planning to go to the service station in Halifax for the motorcycle's scheduled check-up. The mileage on the motorcycle was already almost 30 000 km. That wasn't much for it, considering my plans for it.

While tanking up I heard someone ask, "Where're you going with so much equipment?" Not expecting the question, I looked at the man in uniform, filling his tank.

"Home, home to Croatia. I'm just going to circle the world first." I answered with a grin.

"Very nice. I also have a motorcycle. Bon voyage!" he answered, smiling.

"Thanks!"

At the service centre in Halifax, I gave a short presentation about my travels (as the employees wanted to hear about my journey), and then the mechanics got to work. They had never seen this motorcycle model before, since it wasn't designed for the North American market. They needed to change the oil and replace the oil filter. Luckily my bike used a universal oil filter, so the guys easily found a replacement. Of course, they didn't know where the oil drain was, so this first service I mainly performed by myself. Once we were done, I could relax. Or at least for a while. Though Yamaha says it is enough to change the oil and filter every 10 000 km, I decided to do it twice as often because I figured it was better that way. I forgot to mention how on the way to Halifax and at the entrance to the province of Nova Scotia, the wind had picked up. At times there were heavy gusts, so I had to really slow down, especially when crossing bridges. I didn't stay long in Halifax. Actually, I spent more time in the service centre than in the town's centre. Only once, around ten o'clock did I go out for a walk. I climbed up some hill and caught a glimpse of the city lights from the top. I would have loved to have stayed and relaxed, but the wind and the cold made me leave.

The strong wind followed me to Sydney, some 400 km from Halifax. By Sydney, I mean the windy and lively Cape Breton Peninsula, and not the one in Australia. After the Vikings landed here in the tenth and eleventh centuries, this rocky coastal region was explored more closely towards the end of the fifteenth century by the seafarer, John Cabot.

I had arranged accommodation at the home of Nick, a guy that worked at the city library. When I arrived at his address, he wasn't home. The irritating sound of a vacuum cleaner was coming from a green Dodge pickup parked in front of the garage. When the girl who was cleaning the truck, whose name was Marie, noticed me approaching, she said that Nick would be home from work soon.

"Get your stuff in the house before Nick comes home!" she said.

"Of course."

Marie came from Montreal and was travelling through Canada. In the evening she was to board a ferry for the island of Newfoundland, also a Canadian province. Newfoundland interested me, too, but I decided to spend more time in the western and northern regions of Canada. These regions attracted me the most.

Just as I was imagining myself racing with the bears in the Yukon, Nick came in. He was carrying a bag on his back that looked like it was about to burst at the seams. The load was, not surprisingly, since he worked at the library, books and a few DVDs of old movies. He took his glasses off and wiped his eyes. Obviously tired, he nevertheless welcomed me to his home. In the meantime, Marie had prepared risotto, so during dinner we talked about travelling. It really is a great feeling to spend time with people who think as you do. Each of us talked about personal experiences until Marie had to get going to catch the ferry. Though it was late, amazingly, I was not tired. So I asked Nick about the route for the next day. He recommended going to Cape Breton Peninsula from Sydney.

"You could take the motorcycle all the way to the edge of the peninsula, then across the national park. There you'll see the Atlantic Ocean, and maybe, if you get lucky, you'll come across a bear or an elk." he said, while we were looking at the map and noting its position and size.

"Sounds interesting. I'll get going tomorrow morning."

In the morning I removed the luggage from the motorcycle, leaving only the tank bag into which I threw my camera and something to drink. The others had already left the house. Somehow, I just couldn't manage to lock the front door. Actually, to be precise, I didn't know how to lock it. I had a key, but I couldn't figure out what the deal was. I tried inserting it at various angles and positions, but nothing worked.

I sat on the front steps and looked at the lock that was preventing me from carrying on with my trip. Starting to lose my patience, I went back in the house and drank some juice. When I returned to the front door, I noticed a button on the doorknob that locked it. I was happy to have discovered this. Instead of leaving at eight o'clock, I sat astride my motorcycle around nine o'clock, and headed for the peninsula. I managed to miscalculate my fuel consumption, and was already running on empty. So I recalled where I had seen the last gas station, some 40 km back the way I had come. The light had started blinking just 5 km ago, which meant I had enough for another 100 km. I guessed that would be enough to just keep going, and eventually come across another gas station for my thirsty motorcycle. I was right.

Who wouldn't enjoy driving along winding coastal roads? Idyllic scenery with small towns in harmony with the landscape. And once in the national park, beautiful all-encompassing wilderness. I turned off the road and started down a gravel trail in a forest, stopping often to enjoy the forest and view of the endless ocean. The shadows became stretched out and it was getting chilly. Full of impressions and encompassed by silence, I cruised slowly back towards Sydney. When Nick asked why I had such a late start in the morning, I just said that I had awoken late. I didn't tell him about the interesting experience with locking the front door. My host would have probably choked with laughter.

RETURN TO ONTARIO

In the morning I did some push-ups and sit-ups, then got ready to travel. I said goodbye to Nick and continued towards Edward and Alexandra's house in Oromocto where I had stayed earlier, and where I was to stay again for a few days. I took a side road, but soon got on the main road in order to get there in time. I planned on visiting the Bay of Fundy, known for the highest tides in the world. Numerous tourists flock daily to see this spot where the sea level rises some sixteen metres. I reached the city of Saint John, but I didn't make it to the Bay of Fundy. I continued onwards, leaving that for next time.

ABOVE: Parliament
Hill, in Ottawa.
RIGHT: View of the
Atlantic Ocean
from the Cape
Breton peninsula.

ABOVE: Traveling through Ontario.
LEFT: Terry Fox memorial.

The bad weather forecast for the rest of the day and the heavy dark clouds rolling in convinced me to hurry on. The storm started just as I knocked once again on their door.

"Seems you got here just in time," Edward said.

"It seems I did."

"OK. You'll sleep in the room you slept in last time."

"Great."

Edward and Alexandra also had guests from Montreal staying with them, and after entering the house, I introduced myself to them. As I went down the hallway, I looked to my left, where the kitchen was. Just like the last time I had been there, the kitchen was pretty crowded. But this time, for a different reason. They had prepared sushi for dinner, something I had always wanted to try. And now the opportunity had arrived. We settled in the living room. I dug in first, taking sushi made with wasabi sauce. At first it was good. But a few moments later, my eyes started watering, my vision became blurred, my nose started running, and I can't even describe the redness and heat.

"Who put so much wasabi in the sushi?" I barely mustered, while the guys were laughing.

I went to the bathroom and splashed my face with icy water. Several times! I don't want to try anything so hot ever again. As the night progressed, I ate my fill of sushi without wasabi, so I didn't have room for dessert. Actually, I'm not much of a cake eater anyway, so even though that was the high point of the evening, I didn't join in. The crowd went on hanging out and talking, while I went on the Internet to write to friends and to check out local web portals to see what was going on in Croatia. I fell asleep by the laptop.

Next stop, Montreal. As soon as I opened my eyes, I got up. Or maybe it was the other way around. Sunlight was barely shining through the window. A rainy and cloudy day awaited me. Just lovely. No one else had awakened yet, but they sure did wake up when I started packing my stuff and walking around in my motorcycle gear. Those heavy boots made a lot of noise, even though I tried to walk down the wooden stairs as quietly as possible. In an instant, everyone was lined up outside the bathroom. Some couldn't wait that long, and went out to the backyard. Out front, I began loading my stuff on the motorcycle. This time there weren't flashes of light and explosions from the military base nearby, just heavy grey clouds looming. I said goodbye to Alexandra, Edward and the guests, and got going.

So far my timing was according to plan. The rain kept me company all the way to Montreal. Along the way, I didn't come across any cars. Obviously many people had changed their plans because of the rain. But a little rain wasn't going to stop me, so I got going, stopping only once at a gas station. I couldn't wait to travel across Alberta and the Yukon, but I'd be doing that when the time came. Cold water was dripping down my back, and especially into my boots. I felt as if I was carrying weights around my ankles. Despite the quality gear I had, after riding all day in the rain, the water found its way in.

I easily found Daniel, who was to be my host in Montreal, on a quiet street near the centre of the city. "My girlfriend isn't home at the moment, so you can dry your boots in the kitchen," Daniel laughed. So that's how my boots were given a great place to dry: in the kitchen, between the heater and the microwave. I set out the rest of the gear to dry in the bathroom. Since the apartment was on the ground floor, I placed towels on the floor to avoid flooding the place. After 850 km, a shower and warm meal lulled me to sleep. Montreal is located at the foot of a mountain, called Mont Royal. Once the centre for the fur trade, it is the second largest city in Canada, and is the largest city in the province of Quebec. English is much more common here than in Quebec City. I took a walk through the downtown, and then got back on the road towards Canada's capital.

OTTAWA

I was planning on spending just one day in Ottawa, but ended up staying for two, sightseeing, visiting the Museum of Civilization, and many other tourist attractions. Walking the streets of Ottawa, I noticed flags with the emblem of the province of Quebec waving from street lights. I was accompanied by my friend, Melodie, whose place I had stayed at in Kingston, and she answered my questions about this.

"We're on the bridge that leads to the Museum of Civilization, in the province of Quebec, and right now we're in Ontario." Melodie said.

Great! I didn't realize Ottawa was so close to the province of Quebec. Apparently, Canadians couldn't agree whether the country's capital would be Montreal or Toronto, so they decided to declare Ottawa the capital instead.

The museum was visible from the bridge. It seemed big, but only when I entered did I realize it was, in fact, huge. Tall totem poles built by First Nations peoples were set in the Grand Hall. After we paid our admission at the entrance, we slowly walked around, studying the exhibits. The first part of the museum we visited contained exhibits about human evolution. There were so many rooms filled with the tiniest details, so many floors, halls, that I just skimmed through many of them. Although this all interested me, there was too much to see in so little time. I spent the most time in the Egyptian history exhibit, since I hadn't yet had a chance to see mummies of pharaohs. I could have spent hours there.

We left the museum and went back the way we had come. Once again I crossed the bridge and entered the province of Ontario. We headed for the Parliament Buildings. From a distance, they reminded me of old British buildings. Up close, they reminded me even more of old British buildings! Parliament Hill is a whole complex of buildings, with the Ottawa River along its border to the north, the Rideau Canal to the east, Wellington Street to the south, and the Supreme Court of Canada, Canada's highest court, to the west. The Parliament Buildings attract some three million visitors annually. The bridge I mentioned spans the Rideau Canal—or as it's also known, the Rideau Waterway. It's a canal that connects the city of Ottawa at the Ottawa River with the city of Kingston at Lake Ontario. The canal was built as a strategic site in case of war, and still functions with most of the original structures. It was designated a UNESCO World Heritage Site in 2007.

Since I had left my motorcycle in a paid parking lot, and almost the entire afternoon had passed, I went to pick it up. Thoughts came to mind while I was walking: how I had already been in Canada for about twenty days, and I still hadn't camped in a tent, hunted wild animals with my camera, or ridden more seriously off road. Yep, it was time to go west. When I reached the parking lot, I could see a group of people gathered around my motorcycle, examining both it and the equipment. There were four of them, if I recall correctly. One was looking at the pannier. Another was studiously examining the front part of the motorcycle, while the other two were watching someone who was watching them.

"Hello. You ride this motorcycle?" the examiner of my homemade pannier asked.

"That's me."

"Bravo! I see you're from Europe, where from exactly?"

"From Croatia."

"Are you travelling alone?"

"Yes, I am."

"Way to go! My guys and I also tour by motorcycle, but never alone. What's your route?"

"I'm travelling around the world. I started in Croatia, went west to Portugal, then had the bike transported to Toronto. From there I rode to Halifax, then west to Ottawa. Next I'll be going to Vancouver, then to Asia, which will be interesting, then back to Croatia."

"Great, hang in there."

"I will." It was good, and it's always good, to meet people who think like you do.

I headed northwest from Ottawa towards Sudbury. Cruising along, with long breaks for meals and enjoying the wilderness, I travelled through the breathtaking Algonquin Park. Then I picked up speed. Almost 30 per cent of Canada's population lives in Ontario. What's good is that forests make up about two-thirds of the surface area of this province. Algonquin Park is the largest protected region in Ontario and a popular retreat for nature-lovers.

I saw fewer personal vehicles on the road, and more and more all-terrain vehicles, especially my favourite, pickup trucks. Road conditions were also worsening. A significant drop in temperature combined with the destructive nature of freezing water sometimes causes the rock face lining the highways to crumble into pieces—even into sand, and roads are not spared from being "toyed with," either. These natural forces are a major consideration in road construction here. The previous winter had lasted pretty long, so the rough conditions served as great training for me and my motorcycle, and that was just an introduction to what was awaiting me, or better said, what I was waiting for.

THE GREAT LAKES

After having travelled some 500 km, I reached Sudbury. This time I stayed at the home of my friends, Alex and Neil. They were glad to see me. We talked about familiar topics, while enjoying their favourite dish for dinner, lasagne.

By the way, compliments to the hosts! The previous year, Neil and four of his friends packed handsaws, tools, rope and all other necessities, and went to Dawson City, Yukon. There they spent a week building a raft for a trip down the Yukon River. All of this was documented, so they showed me the photos. That's something I should think about doing.

To reach the next-to-last stop in Ontario, the city of Sault Ste. Marie, almost 300 km away, I took the road that followed Lake Huron. Smaller lakes gradually increased in number. Actually, quite a number, as did long haul trucks. Though there were often signs warning about the wild animals in the vicinity, I still hadn't seen a sign of a bear or elk.

Sault Ste. Marie is a city on the border with the United States. I decided to stop there, since riding from Sudbury to Thunder Bay in one day would have been too much. While I was stopped at an intersection, waiting to turn right and looking up the address where I was to stay, I felt something bump my motorcycle. By instinct, I turned around, and saw a man raise his arms. He looked as if I was threatening him with a firearm. I checked the motorcycle, turned around, and left. I didn't even stop to see if there was any damage. He hadn't hit me hard anyways. The only thing that could have broken was the licence plate frame. When I reached the place where I was to stay, I got off my motorcycle, and saw there was no damage.

My host, Jody, an aeronautics student, lived in a big house. However, a big house becomes a small one if there are a dozen people living in it, or even more so, if these people are mainly college and high school students. Even though I'm 192 cm tall, and can have a long stride, the first step inside the house was impossible. There was no way I could step over all the shoes, flip-flops, high heels, boots and rubber boots clogging up the entrance. I somehow managed to jump across, then took my motorcycle gear off and changed into something more comfortable. An unusual noise was coming from the living room, so I went in. It was minor conflict between two roommates about something I didn't understand. I managed to secure myself a seat, and watched what was going on. Almost all of the people in the room were taking turns playing *Call of Duty* on PlayStation 3. Only the dark-skinned Turkish guy didn't lift his eye from his plate of lasagne. When he finished it all, he added his plate to the pile on the floor. The way it looked, that pile had been there for days already. Great, I thought. I'd rather go on the Internet to see what mood my people in Croatia were in, and to say "hi" to my friends on Motori.hr, and, what's most important, to check the weather forecast. The sofa in the living room, which I had found out would be my bed, was just the right size for me, were I still 13. Nevertheless, I had no reason to complain. The motorcycle was taken care of, I had a roof over my head, I wasn't hungry, and I had Internet access. The perfect accommodation!

I have no idea how, but I woke up at ten o'clock. Not a soul was in the house. Everyone had disappeared. Even the plates from the night before were gone. How did so many people succeed in passing by me, and not waking me? I didn't know, and it didn't matter. So I took care of my morning business and got ready to go. That day I was to go to Thunder Bay, located along the northwestern shore of Lake Superior.

I took the road along Lake Superior, which is the largest of the Great Lakes. Mostly small towns dotted the landscape. I often stopped to take pictures. With the lake to one side and the thick forest to the other, these were images not to be missed. I could just imagine what autumn is like here, when the leaves on the maple trees turn to red and gold. A swarm of mosquitoes soon gathered around me, trying to attack me and my motorcycle. Documentaries about the Canadian wilderness usually forget to mention these little buggers. They were forcing me to retreat and leave. I was also getting impatient to see the western part of the country, so I picked up speed.

When driving long distances, I get carried away with the ride and eat less often. But when I get as hungry as a wolf, I stop, devour something, pour some liquid down my throat, and then when my "batteries" are recharged, I get going. About 100 km before Thunder Bay, I noticed signs along the highway about Terry Fox.

Terry Fox was a Canadian humanitarian in the fight against cancer, and an athlete. After a car accident, he was diagnosed with osteosarcoma (a bone tumour). His right leg was amputated. He wanted to raise money for research in order to find a cure for his type of cancer. It was on this very highway, where I was driving, that Terry had run his last kilometre before having to give up because of his poor health. He ran 5 373 km across the provinces of Newfoundland, Nova Scotia, New Brunswick, Quebec and Ontario. He passed away soon after. There is a memorial to Terry located just before the entrance to Thunder Bay, which I visited. Terry, with his great heart, undertook this marathon (which, today, is known as the Marathon of Hope) and succeeded in showing how you can do more than you think you can.

After visiting the memorial, I entered Thunder Bay and headed straight for my accommodation, where a friendly student named Kelsey awaited me. Besides the travel stories and "who knows what else," I think she remembers me for the amount of bread and peanut butter that I devoured. She was probably thinking to herself, "Does this guy even eat every day?"

THE PRAIRIES (7/6–12/6/2009) 2 300 km

After a nice evening in good company and a restful night, there I was on Highway 17, rushing towards Winnipeg, the capital city of the province of Manitoba. The weather was sunny, and the numerous lakes of Western Ontario were slowly giving way to the rolling plains of

Manitoba. At the entrance to the city stood a sign with a bison on it. Great herds of bison once roamed through this area. And because of human depradation, these animals have almost become just a memory. Today, though, this large bovine is a protected animal, and luckily, their numbers are increasing.

WINNIPEG

As soon as I reached Winnipeg, I began looking for the place I was going to stay, Couchsurfer Brock's address. I typed up St. Mary's Road in the GPS, the way the Couchsurfer had sent it to me. After having spent the whole day in beautiful expanses of space, I once again found myself in a city among crowds of people. I soon found St. Mary's Road and parked the motorcycle next to the building at the address, which turned out to be a restaurant. Realizing that this wasn't the place I was looking for, I walked around to see if someone was waiting for me or maybe looking for me. I walked and walked. Slowly losing the will to wait anymore, I thought about looking for a hostel. I went back to the motorcycle. A huge green pickup truck stopped beside me. Noticing my wide-eyed state, I guess the driver figured I was looking for something. A cheerful middle-aged man got out of the truck and came up to me. A fellow biker himself, he helped me find the Couchsurfer I was looking for.

"Where are you from?" he asked, just like many others before him had.

"Koprivnica, actually, from Croatia," I answered, assuming a familiarity that couldn't have been there, as if he knew the street I lived on.

"Interesting. Where are you planning to go?"

"I'm looking for an address and I thought I found it, but this isn't it. Obviously the guy I'm looking for gave me the wrong address."

"Do you have his phone number?"

"Yeah."

"Here, I'll give him a call."

The man called, and, really, he *had* given me the wrong address by mistake. "St. Mary *Avenue* is what you're looking for," he said, before hanging up.

"C'mon, follow me. I'll get you there," the other guy said, while walking towards his green truck. I turned the motorcycle on and followed him. Just a few blocks down, we reached the destination.

"That's it," he said.

"Thanks for taking me here."

"It was nothing, enjoy yourself and good luck!"

Brock came out of the building, seemingly out of breath. The first thing he did was apologize for having given me the wrong address. He had just moved into this building, and was still getting used to things. And since he did not own a car, he didn't have a parking spot. The only thing I could do was use the paid parking lot. I covered the bike with tarpaulin and stuck a sticker on it to show that I had paid. It would have been perfect if I could have just jammed my pet into the elevator and kept it on the balcony overnight, but the fact that I could see it from the apartment was something, at least. Just moments later, the sky blackened and it began raining. The rain falling and the thought that I'd need a good night's rest for the next day lulled me to sleep. I awoke on the floor in the living room, in my sleeping bag, on the fifteenth floor of a building, in exactly the same spot where I had found myself earlier that night. The view from the balcony was what I had expected. The rain had probably not stopped pouring all night, and did not seem like it would stop all day. Although I did not really feel like moving on, I decided to pack my stuff, put my "waterproof" boots on, take the elevator down to the lobby, and get to my motorcycle. I uncovered it and quickly put everything in its place, said goodbye to Brock, and got going towards the capital of the province of Saskatchewan.

MOTO TRANS PHILOSOPHY

Photography did not come to mind. The rain was pouring down and not giving up, and my Tenere was "purring" along wide prairie roads with no apparent end. Probably to get my mind off the weather, I started thinking about Canadians, about the ones who had come here a long time ago from Siberia, across the ice. Here they are known as the First Nations. How did they see these regions back then? What ideas did they bring? What thoughts and what hopes did they spread further south? Somewhere in and around Mexico they built pyramids. Did they meet anyone along the way? Carried away by my thoughts, I may have gone too far, speculating that maybe they had met and mixed with the immigrants from Atlantis, or with who knows?

I wondered how today's descendants of the early Canadians—the ones who came earlier, across the ice from Asia, and those who came later, in large boats—see themselves? As immigrant nations, immigrant individuals, or just as Canadians? Maybe I'm wrong, but I am under the impression that in addition to seeing themselves as Canadians, they have a feeling of belonging to the motherland. From what I see, there is a good mosaic of nations here today and the people here enjoy the wealth of this great land.

And how do Canadians see us Europeans? How do we see them? Some of my friends probably think of Canadians as lumberjacks and trappers that have in more recent times started playing hockey. It's possible I wanted to think about that some more, but these thoughts in my mind were being replaced with a thirst for a cup of tea or some other warm drink. Since I was all wet, soaking wet, I decided not to enter any cafés at gas stations. It needed to warm up a little, but not to dry up, so I picked up the speed and continued towards shelter in Regina.

I remember that day because of the rain and the monotony. I didn't write anything in my diary, except:

> With this wonderful rainy weather, I headed for Regina and got there totally wet. I took a shower at the Couchsurfer's place and right after that hit the sack.

I appeared at Paul and his family's front door two days late. Dripping wet and with my helmet still on, I stood at the entrance to their wooden house. My knees were stiff from the ride. The journey to Nordkapp without proper gear a while back was to blame for that. I rang the bell and heard someone approaching. Paul was surprised. He looked at me and asked, "Weren't you supposed to come two days ago?" Luckily, the

ABOVE: Crossing the Prairies.

guestroom was available, so he let it pass. First, I rushed to the bathroom and took a shower. That really felt good after a whole day on the road. This was probably the only time I took care of myself before my motorcycle. Or maybe I did put the motorcycle in the garage? I have no idea. It was that kind of a day.

During the night, my cellphone rang and woke me. I never turn it off, except when it turns off itself. My friend Niven was calling. I thought it was an emergency, since he was calling at three-thirty in the morning.

"Hello?"

"Hey! Where are you? What's up?" he said with a cheerful voice, as if we hadn't heard from each other in ages.

"Well, here I am in Regina, sleeping right now. Is there something urgent?"

"You're sleeping now?" he asked, in shock.

"Well yeah. It's three-thirty in the morning here. You've probably heard of time zones?"

"Oh yeah. I did, yes. Nothing, pal. Go back to sleep. We haven't heard from each other in a long time so I wanted to hear where you are."

"OK. Just next time, try to remember the time difference."

"I will, go on, get back to bed. I'll go get a beer."

"OK. Bye." I mumbled and hung up.

I fell asleep, probably right after the conversation ended. It was not until morning that I tried to remember whether the phone call had just been a dream or had been real. I checked the last calls on my cellphone. A call lasting half a minute at three-thirty in the morning was registered in the cellphone.

While writing this book, I sent this dialog to Niven by email to see what he would say. He called me on my cellphone after reading the email.

"Hello. Hey, I read what you sent me!"

"Good, so what do you think?"

"You wrote 'You've probably heard of time zones?' Like that I sound . . . dumb!"

"Do you really want me to look stupid in my own book? Anyway, that's how it went." I laughed.

"All right, then just put what you want."

"Will do. Talk to you later." I replied, laughing.

Everyone was awake and ready to go to work, while I was just getting to the bathroom to wash up. Outside, a beautiful morning was awaiting me. Thoughts about breakfast occupied my mind—or to put it better—I hardly wait to eat bread with peanut butter. Ever since I had set foot in Canada, I was hooked on peanut butter. A large jar with my name on it was in the kitchen. The only thing stopping me from fully enjoying this simple and delicious breakfast were the two large brown eyes watching me, as if accusing me of thinking only of myself. The dog I didn't even know lived in this house whined and whimpered until I dropped him a bit of bread.

After breakfast, I put everything in its place and prepared to continue my journey. My motorcycle gear and boots were dry enough, if not completely so. I studied the garage door opener, pressed some buttons, and, after a few minutes, managed to open the door. Refreshed, dry, and full of energy, I headed for Saskatoon. The sky was clearing into a nice sunny day in the distance, though soon after I got going, short and strong gusts of north wind kept blowing, trying to throw me off balance. At the gas station I found the chain spray that I use back home. The coconut scent was long gone, but so were the signs of grease on the parts of the chain that ought to stay lubricated while the bike is being ridden. Because of the short distance from Regina to Saskatoon, and the relatively quick speed at which I was travelling, in order to avoid arriving too soon, I stopped by an abandoned gas station. From the tank bag I took out a snack that my hosts had packed for me that morning. While snacking on dried fruit and nuts, I took time to take some photographs.

While at it, I noticed how the exhaust pipe had turned a nice brown colour. Had I been at home, I would've removed that right away, but now that I was on the road, that colour was like a trademark for Enduro driving. I continued on, riding on the gravel parallel to the highway in a standing position. One of the Enduro riders in Canada had told me that riding in a standing position is prohibited. But, if no one sees you, then it isn't. Therefore, I rode down the gravel until I approached a hill with a steep slope that could have posed a problem for my motorcycle and its heavy load. I slowed down and weaved between the piles of dirt to the highway, leaving behind a dirty trail of marks on the road—an imprint from the terrain tires.

SASKATOON

I arrived in Saskatoon with the same question as when I had arrived in Winnipeg: The address situation! Where was I staying? Once again, I didn't know if the name of the street ended with a "Road" or an "Avenue," so I tried to play it by ear, and succeeded. I was honoured to be taken in as a guest in the home of a First Nations family. There were about twice as many people living in this classic house than there were chairs in the kitchen. It was interesting to see how the youngest members of the family had decorated the walls in all the rooms. The adults did not always agree with the youngsters, I concluded, by the occasional reprimands given in what was to me an unfamiliar language. I spent my time there in and around the house hanging out with Ashley. We talked mostly about travelling.

The next day, thankful for their hospitality, we said goodbye and I got going towards Edmonton, in the province of Alberta. While on the road I realized that I was supposed to have tightened the chain that morning. I turned off the road into a small grove. I removed the gear, and from my yellow bag I took out my tools. I "unscrewed" the axle, and adjusted the chain's tightness. I put the tools back in the yellow bag, put my equipment back in its place, and got going once again on the road to Edmonton.

Absorbed in the surroundings, I was enjoying myself, until a thought came to mind: I hadn't tightened the screws in the axle! I thought about what could have happened, stopped along the gravel shoulder, and took the tools out once again.

EDMONTON

After a few thousand prairie kilometres, the landscape in Alberta seemed livelier. Here, I could surely spend a few months enjoying the variety this province had to offer. During the time of my visit, Alberta was the province with the fastest economic growth in Canada. The capital city, Edmonton, towards which I was travelling, is situated near the geographic centre of the province, near most of the crude oil fields and refineries. Over here, crude oil is one of the major economic factors.

When I reached Edmonton, I headed across the city's centre and reached the home of the two roommates who I was to stay with, and who were expecting me. One was from the Ukraine, and the other from Belarus. This was going to be good practice for the next continent on my itinerary, I thought, while waiting at the front entrance. The shiny door knocker was protruding from the flat surface of the door, beckoning me to knock. So I knocked. Anton, the Ukrainian, opened the door. A few moments later, the Belarusian guy, Oleg, raced over on his bike, introduced himself quickly, and then asked me what I drank. They meant alcohol, of course. I'm not too crazy about beer or wine, and as far as champagne is concerned . . . I don't even see its purpose. So only liquors were left, which the two of them, of course, had plenty of. Never having had an urge to drink much, I had never been drunk in my life. Sometimes I did drink a little, but rarely. This was one of those rare days. Soon, a glass with some vodka in it found itself into my hand. While talking about travels, mine and theirs, I noticed they were looking at me strangely. Aha, I got it, I was drinking too slowly. I drank half, and "saved the rest" for later, say, in the morning, for my empty stomach. Soon, my hunger overcame me.

I was told to just make myself at home, so I went to the fridge. This relic from the Soviet era was humming an irritating melody that just magnified my hunger. With great curiosity, I opened the fridge. The first three shelves were empty; only the bottom shelf contained any food. I took a closer look and saw that there was a big pile of sliced cheese and a pile of sliced bread. Not much of a choice, but cheese and bread are cool. I ate a few pieces of one and the other, put the rest back, and went to sleep.

The morning in Edmonton began with a noontime wake-up. I left the rest of my drink from last night. I'll never forget the preparing the motorcycle to leave because of the garage sale that was going on at the house next door. The whole front yard was loaded with stuff from basements or attics. Everything was probably a bargain, low-priced. With one push of the starter, the Tenere started right away, as it always did.

CANADA, WEST AND NORTH
(13/6–16/7/2009)
8 400 km

I was back in the saddle, heading for Calgary, some 300 km away. Riding the main highway, I felt as if I were on the most congested road ever. Cars were lined bumper-to-bumper. Later I found out that 80 per cent of Alberta's population lives along the corridor between Edmonton and Calgary, so that could explain why this stretch was in such a state. I stopped about halfway, at Red Deer. Wanting to eat some greasy "health food," I parked in front of a restaurant. There I recharged my "batteries" with a chicken sandwich and then continued further south. Soon, near Calgary, the queue of cars from the other direction seemed to be trapped. A collision had disrupted the freeway's harmony. By the way they were reacting, people in the drivers' seats looked pretty hot-tempered and angry. I thought such reactions were unique to my homeland, but obviously, people are people, and when stressed and in a hurry to reach destinations, they tend to explode easily, especially when protected in the armour of their "wheeled pets." Outside the confines of their armoured shelters, they actually aren't as bad as they may have seemed to be at first glance.

IN RODEO CITY

I was standing in front of the entrance to the city known as the home to the greatest rodeo in the world. The rodeo is held every year and during this week-long festivity, most citizens dress as cowboys and cowgirls. Calgary is also known as a popular destination for eco-tourism and winter sports. In 1988 it became the first Canadian city to host the Winter Olympics. And most importantly, it is the city where I had a great time and met two Canadian bikers planning to go on their own trip around the world.

I had met Tim online a few days earlier through Couchsurfing, and decided to send him a request for accommodation. He was surprised and amazed by my journey. Right away, he gave me his address. At first, the wide and calm streets did not look like a neighbourhood where Tim would live. I stopped in front of the house at the address he had given me, and with my helmet under my arm, climbed up squeaky steps to the front entrance. No one answered, although I knocked a few times, so I thought about alternatives. Maybe find some other accommodation? Back by my motorcycle, I took my cellphone out of the tank bag and called Tim. It rang a few times before the voice mail kicked in. I left a short message, got on the motorcycle, and headed down the street. I'd come back in half an hour, I thought, maybe he'd be home by then. I went to a hill just outside the city and admired the view.

My cellphone rang. I got back to the house. On the lawn was parked a very popular Bavarian BMW 1200 GS Adventure. So this was his house after all. I got off the motorcycle once more and climbed up the squeaky steps again. The door opened, and Tim came out with a camera in his hand. We shook hands and introduced ourselves. Right away he went about taking pictures of my motorcycle from different angles, all the while comparing it with his own. I removed all the equipment, including the panniers, since I was planning on staying for two days. I parked the motorcycle next to his, and then, at Tim's request, went around to the back of the house. He opened the wooden gate, and there I could see his favourite toy. What was it?

Well, on the patio between the garage and the house was a parked Mercedes Unimog that Tim used as his personal vehicle. The mean machine of a truck had a huge boulder in the cargo space, tied down with bungee cord. The boulder was there as a counterweight for riding in winter conditions. After I examined every detail of the Unimog, Tim opened the garage, which held a dune buggy that he had been working on in his free time for several years. Next to the buggy, in a wooden crate, was dehydrated food that the guys were planning on taking on their journey. That was one huge pile of food. I thought to myself, "Where are they going to pack all of that?"

Tim was allergic to certain kinds of food, which additionally complicated their journey, especially across the regions where there wasn't much variety of food available, so "eating what the locals eat" was not an option. That's why his motorcycle needed enough space for 120 bags of dehydrated food. After examining those bags of food, we concluded we were hungry so he suggested we eat at a restaurant near his home. We'd get there by Unimog, of course. Tim put on a show for me while manoeuvreing that humungous Unimog out of his little patio. Scratches from previous rehearsals were evident on the bent wooden fence, and on the corner of the garage door, which was partially chipped. Nothing serious, though obviously unavoidable. So that's how we drove the beast of a truck to the restaurant. We hardly managed to turn into the parking lot. Making a turn without having the last wheel climb on the sidewalk turned out to be mission impossible.

The restaurant we were at specialized in chicken, which suited me. While eating, we talked about my preparations for the trip and about interesting situations and occurrences that I had experienced while on the road. Tim wanted me to meet Cory, his expedition partner. Cory worked as a bouncer at a nightclub so that he could save as much money as possible for equipment and travel expenses. About one month ago, he had applied to work for the police department in Winnipeg, but had failed a test that was part of the hiring process, and so did not get the job. When he found out that he hadn't passed, he became angry and called Tim. He said, "Remember a few days ago we were watching the show *Long Way Round*? Let's do it! I've had enough! I didn't get the job, let's hit the road!" Later, Cory said that he just wanted to get away from everything for a while. Although, to me, it looked like what he wanted was more of a new beginning.

And there they were, about to put everything into action. Cory needed to sell a lot of his belongings in order to finance the trip. He sold almost everything he owned, bought a motorcycle on credit, and then there he was, standing out front of a club talking to me. He was dressed like a cowboy, like all the employees in the club, including the cowgirls, of course. Since I was not much older than the legal drinking age of 18 at the time, they asked for my ID and for me to sign a piece of paper three times. Inside, everything was cowboy style. We played some pool, but I had no luck with it, even though I had played billiards back home in Koprivnica almost every Saturday before heading on my trip. This bad luck was probably because of the cute cowgirls in the club!

After playing some more rounds of pool, we headed home at about three o'clock in the morning. I wasn't tired, but it was time to hit the sack. We got out of the club, got into the Unimog and got going. It's a great feeling riding in a vehicle that's a lot bigger than your average car. After just a few blocks, though, Tim realized his wallet was missing. He made a U-turn right away and sped back to the cowboy club. However, as we could have guessed, the wallet could not be found. Someone must have taken it. Bank cards, money, and documents were all lost. Just great. I didn't notice any special anger in Tim's expression, however. He repeated a few times how stupid he was to let something like that happen. And that was it. When we got to the house I suggested he call the bank to cancel the cards. "Good idea," he answered. I went to bed at about four o'clock in the morning.

A noise from downstairs woke me at about nine o'clock. Tim had woken up and was preparing breakfast. Driven by my appetite, I went downstairs towards the commotion, avoiding the mess and stuff lying around the house on the way down. Quite some agility was necessary, but I managed to make my way somehow. Probably such tidiness and order decorate most bachelors' homes. I hope he doesn't mind these words—he took me in and this is how I return the favour. This hefty guy with a few kilos to spare proved to be a great cook. He made a Canadian specialty: pancakes with fruit and the infamous maple syrup. I liked the taste of the syrup, but the amount poured over my pancakes was way too much. During breakfast, my host suggested he take me to the motorcycle shop where I could buy some things I needed. Of course, sure. Start up the Unimog, and get going!

Again, For Bikers ;-)

The shop with motorcycle gear, motorcycles and everything else that has anything to do with motorcycles—was huge. And still is! Blackfoot Motosports is a dealer for BMW, Yamaha, KTM, and Kawasaki. I was most interested in tires. In terms of the terrain tires I was looking for, I could choose between TKC 80, from Continental, and Karoo, from Metzeler. I bought the Metzeler tires for a couple hundred dollars, knowing they'd do the job just as well as a TKC 80.

While there, I checked out hand warmers, and bought some without giving it a second thought. I had already experienced cold conditions in the past, as well as riding in the rain, and the gloves that I had weren't warm enough.

Training for the
journey: lifting the
loaded motorcycle.

We lifted the tires into the cargo space of the Unimog and then went to the Simply Computing store, on West Broadway, where Tim worked as a manager. Tim had ordered shock absorbers, which had been shipped to the store. In Europe, I had never heard of Elka shock absorbers. But from what I could tell by the stories I heard from those who use them, they are among the best. I immediately felt the difference when I drove the BMW with serial and non-serial shock absorbers. The difference was obvious, especially when I tried to ride the motorcycle overloaded with equipment. It would have been better had I put other suspension on my bike, but I'd make do with the generic ones. We reached the house and immediately began mounting the hand warmers on my motorcycle. I made a deal with Tim to send my tires to his company's store in Vancouver, so that I wouldn't have to carry them as cargo, in case I decided to visit the north of Canada. I used these tires later, when I crossed Siberia and Mongolia.

We went back to the garage housing all the dehydrated food. I really didn't know whether all that food would fit on Tim and Cory's motorcycles. They probably didn't even know how much food they were going to end up with when they ordered it. While reading some of the ingredients, I heard a motorcycle park in the front yard. I put the package back in the box and went around front to find to Cory with his BMW GS 800 motorcycle.

His motorcycle was visually better looking than the bigger GS; it looked more symmetrical. He was already equipped for the journey: front light protectors, crash bars by Touratech, which were additionally strengthened and widened, plastic panniers that, to my surprise, proved to be great, and two canisters of fuel in front of the panniers. Maybe they were set in an awkward position, but because the original fuel tank held only 16 litres, these additional canisters were definitely necessary. The other minor stuff, like the tank bag, hand protectors, cooler protector, maybe weren't worth mentioning, since all that was necessary for such a trip.

When they saw my trademark climbing rope wrapped around the handlebars and the protruding parts of the crash bars, they decided to do the same, as did several other motorcyclists along the way. I had obviously begun a trend in Enduro motorcycle equipment.

Cory had come over so we could watch *Ultimate Fighting Challenge*. After Cory, Tim's friend Zack arrived. Since we couldn't watch *UFC* on television, we watched it on the computer, while drinking chocolate milk from a canister and eating mint-flavoured Mentos. We soon got bored with it, however, because even though the matches were interesting, we couldn't stare at that tiny monitor for long, so we decided to go to the movies.

Hit the saddle and ride to the cinema. The only film we could watch was *The Hangover*, since all the other films were sold out. We had to watch it sitting in the front row, since those were the only seats available. This was my first time watching a movie as if I were watching a tennis match. We were so close to the screen that we had to move our heads from left to right in order to see what was going on. After a while we even got used to that, but by the end of the movie we had sore necks. Our plan for the next day was to go camping at Banff National Park, a popular destination. This was going to be my first camping experience on this journey, since up till now I had always managed to find accommodation. For Tim and Cory, this was going to be a test ride with their motorcycles completely loaded.

It was morning and I got ready in a hurry. I left the unnecessary stuff that I had been pulling along in Tim's garage. Maybe they'd need it. I left the tripod for my camera, which I hadn't used at all, some papers and instructions, a plastic pump, and one yellow transport bag.

THE ROCKY MOUNTAINS

We headed west across the city towards the Rocky Mountains, then climbed towards Banff National Park. Tim and Cory filmed the whole stretch on video, with a camera positioned on each motorcycle, each helmet, and the best one in the tank bag. Five cameras total. I cruised, relaxed and enjoyed, while the Tenere got used to spinning at a higher rpm because of the new tires. Alone, I surely would not have been driving over 120 kmph. We approached a rest area, and the guys slowed down and turned in to the right. There was a scale for weighing vehicles there. Tim weighed his motorcycle first. I remember it weighed over 300 kg, even though it wasn't yet fully packed. Cory's motorcycle weighed about the same, but my Tenere weighed only 250 kg. So, my motorcycle, fully equipped, without spare tires, weighed about the same as Tim's motorcycle without equipment. Just as I thought we were going to leave and continue driving towards Banff, Tim started his motorcycle, moved forward a little, turned it off, and then laid it on the ground. He wanted to see if he could lift it without any help. Cory did the same, while I took my camera out and documented this idea that I had never thought of myself. We got going with new photographs in our memory cards and with new knowledge about how much our bikes weighed.

BANFF

The closer we got to Banff, the more we were enjoying ourselves. Actually, I'm speaking for myself, since for Tim and Cory, this half-hour trip from Calgary was one they'd done before. As we paid the entrance fee to the park, I thought about whether I'd go to the Yukon, too, since that's where the true wilderness is, and that was what attracted me. We reached the town of Banff, a very popular tourist destination.

We stopped in a parking lot and took out some packages of dehydrated food. Preparation is a piece of cake. You just pour a pint of boiling water into the bag and then wait about ten minutes. That's the whole philosophy. The food may even be tastier than in some restaurants. While browsing the grocery store in search of the best pineapple, I could hear German, Japanese, Spanish, French, English and even Croatian, that is, myself, while I mumbled my shopping list aloud. The campground we were staying at was near the store.

To keep bears out of the campground, electric wiring was rigged up around the entire property. We put up our tents. We weren't hungry anymore, so we took the luggage off the bikes and went to Lake Louise. It was pure enjoyment to ride without the weight of the luggage along the winding roads, where after each turn, we'd reach higher and cooler zones.

What a majestic lake! Its calm green surface reflected the surrounding woodlands and high mountain peaks. All year long the peaks are covered in snow that melts little by little, pouring cool clear water into the lake. No words could describe this beauty. The place is so breathtaking that

I could have stayed there for days. The past winter had been harsh and long, so there was still a lot of snow. After we returned to the camp, it started to rain. As we lay in our tents, the hum of the wind and rain became the music we listened to as we fell asleep.

Morning. Time to say goodbye to this place and to these great guys. *But without parting there's no meeting again!* We'd stay in touch and maybe meet again in Mongolia. That was a thought we shared.

I continued across the mountains to the north towards Jasper, accompanied by a moody weather characteristic of high elevations. I often stopped to take pictures and enjoy the wilderness. Huge ice caps, lakes, forests, mountains, animals, ice, waterfalls, hot springs, streams and rivers: all of this surrounding me, and me a part of it. This was the most impressive part of my journey so far, definitely. Not knowing what awaited me ahead of the next curve, I decided to slow down.

Cruising and enjoying the landscape, I came upon some sort of hotel-restaurant and decided to stop to get a bite to eat and to buy some batteries. I couldn't take my eyes off of the view of the huge glacier squeezed between two mountains in the near distance. Pictures on a wall in the hotel portrayed how the glacier had changed in size over the years. Though still huge, the glacier had shrunk greatly in size. I decided to go see it up close, so I grabbed my stuff and returned to my motorcycle. A man, also a biker, was standing next to it. We introduced ourselves. Ralf, a German with a Ukrainian last name, lived in San Diego, California, and was riding to Alaska. When I told him about my views on travel and what I was doing and how I was living, he was astonished.

"You're nineteen years old and you're already travelling around the world? You're really brave," he said.

We said our goodbyes, exchanged contact information, and I continued up the side road towards the glacier. When I reached terrain that I couldn't cross on my motorcycle, I continued on foot, leaving the equipment on the motorcycle behind. Hiking uphill in motorcycle gear is "interesting" (in other words strenuous). I got all heated up and unzipped my jacket.

While searching for a way to the lake, to the west I could hear a stream flowing, partially under, and partially alongside the glacier. I came across a sign warning about the danger of walking along the glacier on that side. Nevertheless, I decided to walk with caution along the stream. As I hiked, I tested the surface carefully before each step and avoided deep cracks in the ice. Soon I reached the edge of the glacier and jumped up onto a boulder that was poking above the ice. There I lay down on my jacket. While listening to my pulse and the sounds of nature around me, I gazed at the clouds above.

I don't know how I fell asleep, but I woke up feeling warmth on my face. When I got back to my motorcycle, I noticed a red face staring back at me from the rear-view mirror. This happened because the sun's rays are stronger at higher elevations. I put my helmet on and got going. At one lookout point, the whole world could be seen. I stopped to stretch my legs and take some pictures. Ralf was there, too.

JASPER

Since we ended up meeting a few more times along the way, admiring the landscape and the wonders of Canadian forests and mountains, Ralf and I decided to travel together for part of the way. Once we reached Jasper, we saw a campground to the left. But first we needed to get our "mustangs" to a watering hole, so we rode past the campground and stopped at a gas station. Our next stop was a store for some food.

The campgrounds that I visited in Canada charge according to the amount of space you use, so the price is the same regardless of whether you put up one or more tents. I took a ten-metre climbing rope, tied it between two fir trees, and used it as a clothes line to hang the wet tent that I had packed in my transport bag earlier that morning. While the tent was drying, I removed the panniers and used them as an improvised table and chair. A squirrel noticed I was eating nuts, and joined me. It trusted me and wasn't scared at all. Oddly, it almost ate from my hand, taking a few smaller nuts and eating them. It was interesting to watch how it ate. I gave it a Brazil nut, which is bigger than ordinary peanuts, hazelnuts or ordinary walnuts. The squirrel took it and scurried up the

ABOVE: **It's going to rain!**
RIGHT: **Roadwork ahead.**

ABOVE: Lunch break.
BELOW LEFT: I offered food
to one critter . . .
BELOW RIGHT: . . . while
another helped itself.

DOGS PROHIBITED

THE CONSUMPTION OF LIQUOR IN PUBLIC PLACES IS PROHIBITED

GATES CLOSED AT 10:00 PM

ATTENTION
Bear Activity in this Area is High
Visitors must stay on boardwalk and use caution

tree with it. It looked like that little critter had had enough for the day.

The tent was dry, so after filling my stomach, I got it ready for the night. Ralf had just finished cooking a quick meal and started eating. Darkness would fall in three hours, and I wasn't sleepy, so I decided to take a walk around the camp and see if there was anything interesting going on. After walking down a paved path, I reached a dirt path. Signs warning about the presence of bears could be seen all over the place. We were situated in a region with high bear activity, and were given instructions by the campground staff, and others, on how to avoid encounters with bears, and what to do in case of a close encounter. The main preventive action is not keeping food in the open, and dispensing of trash in bear-proof containers.

Ralf always carried with him a spray for repelling bears that is supposedly effective. The spray costs about fifty dollars and can probably be found in every vehicle from here all the way to Canada's Far North. After the walk, I zipped up my tent wing. The last thing I remember was Ralf sitting and typing up notes on his laptop. He had managed to somehow make room in his BMW GS Adventure for another battery, so he wasn't worried about draining all the energy from the "main" battery.

The morning in Jasper would have been nicer had it not started with a search for Ralf's key to the motorcycle. The tent was searched and scanned meticulously, as well as his jacket and pants, and the space around the tent, but the key did not show up or call out from where it was!

"Check your sleeping bag, maybe it's there?" I said to Ralf several times. He didn't listen. Instead, he continued with his detective work of searching for the key near the motorcycle. "I have a spare key, but I won't use it because I know the key I'm looking for is here somewhere."

Determined, Ralf did not give up! And after searching through everything one more time, he decided to lift the sleeping bag up. The key fell out. A smile spread across his face. Relieved, he could finally continue packing our equipment. My motorcycle was already ready for new challenges. We planned to ride together to Watson Lake. From there, Ralf would go north, and I would go south through Vancouver along the Stewart-Cassiar Highway. That stretch of road, from what I had heard from those who had travelled it, was even more interesting. People could

BELOW: A grizzly's signature.

Watson Lake.

almost guarantee I'd come across a bear, and said that some parts of the road were missing. I needed to be careful with fuel consumption, since gas stations were scarce. Sounded good. With that ride, I'd at least touch part of the Yukon Territory, and maybe catch a bear or two, with my camera, of course.

We left Jasper later than we had planned, so we decided to ride to Dawson Creek, and if there was enough time, go even further.

We rode north, towards the Yukon! I was reflecting while driving. The weather was sunny, yet humid. Though I had opened all the vents in my jacket, I was working up a sweat. We were riding at about 110 kmph. There were longer stretches of straight roads, and the curves were also longer, so I didn't have to slow down too much. After an hour, we stopped by a gravel parking lot in front of a wooden house.

A yellow school bus was parked not far from the motorcycle, so I took a picture. Hundreds of these buses had passed by already, but each time I had tried to take a picture of one, it hadn't worked. A lady came out of the wooden house and said we had come at the right time. Elk had just been spotted nearby, so if we wanted to, we could go look for them. Sure! Let's get this "hunting season" going.

We trekked through the forest. I descended down the left bank, and Ralf went right. While walking down the trail, I tried not to make too much noise and scanned the area in all directions, in order to catch a glimpse of any motion nearby. I came to the lake and could see Ralf tiptoeing along the shore. Apparently he wasn't having any luck either. Rustling could be heard as something approached. I turned around in a half-squatting position, straining hard to see what was causing the commotion, and saw children running through the forest. No catch this time, I figured. The children had probably driven the elk away with their noise. Well, good luck to them, then! I went back to my motorcycle, not expecting any surprises. And there weren't. Ralf also came back without any "catches."

We got our gear back on, put our helmets on, and continued into the unknown. I always prefer riding last in a line, or second if there are just two of us, because then I don't have to keep checking in my rear-view mirror for the biker behind me. All of a sudden, Ralf sped up, which confused me for a moment, but I continued riding at the same speed. Not only was his motorcycle twice as powerful as mine—I'm not sure how well mine would have performed at the faster speed—and besides, if you drive too fast then you don't have time to enjoy the view or the wildlife—for instance, a porcupine that I noticed and had carefully circumvented. In my opinion, Ralf was going about 160 kmph. He disappeared in the distance. At a bend later on, I saw him. He later told me that he had sped up so that he could drink some water and then continue driving without me having to stop. Or maybe my slow driving was beginning to bore him.

More and more, I was thinking about how to transport the motorcycle to Asia. I still hadn't solved that dilemma. I had some names and numbers of cargo agencies in Vancouver, but they were too expensive. Still, it was important to me to get to Asia; actually, to Siberia. In that part of the world, living expenses were much lower. If I got stuck somewhere along the way, I thought about how I could just spend the winter in that region. But since I wanted to get back to Croatia before winter, I needed to figure this out in time. I wasn't limiting myself or worried; I just needed a plan.

Often, good expeditions—mine included—are successful, despite a lack of funding. Some of the sponsors who had promised to donate money had obviously forgotten their promise, as well as forgotten me. Through Motori.hr's initiative, some motorcyclists from Croatia donated money to support me. I tip my hat to you guys, the donation helped, thanks!

I wanted to continue going north, across the Arctic Circle, but how? Maybe my practical Western friends, Cory and Tim, had a better solution for transporting my motorcycle. Why hadn't I thought of that earlier when I was still at their place? I sent Tim a text message asking about transportation options from Vancouver to Asia. He answered that they were going to send their bikes to South Korea, then by ferry to Russia, which was much more affordable and simpler than my idea.

We decided to send our bikes together and travel through one part of Asia together, also. With this, my trip became cheaper, simpler, and more interesting. Even though I liked being alone, I was looking forward to the company. And the only thing that mattered to me was that we all got along. For instance, back when I had announced my plans for the trip, AROUND THE WORLD, a guy came to me with the idea to join me. From his message "I'm crazy enough to go with you," I sensed his high adrenalin and affirmative motivation, but I politely "explained" that I do and see things a little differently. But Tim and Cory, the two guys with whom I had spent some time, and who were also planning a trip around the world, seemed cool and were skilled bikers.

The solution I had found to transport my motorcycle to Asia left me with enough time to travel to the Arctic Ocean.

Great! I told Ralf the news about my new plan. Now we could travel further north together.

We reached Dawson Creek during daylight and decided to keep driving north. But first, we stopped at a store so that Ralf could buy a jumbo-size pillow. From then on he didn't let go of his pillow, and every day I listened to him brag about his pillow. It was a bit funny. I believe no one will tell him that, though. We stopped at a Shell station and were trying to figure out how to fill the tanks with fuel without dismounting from our bikes. I lifted the nozzle and put it in the fuel tank. I pressed the lever several times, but the fuel wouldn't begin to flow. As I put the nozzle back, I noticed how others were paying at the register and then filling their tanks. So I got off the motorcycle, went to the cashiers, leaving my ID as a guarantee that I wouldn't disappear until I paid. I filled it up, paid, and took my ID back. Ralf started laughing when I told him what I had learned. Just as we were about to get going, another motorcyclist showed up.

"I'm lost!" he said, "Are you guys also lost?" he asked, laughing at himself.

The motorcyclist, whose name was Paul, took a map out of his tank bag so we could show him where he was at that moment, and in which direction he needed to go. Ralf showed him where we were, approximately, and gave him some directions. We said he could join us, since we were going in that direction also, but Paul decided he'd had enough of driving for the day. He lived in Utah, in the United States, a state I had originally planned to visit, but couldn't because I didn't get a visa.

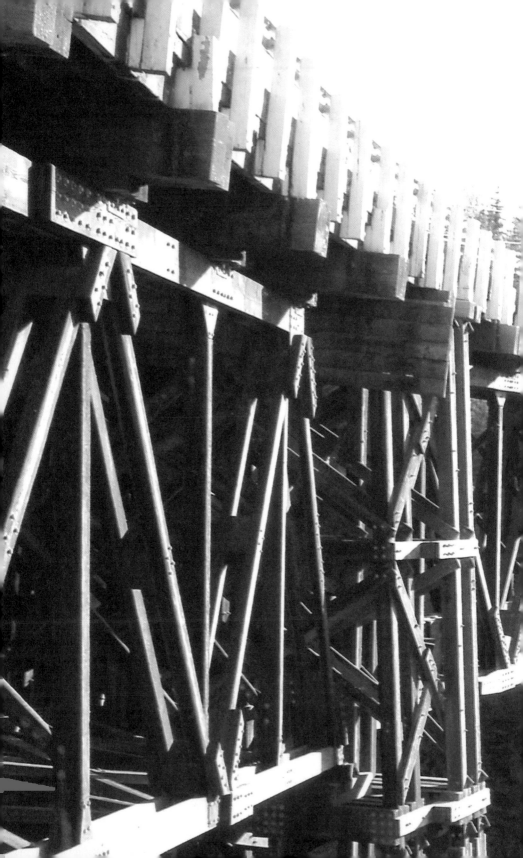

THE ALASKA HIGHWAY
(Dawson Creek–Whitehorse)
1 450 km

An old bridge, part of the Alaska Highway.

The famous Alaska Highway runs from Dawson Creek to Alaska. A few kilometres outside Dawson Creek, just as we were getting underway, we noticed an old sign for the Old Alaska Highway. Without thinking twice, we turned. The road worsened and soon became gravel, and as we both sped up, huge clouds of dust lifted. The road was paved again further down, where we came across an old wooden bridge that definitely deserved our company and photo session. I leaned the motorcycle against a wall, since the side kickstand didn't take leaning from the left to the right side too well. I went underneath the bridge to get a better look at that massive construction. I think most travellers miss this bridge because the sign isn't clearly labelled. All that's written on it is the name of the road and its length. Several times I walked to the middle of the bridge, admiring and examining that sturdy construction, which stood as a monument to manual labour. My eyes followed the river as I stared into the depth of the abyss below.

Driving onward towards Alaska, we left Alberta behind and entered the province known for its wealth of primordial wilderness: British Columbia. Since we had spent so much time at the bridge, we had to find a campsite or affordable accommodation soon.

Towards the entrance to Fort St. John, we found a few motels with prices we could afford. My priority was Internet access; everything else came second. Oh yeah, and I have to mention the shower that I jumped into right after I threw all my stuff on the bed. The Internet wasn't working in the room, so I took the laptop in one hand and a chair in the other, and walked around the parking lot in search of a signal for the wireless. I wrote to my family and friends back home, who woke every morning and fell asleep every evening with an atlas open beside them. I guess after this journey, they'll be much better at the geography alphabet game kids play on car trips.

Driving northward, we stopped at almost every gas station we came across, since they were getting fewer and farther between in these parts. Though British Columbia has a population of nearly four-and-a-half-million, this region is mountainous, with numerous forests. The few times we talked with the locals, they'd laugh at us as soon as we'd mention how we were armed with sprays in case of bear encounters. More precisely,

Ralf was "armed and dangerous." The locals said they trusted their rifles the most, and did not even trust their women as much. Pickup trucks, weapons and husky dogs were now part of the everyday scene. Crossing bridges the first few times needed some getting used to. Crevices along the lengths of these bridges were wide enough for the front tire to fall into, which could cause the motorcycle to lose balance. We drove carefully, and managed all right.

THE GRIZZLY'S GREETING

After a night's rest and another 50 or so kilometres, I was riding in front of Ralf, taking a long right curve at over 80 kmph. All of a sudden to my right, I saw something large trying to run across the street. Grizzly! I hit the brakes and leaned, making the motorcycle swing. I missed falling on my side by a hair. The bear, confused, ran to the middle of the road, changed directions, and then began running next to me. I could hear its panting and the thumping of its heavy paws on the road. Ralf was also confused. Unable to see what was going on in front of me, he hit the brakes and went to the left. The big furry teddy, however, decided to give up and went back, running. It was a close call! I slowed down a bit more, and, overcome with awe and grateful for the chance to see this wild beast, I stopped to watch it. With a long gaze, I followed the amazing animal. I was impressed and happy! "That's it!" I shouted to Ralf, filled with delight. Everything happened in the best way that it could have. I hope the "king" of the Canadian woodlands was not too traumatized by this experience. After all, we were guests in its land. Later, after all these impressions settled in my mind, other than the feeling of satisfaction for having had that contact, I was overwhelmed with a feeling of concern for this beauty that is cut off more and more by growing roads, and whose basic interests are, apparently, inferior to those of human beings.

Suddenly, black clouds formed in front of us. They had been hiding behind the peaks, waiting for us. Ralf stopped to put his raincoat on. I stopped a metre away and did the same. There was no shelter anywhere nearby, and no ideas for improvisation came to mind. We continued driving as if everything was normal. In less than a minute, a hailstorm started.

Through my raincoat, motorcycle jacket and long-sleeved shirt, I could feel the bits of ice massaging (in other words, beating) me. The blows to the helmet produced a unique melody. The windshield was vibrating and ice was bouncing off it in all directions. Properly punished for "who knows what sins from the past," we continued driving. The hailstorm turned into a rainstorm, probably to console us and, additionally, to cool us. The storm didn't last long, but it will definitely be remembered as a very interesting travel experience.

Since our sins had probably been "washed away" by the rain, and since the weather changes so suddenly in the mountains, the sun warmed us and then dried us in the end. We took our rain gear off. Personally, I would have kept riding in my rain gear, but seeing Ralf take his off, I did the same. A few minutes later and a few kilometres further, there the clouds were again. Ralf obviously had a lot of sins to wash, I thought! And that's how I, next to Ralf, according to military talk, became collateral damage. An innocent victim! We stopped once again and put our rain gear on. This time we were spared the beating, and after the rain fell for a short while, the sun shone. As a reward, we were given a unique view of a double rainbow, with the mountains in the background, one under the other. I had seen such a sight only a few times before. I stopped at the side of the road, looked behind me, and there was Ralf with his camera in his hand. He took a few great pictures.

We continued on and were treated to something you don't see too often, a beautiful demonstration by nature. Beyond the lake were mountains with snow-covered peaks embraced under the arc of another double rainbow. A miracle!

I watched in silence, feeling a breath of freshness from the north wind. A flock of birds in the distance joined this harmonious scene. Already accustomed to miracles, we continued, without saying a word.

Further along, we came across an elderly couple who obviously knew how to pick a good spot. At the moment, however, they were looking for their cat, which had escaped from their camper. We joined in the search-and-rescue action. Their four-wheel camping trailer, which was about a dozen metres long, and the truck that was pulling it, loaded with a jeep, were all meticulously searched. Every single corner! And then in the end we realized the cat was lying next to our motorcycles. That made this interesting couple smile, and us too. We couldn't figure out, however, how the cat had managed to pass by without us having seen it.

A sign for a gas station was nearby. We filled the tanks at every station, so this one was no exception. Selling fuel did not seem to be the owners' priority, though, since the parking lot was full. Cameras watching my every move reminded me that I had to pay first, then fill, then go back for the change, if there was any, of course. Not losing any time, since we could still ride, we decided to continue.

I was glad we decided to keep going because we then had several more encounters with wild animals. Just a few minutes after we left the gas station, I noticed a black bear running across the road, and then two more that had crossed moments before and that were eating grass on the other side. I watched them and slowly approached. They were just a dozen metres from me and their eyes were on me. I slowed down some more to reduce the noise from my bike, and coasted past the furry gang. Nevertheless, they decided to quickly disappear into the bushes.

Further down the road, a confused elderly man, who had come out of his parked camper, stopped me. He was totally lost. He didn't know where north or south was, nor did he know where the road that we were on led. He took a map out of his pocket and asked if I could show him where we were. Actually, he was looking for the way to Fort Nelson, which we had just passed. His camper was facing in the right direction, so I told him to just keep driving. To further reassure him, I turned my GPS on and showed it to him. The man thanked me.

Until the previous day, I hadn't seen a single bear. And this day I was really lucky. However, that wasn't it for the day. A bison was lying motionless in the grass, and we almost missed noticing it. This sight was a nice surprise. Since it was resting a distance from the road, and my camera didn't have a big enough zoom, I had to approach closer to it in order to take a picture. In case of some unpredictable situation, I was ready to shift into first gear and disappear in a split second. Then I noticed the heightened whites of its eyes, which showed the animal was alert. Better get going to avoid being chased around. Probably while escaping the throttle cable would snap, which would make for a fun situation.

LIARD HOT SPRINGS

The last rays of sunlight were just about to disappear. It was pure luck that we came across a small tourist attraction with a campground, the Liard Hot Springs. With the hot springs nearby, this campground is almost always full. Just what we needed! We went in and started looking for a spot to set up our tents. It was almost impossible to find a place; everything was full. The campground staff started looking around also, and would have probably sent us to another campground, had we not seen Paul, from Utah, whom we had met back at the gas station in Dawson Creek. What I couldn't figure out was how Paul had managed to pass us without us noticing. All day, we hadn't seen him on the road. Maybe he had passed us while we were hunting bears? His tent was at the last campground, and he was camping with a guy named Chuck, from Colorado.

"Well, looky here." Ralf said.

"Whoa guys, where'd you come from?" Paul answered.

"We're looking for a place to set camp, and can't find any. Everything is full."

"C'mon, set up your tents next to ours. We'll move the bikes a bit and make some space for the two of you."

"These two are with you?" the guard asked.

"Of course, they're always late," Paul answered.

We moved their bikes and set up our tents. I grabbed my swim pants and trotted down the wooden path across the forest towards the hot springs. Along the way was a sign warning about the possibility of meeting bears. Since bears also like playing in the hot water, there had been cases of people finding themselves in the company of a bear in the pool. Night fell. The closer I came to the hot springs, the thicker the underbrush was. Steam was rising from the pools, and the moonlight was the only light. The size of the hot springs surprised me. I went in and thought about how it would be nice to dip in and enjoy a hot soak after each day of riding in rainy weather. My muscles relaxed immediately, which felt good. Hot water surfaced at one end of the "pool" next to where cold water flowed, making for a perfect temperature for relaxation. Since it was already late, I got out after about ten minutes and hit the sack. Rain fell almost all night long. It is definitely better when the rain falls during the night, and not during the day while I'm on the road.

In the morning, I packed my stuff quicker than all the others so that I could squeeze in a dip in the hot springs. Once again on the path I stopped to read the yellow sign with the black letters, "Bear activity in this area is high. Visitors must stay on boardwalk and use caution." After a few minutes, Ralf jumped in too, while Paul and Chuck left and headed towards the capital of the Yukon Territory: Whitehorse. Our plan for the day was to pass Watson Lake. According to my old plan, from there I would have taken another route back towards Vancouver, and ended my stay in Canada. But, Inuvik was awaiting me!

YUKON: LARGER THAN LIFE

Several times already that day we had had to stop because of roadwork. I liked how there were a lot more warnings ahead of time about roadwork or even about damaged spots on the road, in order to avoid disappointing surprises. Before we arrived at Watson Lake, we came across a sign that read "Yukon–Larger than Life." Of all the pictures I had taken so far, the one of me in front of that sign is my favourite. It is said that this sparsely populated region, which stretches north to the icy ocean, has more bears than people.

Watson Lake, where we were heading, has a population of about twelve hundred, and is known for its Sign Post Forest, with numerous signposts, signs from other cities, and licence plates from all over the world. This "signposting" activity started back in 1942, when an American soldier working on the Alaskan Highway posted a sign with the name and distance to his hometown. Many others followed his example, and the tradition continues today. Over seventy thousand signs decorate the entrance to Watson Lake. I took a walk around to see if I could find one from Croatia, but didn't succeed. Maybe there is one somewhere, but the search could take a while. I noticed a lot of German signs, which didn't surprise me,

since I always meet someone from Germany on each trip I take.

Paul and Chuck who had left two hours before us that morning, were also there. Either they rode slower or stopped more often. I believe they stopped more often, though, since we met them again at the gas station some 100 km before Whitehorse. This time they were having lunch, so Ralf and I joined them. I grabbed a sandwich, ate it in a hurry, and then went to lubricate my chain because it was as dry as a bone.

A jeep with a map of a travel route painted on its side caught my eye. The route was from Ushuaia (Argentina) to Prudhoe Bay (Alaska). I didn't get too good a look at it, though, since the jeep was just pulling out of the parking lot. It was an interesting route I'd like to try some day.

A man showed up and asked about our motorcycles. He was interested in my motorcycle and where I came from.

"I'm from Croatia," I answered.

"Croatia? Never heard of it. Where's that?"

"That's a country between . . ."

"Yugoslavia," shouted someone who had joined in.

"Yes, we used to be part of Yugoslavia, but not any . . ."

I was interrupted once again.

"Aha, now I know where that country is and where you're from."

"Great." I answered.

This wasn't the first time I had had to explain to people Croatia's location to people I met. Once I even explained this to a man who had spent a few months in Trieste, Italy. He repeated several times that he had no idea where Croatia was, which surprised me a bit. Where do you live, man? Go figure. So I managed to draw a map of the world in sand using a stick and showed him Croatia's position in respect to the universe.

Time passed and we all got going towards Whitehorse. We decided to ride the remaining 100 km together. I drove first, and the others followed. We didn't stop until we reached some road construction. A bridge was being repaired, so there was nothing we could do but turn off our bikes and wait. The soft sand by the side of the road lured me to try out the bike on that kind of surface. But, I thought, I may get stuck in it, and I didn't feel like pulling my motorcycle out. The rest of the team probably thought the same. Once we reached Whitehorse, I called my Couchsurfing host and said I'd be a day late, since I was with some great company and would probably camp for the night.

Upon entering Whitehorse, we turned right after we passed the airport. We followed our noses and the instructions of passersby on how to reach the campground. It was large and filled with motorcyclists, so an exchange of stories was guaranteed. We got a spot surrounded by trees. I leaned the motorcycle against one because the kickstand wouldn't hold on soft terrain. Somehow, we managed to set up all our tents in a camping spot reserved for one person. We removed the panniers from our bikes and rode into town to get something to eat. I cruised around and found a few restaurants, but they were closing for the night. The further north we went in Canada, the longer the daylight lasted. The nighttime seemed to be disappearing. Our hunger was reaching a critical point. We convinced an Italian restaurant to work overtime for us, and ordered two jumbo pizzas. We let the waitress choose our pizzas. When I insisted they not add anything hot on the pizzas, the others shut up in surprise. I recalled the incident with the wasabi sauce, the tears and watery nose, and did not want to go through that again.

It occurred to me that most of the people I travel with are middle-aged or older when they start touring on motorcycle. They probably undertake this after their kids reach a certain age, allowing them more freedom to combine their abilities with their wishes.

The hot pizza got my stomach growling louder than ever. I don't even remember the last bite. I looked out the window and saw that darkness still hadn't come. I felt as if it were a lot earlier than it actually was. We returned to the camp after a great dinner. Satisfied and with a heavy feeling in our stomachs, we sat around the fire. Probably inspired by the primordial warmth, illuminated by the flame's glow, we started the usual "philosophical biker talks" about the meaning and meaninglessness of life, about everything, from Plato, Gurdjieff, Zen Buddhism, Baha'ism, Descartes . . .

Even more motorcyclist-adventurers arrived at the camp. All on Enduro bikes. I have to note that I didn't see any other kind of motorcycle in this great region. Except, of course, for the rare chopper that wandered into Northern Canada.[1] And it was present in the more southerly parts of the country, too. While walking in Kingston, Ontario, I was surprised to see many bikers on choppers taking part in a motorcycle caravan. About five hundred chrome motorcycles must have passed me. Many of the people on the streets, who were going about their daily business stopped to watch, wondering where the loud rumbling, which was disturbing the peace of their town, was coming from.

Let's get back to Enduro. During the previous night's congress of biker philosophers, I met a group planning on attending the adventure meeting, Dust to Dawson, or D2D, in Dawson City, at the border of Canada and Alaska. The D2D is a meeting of people that tour longer distances by motorcycle. They're probably all "philosophers" like us. I asked Ralf if he knew anything about it.

"Of course! I plan on being there during the meeting. Actually, I plan on being there a day earlier so that I can get myself a T-shirt with the logo." He answered quickly in one staccato breath, like an automatic machine gun.

Sounded interesting. Actually, it could be interesting. I was the first to hit the sack, because in the morning, I needed to get to the Yamaha service centre. I had to go mainly in order to change the tires, since the Metzeler Tourance that I had been riding back home, even before the expedition began, were already completely worn out. The front tire could go another thousand, but the rear one was done.

For motorcyclists ;)

As far as the longevity of Tourance tires on asphalt is concerned—I'm satisfied. I could travel over 20 000 km with them, which is good mileage. In order to make sure the guys at Yamaha Yukon (that's the name of the service station), had the tires with the right dimensions for my motorcycle, I called in advance and ordered the most affordable ones, whose brand I couldn't remember. Later I read the name: Kenda.

---

1 A chopper is a type of motorcycle that is either modified from an original motorcycle design ("chopped") or built from scratch in order to give it a unique, handcrafted appearance.

Once again, for everyone

In the morning, Paul and Chuck headed for Alaska, and I went to the Yamaha service centre. As soon as the store clerks saw me and my motorcycle, they knew what I had come for, since I had called ahead. They set the tires on the counter. At first glance, the tires looked all right, and they were, actually, what I had paid for: off-road tires that could be used on pavement also, but they seemed really soft. I could have waited a couple of days for them to order some other tires, but then I'd be taking up time that could be used for this interesting stretch of road. I was satisfied with the way things were going, and was glad to be where I was.

"All right then, put them on my motorcycle." I handed over $104. These separations from my cash were getting harder and harder for me to take.

While waiting for them to mount the tires on my bike, we decided to stay one more day in Whitehorse. To save some money and lessen my expenses, I went to sleep at a Couchsurfer's place while Ralf stayed in the camp. In the morning we could head for Dawson City. There, an interesting route awaited us: the Dempster Highway. I bought chain lube and oil, which I changed myself. After just 40 000 km, with new tires and new "blood" pumping, the Tenere got a second wind. The bumper stickers with the store's logo were placed on the panniers, and are still there today, with just a few scratches earned. I shifted into first gear and headed down the gravel road, then turned onto the paved road on my way to the Couchsurfer's home. This was my first time riding on such soft tires, and I felt as if I was going to fall at each curve, as if this was a whole new motorcycle. It swung a lot at the curves. Somehow I managed to reach my host's home and park the bike.

I knocked on the white door and Vincent opened it. I was planning on leaving some stuff at his place (read: heavy loads) so that I could ride burden-free to Inuvik. After a good rest in his guestroom in the basement, I prepared the motorcycle. According to Ralf's stories, the leg from Dawson City to Inuvik might be strenuous, especially after passing Eagle Plains, a large, rolling region of hills between the Ogilvie and Richardson mountain ranges, about 365 km from Inuvik. I needed to load as much fuel as possible, because, apparently, Eagle Plains might not have any, which could turn our adventure into a mission impossible. So I loaded two one-gallon canisters with fuel, and in the panniers, put tools, my first aid kit, the laptop, and some food and clothing. In my yellow transport bag I stuffed the tent and sleeping bag.

Off I went to Dawson City on my motorcycle, which was now about twenty kilograms lighter. The tires still danced their dance on the curves. I didn't have much off-road experience and was looking forward to finding opportunities for practice. The road to Dawson City was not paved all the way; some parts were gravel. We didn't even notice the stretches of gravel that were just twenty to thirty metres in length, and just raced through, as if they were paved. But then we started riding only on gravel, and caught up with a camper that was choking us with the clouds of dust spewing in its wake.

We put up with it for a while and just swallowed the dust before Ralf finally passed it. Well I wasn't going to stay behind and eat the dust, so I hit the gas.

A few larger stones projected from under the camper's wheels and hit my right leg, which, in combination with the new tires, caused me to swerve sharply. I was going 80 kmph and began wobbling from left to right. Someone watching would think I was about to fall from the motorcycle, really badly. I even thought I was, but by releasing the gas pedal I managed to calm the motorcycle and stop. I'm all right, I thought, and continued driving behind the camper, this time not too closely. When I reached the asphalt again, I noticed that I was more confident at curves. Still, I took care when I passed the camper, as if I was taking a driver's ed course.

Fuel was at the horizon. The motorcycles were thirsty, and so were we. I think I sweated out all my bodily fluids after having successfully calmed and stopped the motorcycle while trying to do something I wasn't yet confident enough at.

Three BMW GS Adventure motorcycles were also refueling at the gas station. One had a rear tire as bad as my old one. The biker had obviously miscalculated. Money was not the issue; he would have bought a new one, but they weren't available anywhere nearby. He would have had to order it ahead of time and had it shipped to an address for him to pick up. Since

ABOVE: **Hot springs.**
RIGHT: **Having fun with the motorcycle.**

Ralf was planning on changing the tires that he had had since California, he promised to give the unlucky biker his rear tire. That was actually the only solution. So we agreed to meet in Dawson City for a tire swap.

We stopped at a gas station some 40 km outside Dawson City. We didn't stop to fill the tanks; rather, to take a look at the road that awaited us: the Dempster Highway, measuring 740 km in length. This meant we had 1 480 km of gravel to Inuvik and back, which was going to be great training for my trip through Asia.

Near Dawson City, while passing abandoned buildings, I thought about stories of the Klondike Gold Rush. The gold rush changed the way people lived in these parts, and nowadays about 60 000 tourists flock here every year because of the city's design and its interesting history. In this town without asphalt—only dirt roads—situated along the upper part of the Yukon River just at the border with Alaska, time seemed to be standing still. With its small size, getting lost was impossible. Everything was built like out of some old Western, including the buildings, the streets, porches and the hotel. People carried rifles in their vehicles. First, Ralf and I headed, of course, towards the campground. We set up our tiny tents between some huge campers, most of which were from the United States. These campers were as big as buses. Americans do overdo it sometimes. I was glad I could use my laptop and wireless connection in the camp so I could contact my friends and family in Croatia. Once the tents were set up, it was time for lunch.

We got ready to manually change the tires on Ralf's motorcycle, since we couldn't find a repairman anywhere. Of course, the hotel restaurant was also in cowboy style. The swinging doors at the entrance were made just like those in old saloons. Besides the inevitable billiard tables, there was a piano in the right corner, and across from it was a dartboard. We sat by the counter.

While flipping through the menu, I noticed once again how the prices up north are pretty high. However, I needed a warm cooked meal and not the dry sandwiches that I'd been munching way too often. I chose fish and chips, hoping it would be good, and yes, it was! After washing it down with a glass of iced tea, I was bursting with energy. Of course, I had to have a short nap first, since after all, that meal was heavy.

The next assignment was "do-it-yourself" tire changing. We decided to change the tires at the gas station, since their air pump was much better than ours. Ralf put some gloves on especially for this event, and started removing the rear tire. Then the guy on the BMW, whom we had met a few hours earlier, showed up. His tires were already in bad condition. He also began removing his rear tire, and seemed, if you ask me, insecure. Two rear tires removed. Now it was time to remove the rims. We used the kickstand from my motorcycle, thinking it would help pry them off, but because it was so light, it barely helped at all. So for the front tires, the guys decided to use the kickstand from the much heavier GS.

This was my first opportunity to install tires using the mount. Of course, back while preparing for the expedition, I had realized this know-how would be useful, so I asked where I could learn something about tires. AnteK, from Motori.hr, recommended I go to Moto Jakopec, in Samobor. So I went to Samobor and the mechanic generously explained everything he thought I should know when going on such a great journey. Though not on my own motorcycle, I was now applying what I had learned, sure that this experience would be good practice for what was awaiting me.

Ralf had already manually changed tires on his hard Enduro bike a lot of times, so he was finished quickly. The motorcycle now looked more aggressive with its new TKC 80 tires. As a token of his appreciation, the man whom Ralf had given the tires to bought us cocktails at the café. The guys thought I'd be hanging with them, but they didn't know I was hungry again. So I gulped down the cocktail, thanked the man, and went to eat. Same place, same meal. Then, I retreated to the camp to sleep.

Before falling asleep, I thought about the distance between my homeland and the place I was at the moment. Actually, it wasn't much of a distance. The globe isn't that big. You could circle it in just a few years. Of course, not if you visit all the villages and go down all the streets in all the capital cities. But, if you spend a month or two in each country, then surely after a while, you could start investigating other parts of the universe.

THE DEMPSTER HIGHWAY
(DAWSON CITY–INUVIK)
750 km

On the way to Inuvik.

In the morning, after checking emails and folding up the tent, I did some push-ups to get my muscles going in a hurry, and then left Dawson City. We rode the same road as the day before, but in the opposite direction. Once again, I thought about ghost towns and the gold rush, but I also often thought about the road to Inuvik. It'll surely be interesting. I was glad that instead of the short visit to the Yukon that I had planned, I had decided to go further north. We reached a gas station at the intersection that led to Inuvik. Though we had refuelled in Dawson City and had only travelled 40 km since then, we filled the tanks once again to the brim, so that fuel was almost pouring out of the fuel tanks.

Two motorcycles were parked next to ours. One was out of the ordinary, a dog was sitting in the passenger seat. The dog's owner was just leaving the cash and was heading back to this motorcycle. He could see his dog posing for others as they took pictures. His travelling companion also returned.

Both of them, actually all three of them, had just tanked up and were heading in the same direction we were. Andrew, Les, and his dog, Sandy, joined Ralf and me, and we liked them, as if we had known each other for ages.

We got onto the Dempster Highway, anxiously awaiting the first signs of gravel. The wait did not last long. After a turn, there wasn't much asphalt left. The gravel and the dirt roads ahead were wet. Apparently, it had been raining here. This didn't surprise me, since suspicious rain clouds had been hovering above us all morning. I can't even explain how I felt knowing where I was at that moment. The landscape there is more interesting than any form of art. It was the end of June, and I could still enjoy the view of the glaciers, even at a temperature of 20°C, or maybe a degree or so cooler.

The glaciers amazed me, so I stopped by the side of the road and hiked towards them. Wide streams were flowing from them, but by jumping from stone to stone I somehow managed to reach the big blue wonder. The blue hue radiating from the glacier was going to disappear soon, since the melting process was at its peak. Luckily there was a huge mass of ice that endured the sun's heat long enough for us travellers to enjoy it.

Actually, our new friends, Andrew and Les, weren't particularly overjoyed. In response to my curious question "Why?" Andrew answered:

"Les and I live in Dillingham, in Alaska. The only way to get there is by plane or boat. Six months a year we've got ice, so this isn't any wonder to us."

Now it was clear to me. Lucky them, I thought. We continued our travels soon after the short conversation.

The sky partially cleared up, which was incentive enough for us to get going, and the numerous mosquitoes gave us an added impulse. Les stopped after about a dozen kilometres, because his dog, Sandy, wanted to stretch its legs again. I felt as if the same mosquitoes that had made me walk faster when photographing the glacier were now following me while I was riding. They made stopping for short walks impossible. Without warning, they would attack in great swarms. With improvised protection—a hat, bandana, and glasses—I managed to lessen the frequency of the attacks of these bloodthirsty buggers.

Ralf took a picture of me with whole families of mosquitoes, several generations of them, gathered on my hat. There were about fifty mosquitoes on my hat searching for any opportunity to quench their thirst. Later, I noticed how every single picture I had taken that day carried the proud signature of a mosquito—at least one or more. Even Sandy was battling against mosquitoes.

Since Autan and other bug repellents didn't work, the three most efficient measures were: first, riding at speeds of at least 30 kmph; second, heavy winds (which weren't blowing at the moment, so we were sweating heavily); third, rain, which had just started to fall.

The road became a gravel-dirt road, and in some parts was all dirt. Rain was increasing in strength, turning the dirt into pools of mud. Though I had ridden a jeep through such conditions before, I hadn't ridden a motorcycle. But I like taking on new challenges. Each little uncontrolled manoeuvre awoke a feeling of excitement in me, so I had to slow down at times. I lacked skill. Andrew was also riding at my speed, while Ralf rode his big GS as if it was a bicycle. Despite having to manoeuvre with a nervous dog behind him, Les was doing great overcoming the obstacles.

ABOVE: **No comment.**
LEFT: **Dusk in the tundra.**

What was wrong with my steering, then? First, Les and Ralf were riding in a standing position. I tried, but it seemed unstable, partly because the handle was too low for my height, and I hadn't installed an adapter for the handle height before the trip. But that wasn't the only difference. Les and Ralf rode at the same speed continuously, which was faster than mine. This made staying balanced on the bike easier. I tried it. It really did work. I saw that Andrew was also starting to figure this out. We were finally speeding up. The rain wasn't bothering us anymore because, when you're wet to the bone, it can rain all it wants, no one notices anymore. Mud covered the motorcycles, and they all took on the same filthy-grey-brown colour. So did we. Some dynamic terrain was up ahead, with a lot of hills, as if some Enduro master was watching from the sidelines and smiling while assigning us this route.

We rode about 300 km across extremely rigorous terrain before conditions finally improved. There wasn't any more mud and we began riding on asphalt again. According to the mileage, we knew Eagle Plains must be nearby. We stopped by the side of the road to wait for the others to catch up, and then headed for a "watering hole" for our bikes. Since the gas station didn't have any sort of roof or covering, we had to watch to make sure that rain didn't fall into the fuel tanks. Next to the gas station was a primitive service station, and the mechanic there recommended we sleep at a hotel instead of at the campground we had originally planned to stay at.

"We've got a problem with a polar bear," he said, "We saw him this morning around the campground. Maybe it would be better if you slept in a hotel or some other closed space."

I laughed to myself, thinking about how it would be if I owned a hotel around here. Just to fill it I'd invent two more bears. Maybe even pay someone to walk around in a costume. We all agreed to sleep in a hotel. Bear or no bear, I think we would have slept in a hotel anyway because of the heavy rainfall. We were soaking wet, and needed to dry our stuff. Besides that, no one knew I had a secret plan: if a bear did show, I'd let Ralf take care of it.

We parked in front of a hotel just one hundred metres from the gas station. As soon as I entered the hotel, the warmth made my cheeks rosy, and I became drowsy. We got a room for the four of us; two on the beds and two on the floor. Excuse me, the five of us—the dog was in the room with us. After showering, hanging all the clothes up to dry, and repairing a mosquito screen on the room's only window, we went down to get something to eat. The kitchen was closed. Luckily, however, the employees went out of their way to make us some sandwiches. I ordered two thinking that one wouldn't be enough. While waiting for them to prepare the food, I noticed the rain had stopped falling and the sun was beginning to shine.

We were near the Arctic Circle, so the curtains would need to be drawn from one end of the window to the next to create the illusion of perfect darkness, in order for us to get a good night's bed. I managed to finish my sandwiches before the others and went to sleep, since my fatigue was already getting the better of me. Soon the others followed. I fell asleep right away so Ralf, Les, and Andrew were left to decide who would sleep on the only bed remaining. I'm not even sure who slept where, and I don't think that's important anyway.

IN THE LAND OF ETERNAL SUNSHINE

In the morning, with improved skills for riding on rough terrain, we headed for Inuvik. The weather was great; sun-shiny bright! We were blessed with sunshine, with a few puffs of white clouds decorating the bluest sky, and endless tundra spreading the entire splendour of the North before us. Numerous tiny colourful flowers growing close to each other were blossoming from the low brush. Like a living carpet, intertwining and woven together, they resist the harsh winds and Arctic winters. Obviously, beautiful life lives, fights and enjoys, creating an opportunity for new life. The north wind was blowing strongly, keeping us cool. But since these strong winds rocked our bikes at times, we had to ride more carefully. Nevertheless, the wind protected us from the tiny buzzing pests. We reached the mark for the Arctic Circle.

I took my helmet off and felt how my companion, the wind, had combed my hair with its cool arctic breath. It really is rewarding when you can stop and do whatever you want to, unlike the dynamics of the previous day, when I broke into a sweat each time I stopped. The sign for the Arctic Circle, in addition to information about its geographic meridian, contained interesting facts, including the history of this region, tales of some colourful characters, as well as the history of the construction of the Dempster Highway. Of course, the aurora borealis had its own special section. Unfortunately we were here at the wrong time of year for this, so our chances of seeing this heavenly phenomenon were almost nil.

Maybe next time?

It was here that one of our team's motorcycles fell for the first time. Les had left Sandy in the motorcycle, and since the dog was still tied to it, when it jumped off, it pulled the motorcycle with it. Luckily, the hunk of metal, weighing over two hundred and fifty kilograms, did not hurt the dog when it fell over. The motorcycle, built to withstand great stress on the terrain, passed with flying colours, without a scratch. We comforted Sandy a little and continued travelling north. From where we were, the road ahead looked a bit different from the one we had ridden the day before. We had spent the previous day riding on a combination of gravel and dirt. Awaiting us now, after the rain and mud, was well-trodden gravel accompanied by a heavy wind. Later on, we'd unexpectedly stumble upon deeper and softer gravel. With the great speed at which we were riding, this change in the road made for some interesting manoeuvres.

Before hitting the road, we proudly pranced around, posing for pictures in front of the sign. First with one camera, then another. In total, four times.

We packed our equipment and got going again. It really was a pleasure to ride through such regions, especially when the motorcycles could perform well on terrain that they were designed for. Despite the heavy winds, I had a much easier time riding than the day before since my skills and stability had improved. The dust clouds didn't bother anyone in our group, because the wind was sweeping the dust from under the tires directly to the side. At one moment it was so strong, that wind, that it blew Ralf's universally famous pillow, wrapped in a black garbage bag, clear off his motorcycle. He couldn't believe it, because he had tied it down with bungee cord and hooks.

But that's not all. While Ralf was looking for the aforementioned pillow in the bushes, his motorcycle, which was leaning on the kickstand, toppled over from the force of the wind.

Something similar happened to me once, in Norway. This was around the end of September or beginning of October. Most likely the only motorcyclist at the North Pole at the time, I was spending the night at an inn not far from Nordkapp. I was awakened by the wind howling and by something beating on the window. Then a heavy thump sounded. Right away I knew it! So I went outside and saw my bike lying on its side. The motorcycle, covered under a tarpaulin, was supposed to be anchored down as well. I tried to lift it, but couldn't. Already I was soaking wet. The north wind and rain were mercilessly beating on me. I ignored their rage, and activated my own, which helped me lift the Tenere and push it to shelter away from the wind. After returning to bed, though, the thought came to mind: What if the wind changes direction? I knew I wasn't going to be able to fall asleep if I didn't do something about it. So I somehow managed to push the motorcycle through the narrow doorway and park it in the kitchen. Only then could I go to sleep in peace.

But, let's get back to the situation with the pillow and Ralf. The four of us got ready to lift Ralf's motorcycle, and though there was probably one too many for the job, we all pushed and lifted it. Ralf secured his pillow, so we could get going. We rode just a few more kilometres, then turned into an area marked as a campground. This looked like a good spot to camp on the way back, because a stream flowed nearby. Since our Alaskan friends were great fishermen, no one would complain if we had some fish for a meal. But first we'd need to make sure we didn't become a bear's meal.

Moving forward, we reached a ridge that officially marked our passage from the sparsely populated Yukon Territory into the even more barren Northwest Territories. Like the Yukon, winters here are harsh, and temperatures fall below −40°C. The summers here are very short but dynamic, since plants are forced to go through their entire life cycle in a

ABOVE: Les and Sandy.
RIGHT: Tundra.
BELOW: Under the glacier.

Region of tundra
and mosquitoes.

short period. What takes months elsewhere happens within weeks here. Only the hardiest, most adaptable plants survive, and the animals here depend, in part, on the plants themselves, just like everywhere else in this world. Andrew found a stone that the wind had shaped into a perfect sphere. It really is a miracle, the shapes nature creates.

We read on a blue sign up ahead that we had 270 km to go until Inuvik. There were two smaller towns before Inuvik, so we decided to stop and look for a store. We descended down a long hill and came upon roadwork. Even in these parts, the organized Canadians kept the roads in good condition. While waiting for the light to turn green at an intersection, I noticed how layers of brown mud were covering our motorcycles, especially the rear parts. The licence plates were hidden under a mask of mud and dust. I cleaned off the rear lights and blinkers, so at least motorcyclists behind us would be able to see what our intentions were. The light turned green, and the team of "travelling philosophers" continued across the expanse.

The traffic in this region was, as expected, sparse. We hadn't come across anyone going in the same direction as us. Just a few pickup trucks going in the opposite direction. Vehicles coming from the other direction, however, could sometimes be more interesting than you'd think. No one is crazy enough to drive as slow as 30 kmph on gravel. Here, everyone drives as if the road was newly paved and the paint was still drying on the asphalt. As a result, a few pebbles hit my torso, and one even hit the visor on my helmet. Later I noticed dent marks on the fuel tank from flying pebbles. After we passed the section of road being repaired, we decided it was time for a break. Next on the agenda, crossing the Peel River by ferry. I was surprised to find out that the ferry crossing was free of charge. The river definitely was a "bit" that the motorcycle couldn't cross without help, so I thanked the workers for their service when I boarded. After crossing the river, we rode along a dirt road all the way to the first town, Fort McPherson, where we filled the gas tanks and ate in a restaurant connected to the gas station.

At the entrance to the restaurant, we had to take our shoes off. Since guests didn't come often in these parts, we were an attraction. I was the only one wearing high Enduro boots, so they quickly became a fun toy for the little brown-eyed kids. One boy tried to put them on, but he couldn't, because his whole leg disappeared in the boot, it was so big. We filled our stomachs and the fuel tanks, agreed that this had been our last stop for the day, and got going.

We reached the river, where we had to wait for the ferry. I remembered that in the right pannier I had packed bread and peanut butter; my addiction since having arrived in Canada. So I spread a thick layer and enjoyed. The wind stopped blowing, so the mosquitoes returned uninvited. Ralf, Andrew, and Les also dug into the bread and peanut butter, but they didn't have to battle against pests, since they were wearing mosquito nets over their heads. They'd simply lift the nets, take a bite, and then lower the nets again. I tried walking briskly, but that didn't help. So I ate while the mosquitoes ate me and died while at it, and that's it.

INUVIK

We travelled the remaining 100 km to Inuvik without stopping. At the entrance to the city, we came across a large sign, with pictures of the animals native to the region, and a welcome to the edge of civilization: "Welcome to Inuvik NWT, End of the Dempster."

Happy to have reached our goal, and after posing for pictures, we went to look for a campground. Once in town, we quickly found what we were looking for. In order to save money, as usual, we took one camping spot for our four tents. I put some larger rocks on the wooden platform and tied the tent to them. Then it was the motorcycle's turn. After travelling so many gravel roads, I was sure the air filter needed to be checked. I removed the seat and air filter housing, which was full of tiny grains of sand. After cleaning it, I returned it to its place. In order to prepare for the return trip the following day, I stretched, cleaned, and lubricated the chain, since it had loosened quite a bit. Andrew and Les also serviced their chains, while Ralf simply checked his air filter. His motorcycle had a drive shaft.

Les asked the people at the campsite next to ours if they could watch his dog, Sandy, and we went to the restaurant that we had noticed earlier while looking for the campground. I had talked with people further south—Canadians—who were convinced that it is impossible to reach Inuvik even during the summer. They thought this region was eternally freezing cold and covered under ice. But, here we were, at the end of June, wearing short-sleeved shirts.

Here at the edge of civilization, where the mighty Mackenzie River becomes the Mackenzie Delta, and where the Arctic and the north edge of Canada meet, life is unique. The usual rhythm of day and night does not exist. It's eternal daylight for half the year, and nighttime, in the form of dusk, for another six months. The temperatures in the winter get so cold that you can walk on the frozen ocean. The winds are incredibly powerful; in these extremes only a few people can live comfortably, most often the rulers of the ice, the Inuit. Well adjusted to these conditions, they live relatively modest lives, without the need for too many comforts or constant happenings, as in urban parts of the world. Besides the opportunities for winter joys, they enjoy the northern light show known as the aurora borealis.

A modestly decorated restaurant proved to be the right choice for a warm cooked meal. We sat at a table with a view of numerous stuffed wild game animals. While waiting for the food we had ordered, Ralf and I listened to the adventures and mishaps that our Alaskan friends, Les and Andrew, had experienced while hunting elk and bears. The story I remember best was the one about how one of them once found himself standing between a mother bear and her cubs. It was a very uneasy situation that, unfortunately, did not end in the best way.

The food we ordered came relatively quickly. The prices here, for our wallets, were extremely high. The jumbo pizza that Ralf and Andrew ordered cost about $25. After filling our stomachs, we took a walk in town, and then returned to the camp. I took out my laptop and went to the reception area, where I could connect to the Internet. It was great to open Google Maps and see my exact location at this moment: the Far North of Canada. A place further north did not exist. It was already late, but we didn't notice it. The position of the sun—high in the sky—made it feel like it was merely noontime. During the summer there is almost

LEFT: **Strong wind.**
BELOW: Ralf: "I caught the pillow!"

ABOVE RIGHT: Welcome to where the sun never sets.
RIGHT: Dempster Highway.

no way to escape the sunlight. We took some pictures at midnight, and then I worked on the laptop till three in the morning before barely falling asleep under the light from the sunrays that were seeping into my tent from all directions.

RETURN ACROSS THE TUNDRA

Before leaving in the morning, I took a walk around, not really thinking about anything in particular, just absorbing the feel of this place. I was grateful to have had the chance to experience this beautiful region. After the walk, together with the guys, I took pictures of the colourful homes characteristic of the region. The bright and cheerful colours of the façades—yellow, red and others—must help keep spirits up during the winter months. One last look around, then I said goodbye to Inuvik, ready to head south with the guys.

A familiar road and blue skies were up ahead. That meant there was going to be much more dust, especially for the guy riding last in the group. The worst complication we experienced was when trucks would catch up with us, and though we were driving 70 kmph, these trucks would try to overtake us. So every so often we would pull over to the side of the road in a cloud of dust, and wait for them to pass.

And so, while the fine dust was filling our throats and lungs and sand was grinding between our teeth, without being able to see a thing, we continued travelling, exchanging places at the head of the line in order to get an equal share of breathing in the dust.

The best was watching Andrew when he'd ride first. Whenever one of us would pull over, he'd just keep driving. He never looked in his rear-view mirror, and so never noticed when we'd stay behind. Then we would have to just catch up to him, speeding at 70 kmph down the gravel road. By then I had adjusted well to the conditions; the only thing that surprised me was when I'd enter sections with deeper gravel.

We met a group of six motorcyclists also travelling from Inuvik. I recognized some of them from Whitehorse. They were planning on being in Dawson City at the D2D meeting, so we'd see them there again. Returning the way we had come, we stopped at the same place to fill the gas tanks. We were riding much faster, with fewer stops and breaks. We even picked up speed when racing dark clouds suddenly showed up from behind. Soon we reached Eagle Plains. We covered the motorcycles with tarpaulin, sat at the same table as we had previously, and ordered sandwiches. We even decided to take the same room at the hotel as before and spend the night. However, after eating our sandwiches, we looked out the window and saw that the clouds had passed us by. We got out, uncovered the motorcycles and got ready to continue travelling towards Dawson City. Along the way we'd find a campground for the night. Hearing our decision, a passerby spoke out: "It's gonna be dark soon, where're you guys going?"

Ralf answered, "Darkness will fall in about two weeks!" I burst into laughter. It took me a while to put myself together again and get my gear on. We got on our bikes and got going. I noticed how the road was a lot wider at one part, and then realized it was a runway for planes. How cool! This road is built for vehicles, and when needed, is used for the taking off and landing of planes. People of the north are practical. I couldn't figure out how I hadn't noticed this on the way up.

About 70 km from Eagle Plains, we stopped by the side of the road. We could see a good spot for camping in the distance. It was off the beaten track, with enough flat ground, as well as enough mosquitoes. That's just what we needed! We parked our motorcycles and began clearing the area of sharp rocks. Our tents were set up in record time. I went to brush my teeth so that I could crawl into the tent and protect myself from the mosquitoes as quickly as possible. Hundreds of mosquitoes were clinging to each tent, not to mention the ones I was spitting out while rinsing my mouth. With lightning speed, I put my toothbrush away and with a team of buzzing pests accompanying me, dove into my humble home. One by one I took care of them so that they could reincarnate into whatever they wanted to, and placed them all in my baseball hat. I could hear how the other guys were doing the same. And just as I'd calm down and get into my sleeping bag, I'd hear one more mosquito buzz while resolutely searching for something to drink. Smash! Got it! The tent would shake, making my friends laugh. I slept, but lightly. After all, we were in bear country.

In the morning, after folding the tents, we watched grizzlies pass by about one hundred metres away from where we had set camp. It was early in the morning, and we were already wearing our complete gear, including rain gear. The rain had honoured us with its presence and the mud had completely painted our motorcycles. Only the fuel tank still had some "clean" spots. Luckily, the sun appeared and warmed us up so we had dry and sunny weather during the last few kilometres to Dawson City. We reached the gas station where we had filled our fuel tanks just a few days ago on the way to Inuvik. We had successfully finished our journey along the Dempster Highway. Though they did look good all muddy, we washed and cleaned our bikes. This was actually necessary because the mud blocked normal airflow from cooling the motor.

We continued along the asphalt road towards Dawson City. Some bikers on Enduro motorcycles passed by, which indicated there would be a good turnout at the meeting the next day.

D2D

The campground in Dawson City was clearly overcrowded, but luckily for us, Ralf had made reservations and we had just enough room for two tents. We were to stay for three nights, which, after the Dempster Highway, would make for a good break. I set up my tent, took out my laptop, and called home. Around midnight, the owner of the campground came over and reminded me that it was late. Others were sleeping, and I was joking around and laughing with my friends on MSN. However, they had to put up with me a minute more before I retreated into my tent.

I would have slept longer in the morning, but the sauna in my tent wouldn't let me. Motorcyclists were still arriving and putting up tents wherever they could find a bit of free space. One more tent was now set up next to mine. A motorcycle was lying on the ground beside it, and a guy came out of the tent to look for some tools.

It turned out my neighbour and I shared the same name. Pete came from California and was just patching up his tube. During his last 500 km, he had a lot of fun with the rear tire. It had torn three times. Besides that, all the flaws of his Kawasaki KLR had surfaced and shown

LEFT: The colours of Inuvik.

their face during the journey. From what I could understand, the fuel was constantly leaking. Pete tried to fix that, but without luck.

Around noon, Andrew and Les came to the camp. They planned on continuing towards Alaska and stopped by to say goodbye. It was a pleasure to have met them and travelled with them these past few days. Great memories from the trip will stay with us.

The next day—which was also the fifty-fourth day of my journey—began with a meeting in front of the Dawson City hotel, the start of the D2D gathering. Registration for the Poker Run lasted until two o'clock. I asked if the people who were organizing the event could give me a few pointers. I thought it would be good to know the rules of poker, if I wanted to be able to recognize a winning hand. After paying and registering, I was given a piece of paper with all the cards in a deck listed on it, and a map with control points marked. First, I had to pull the top card from a deck and mark that card on my paper. Then I needed to find the other locations by motorcycle—in the nearby forest. This was definitely the best part of the game. I pulled out my last card on top of a hill just outside of Dawson City, where I could enjoy a view of the whole city. After pulling the card, I got a list of coordinates indicating where the joker was located. However, the person in charge of the game deliberately omitted the seconds from the coordinates in order to make it harder to find. Since I didn't have much of a hand anyhow, and it really didn't matter if I found the joker or not, I decided to return to Dawson City and wait for the others. Around half-past six in the evening, we all gathered at the main hall, where awards such as baseball hats, bandanas, etc., were being handed out.

The most interesting part of the evening was the announcement of the winner in the "Ride Hard or Stay Home" discipline. The recipient of this award is the person who has travelled the longest distance to attend the meeting in Dawson City. There were about 200 of us, there. Who had come the furthest? As usual, I didn't raise my hand, but Ralf got up in front of everyone and shouted:

"This guy here came from Croatia!" The rest of our team rooted and supported him. The host then asked me, "Is that true?" I stood up.

"Thanks, Ralf!" I explained my route, "I started in Croatia, then rode to Lisbon. From there I had my motorcycle transported to Toronto. I rode from Toronto to Halifax, and then back to Toronto so that I could make it to Inuvik and . . . here I am now with you guys." And there, without me having even planned this, my name was written at the top of the list on the statue in Dawson City. I appreciated the award. It was great to see such a positive atmosphere in the hall. Almost everyone was interested in the details of my trip. After dinner, motorcycle games were on the agenda. I watched and enjoyed. At midnight we all gathered for a group photo, and then went to our tents. Truly a great gathering and some great people.

TO WHITEHORSE

It was time to head south. I said bye to Ralf and the rest of the guys. The sun was still low when Pete and I saddled up our metal mustangs and got going towards Whitehorse. Ralf left for Alaska. We'd meet again somewhere, maybe at some gas station or who knows where. We rode out of that bit of heaven called the Yukon, and headed south. Several times the rain washed over us, and at other times the still-weak sunshine attempted to dry our soaked selves, which is all part of the chaos along the traveller's road. We passed a group of motorcyclists since we were driving faster than they were, but then they passed us because we stopped more often to enjoy the wealth of wilderness around us. This was good in a way, since these guys were willing to help us out of a situation that followed.

We were going about 90 kmph. Pete was in front of me. About halfway through a right curve, I felt my motorcycle jerk and then I began swerving. The chain broke—darn it! While calming the bike's dance, I heard a rattling sound from the rear tire! The chain was caught up and that pulled me to a halt. Somehow, though it looked like I was going to fall, I managed to maintain balance and stop. I pulled over to the right side of the road, got off the bike, and balanced it unstably on the kickstand. Whoa, that was interesting! I couldn't move the bike forward or backward, since the chain was wrapped around the rear sprocket.

Something similar had already happened to me before. Pete returned, examined the situation, then began unwinding the chain while I held my camera and documented what had happened. At one point, the motorcycle fell over on its right side, which definitely made removing the chain easier.

We transferred the bikes to the other side of the road since we were too exposed and vulnerable to oncoming traffic. We heard the group of motorcyclists we had seen before coming up behind us. They stopped. They had spare chain links, but my chain was damaged in numerous places and it was impossible to repair. We had about 130 km to go to get to Whitehorse, and about 30 km before we would get to the first house. Our cellphones couldn't pick up any signals here, and almost no cars were passing. Pete then said, "I'll tow you and your motorcycle. That's the only way!" I pulled out my blue rope, which I was glad to have since it had already proved useful in other situations. We tied one end of the ten-metre rope to the central luggage rack of the Kawasaki, and the other end I just held in my left hand. That way I could release it quickly, if necessary.

We got going. I expected we'd ride more slowly than usual. Sixty kilometres per hour is a decent speed for two bikes and two riders on one wheel drive. The moody weather continued soaking and drying us. Half-wet, we reached the entrance to Whitehorse. I needed to get to Vincent's place, where I'd be staying again, and where I had left some of my stuff earlier. We tried to improvise mounting my GPS on Pete's bike, but it didn't work. So I decided to lead the way and just wave my arms in the direction to go. A heavy rainstorm did its best to make this story more interesting the whole time. At an intersection, I recognized which way to go, with a little help from the GPS. We turned right. From there it was all familiar terrain. A long incline, roundabouts, and then we reached the house.

Pete decided to spend the night in a campground and head back to California in the morning, so I showed him how to get to the camp. We parted with a *see ya* in Croatian, "*Vidimo se!*"

I needed to get to a Yamaha store to buy a new chain. It was too late that day and the next day was a Sunday. So it seemed I'd be staying two or three nights. I took my pannier, and noticed how my "homemade" boxes were cracked along the edges. It would be good to fix those, too.

My Couchsurfing host, Vincent, spent his free day hanging out with me, showing me the city and its sights. In the afternoon, we loaded the motorcycle in his pickup and solved my dilemma as to how to push it a few kilometres to the service centre.

After we drove it to the service centre and left my bike there. It was harder than I thought it would be to find someone to weld my boxes right away. Most repair places said it would take a few days to fix. Luckily, we found a store that specialized in such service and was glad to help us. The repairman fixed the boxes and strengthened them as I requested.

Sometimes it's better not to find yourself in a situation that requires a lot of thought, although that's also part of the adventure. Unexpected situations allow people to rise to the occasion and show their full potential. These situations, which most people consider to be "problems," then turn out well, and leave behind dear memories to savour later on. I never really understood why some people use the expression "no problem" instead of "all right" or "it'll be OK" or other expressions with a more positive attitude.

The new chain on the old sprocket shone with new energy. The panniers were also visibly sturdier. Because of the high welding temperature used, the edge of the sticker with the names of some of my sponsors on it was partially burnt and looked more authentic than ever. I packed the stuff that I had left at Vincent's before the Inuvik trip, and continued as planned. Actually, without any plan!

I knew I was going to ride towards Watson Lake, and about 40 km before that city, I'd turn onto the Stewart-Cassiar Highway. As the morning progressed, the gloomy grey skies in the mountains gradually changed to low, white hazy clouds that accompanied me to Dease Lake. There I looked for a place to stay and took a room. I got my motorcycle ready for the next day, since it would be good to get to Prince George as quickly as possible, and then to Vancouver.

BEAR GLACIER

At 6:50 AM, the alarm on my cellphone rang. Rise and shine! The gas station, which was also a store, restaurant, service centre, café and local

LEFT: **Ralf:** "I did it!"

administrative office, opened at seven o'clock. My fuel tank was full and I could get going. The Stewart-Cassiar Highway, which leads to Southern British Columbia, differs in many ways from the road that I had ridden when I had gone to Northern Canada. It crosses the western, less frequented region of the Rocky Mountains, and is much narrower.

Thick forests and overhanging trees made visibility poor, so I rode carefully, half-expecting that some wild animal would suddenly run out. Some parts of the road were gravel and muddy, and there were almost no settlements. Trusting the Tenere's large fuel tank, I bypassed a big wooden service complex and gas station where everyone else was stopping and filling up.

I reached an intersection where I had to choose whether to go towards the town Stewart, at the border with Alaska, or to go towards Prince George. Of course, I decided to ride according to plan. The whole time, though, a thought kept bugging me: What should I do about the fuel? I realized I hadn't made a good judgment call. I stopped along the roadside and at that moment heard the sound of a motorcycle approaching. A man riding an older sport BMW stopped next to me.

"I was just filling my tank when I saw you ride by. I couldn't figure out why you didn't stop because there surely aren't any gas stations in the direction you're going for a good two hundred kilometres!"

"I have enough for about sixty kilometres!" I answered.

"Then it would be best you go back to the last crossing and head for Stewart. There's fuel there, for sure."

"I'll do that. That's my only choice. Thanks!"

He started his motorcycle and disappeared. I glanced at my watch and calculated how much time I'd need to reach Prince George because of the longer route. About 120 km more than I had planned, but there was enough time.

I drove down the road towards Stewart. In the end, I was glad it turned out that way. Along these sixty-some kilometres, I saw huge chunks of ice, snow, and the Great Bear Glacier, as well as trees that had fallen during an avalanche, and three bears. I wanted to photograph one of the bears up close. It was just a few steps from the road. Aware that the sound of the motorcycle was something unknown to the bear and might scare it, I turned the bike off and carefully lowered the kickstand. As I took my camera out, however, the bear ran away with amazing speed and disappeared into the forest. It didn't matter; I already had photos of his cousins anyway.

I reached Stewart, tanked up to the brim and went back the same way, once again enjoying the wilderness.

On the way back, I stopped at a spot where a large glacier that was squeezed between two mountain slopes was just calling me to come enjoy its company. As usual, in order to avoid unwanted encounters, I took a glimpse around, scanning the surrounding area. First looking nearby, and then further away. When I assured myself that I was alone, I took out some oatmeal cookies and sat on a fallen fir tree. As it melted, the icy tongue of the glacier had formed a turquoise-green lake at its base. The vicinity of the ice mass made for a somewhat cooler microclimate, which felt refreshing. My daydreaming led me to imagine a log cabin with a fireplace, and dogs waiting to be strapped to a sled for some racing about. I lay on my back along the fallen log, watching the blue sky and a hawk gliding in the wind, who surely did not care for me or my thoughts, but, rather, was thinking about its next meal.

Some time passed with me on the log, when, all of a sudden, I heard footsteps, but they weren't human! I held my breath and was all ears. Wanting to get up and stand, I sat up slowly instead. I had no idea where they had come from, but there they were. Obviously I wouldn't notice a porcupine or badger, but a man with a horse? Where'd they come from?

The horse and its master were approaching me. The sounds of human footsteps merged with the hoof-steps. They were already some thirty steps from me. When they reached about ten steps away, the man released the reins and did not heed his four-legged companion after that.

The man, a member of Canada's First Nations, middle-aged with hair braided in a ponytail, continued walking towards the log where I was sitting. He nodded his head and, without saying anything, sat nearby.

ABOVE: Dawson City panorama.
BELOW: Biker gathering in Dawson City.

RIGHT: **Repairing a broken chain.**

The noble animal didn't seem to care much for us, the lake or the glacier. Rather, it began grazing. I noticed it was a grey mare without horseshoes and its mane was braided into several braids. We sat in silence. All that could be heard was the horse grazing and taking a step every so often. The two of us sat without talking, each absorbed in thought and staring into the distance. I did not feel a need to say anything, and obviously, neither did he. It all looked as if we had known each other for ages, and everything had already been said. Using only a hand gesture, I offered him cookies.

The man accepted without a word, and took two cookies. We were enjoying the moment, tuned to the harmony of the environment. It felt good to not hear the usual questions: "Where are you coming from? Where are you going?" After a long while, he tipped his chin up, and with a light and wide sweep of his arm, he pointed at everything around us. I nodded. I felt what he wanted to say.

Sitting in the company of a member of the First Nations, in this interesting spot, where groups of the first inhabitants of this part of the world had once crossed, I asked myself how it would have looked today if Europeans, by chance, had not gone to "discover new worlds"? How would these first inhabitants be living today? What would meeting Europeans with today's level of technology be like if, over here, these people had continued living in their own way and tempo?

Would the experience be traumatic for the weaker ones? I believe it wouldn't. I feel as if opportunities and the level of consciousness are now different . . . or does that only seem so? And how would people from these regions have treated Europeans had they been able to sail to Europe's shores? Isn't all of this part of some plan? Or maybe there isn't any plan? *Aren't we all the same*, if put in a situation to be able to impose our will on others? This last question reminded me of an experience I had in the Himalayas in January of 2005, when I was about 15 years old. Instead of sitting in a schoolroom and learning superfluous formulas, I was trekking around Annapurna.

There, at the saddle of Ghorepani, I met and talked with a young Buddhist lama. We had reached an elevation greater than three thousand metres above sea level and it was pretty cold and windy. He wore a wool cap that covered his whole head, except for slits for the eyes and mouth. He had come from the valley, Kali Gandaki, from the direction of the remote kingdom of Mustang. It pleased him to hear me say hello with the Tibetan greeting, *tashi delek*, and he wanted to spend a moment with a westerner about his age. At the end of that interesting conversation, I asked the masked holy man to take his cap off so that I could see and remember whom I had talked with. "But why?" he asked quietly, as he got ready to continue his journey. This confused me a bit, and got me thinking. After saying goodbye and taking a few steps, a smiling face and shaven head did turn to me after all, then over his shoulder he called out, *"Aren't we all the same?"* Is this an answer to at least one of the afore-mentioned questions? I believe he believed that it doesn't matter how we look, rather, what's important is how we think, and what's even more important, what we do.

But let's get back to the glacier.

By focusing my eyes on the horse, which was now grazing just a few steps away, I returned to the here and now. The glacier and the lake were still there, but my silent acquaintance was getting ready to leave. He got up and addressed his furry companion with a few words, while adjusting its equipment. He waved to me, and then with a light step, led his pet away somewhere. I waved and watched as they disappeared into the distance. This meeting had affected me. I thought about this man, his people, their past and the events that had occurred. For a moment, I felt a knot in my throat. That happens to me sometimes. I took a deep breath and returned to the lake. "Why think about things we cannot change?" I repeated this to myself for the hundredth time. The present moment is here and by living the best way we can we can create a good future for everyone.

Of course, the thought of taking my camera out had not crossed my mind. I like photos as keepsakes, but the value of a personal impression and recollection as a keepsake to me are much more valuable. I rarely take pictures of people, unless the right moment for one comes.

JASPER - FORT ST JOHN -> 600 KM

FORT - ST JOHN -> WATSON LAKE
895 KM

WATSON LAKE - PRINCE GEORGE -> 1372 KM

PRINCE GEORGE - VANCOUVER -1000 KM

PRINCE GEORGE

The sun began settling behind the mountains, and a cooler wind reminded me that I should continue my journey towards Prince George. Because of the unplanned additional distance I had travelled that day searching for a gas station at Stewart, and also because of my stop at the glacial lake, I reached Denise's home in Prince George later than I had planned; a little after midnight. The next morning when I looked at the visor on my helmet, it wasn't clear to me how I had ridden at all. Bug upon bug, it was completely covered, and I couldn't see a thing. Not once had I had to clean my visor on this trip. Until then I had been able to ride carefree since the rain washed it and wiped it for me. This time, however, no natural rainfall would be of any help, so help came from the garage. There I found a Uvex spray for cleaning visors.

My host, Denise, an avid biker girl herself, had to wear protective goggles at work. So she had plenty of spray cleaner to spare. Instead of staying one day in Prince George, as I had planned, I stayed two. Riding for 1 000 km straight the day before had had its consequences, in that I was tired and I still had to endure another 1 000 km to Vancouver.

While eating breakfast, I thought about the sand dunes that I had noticed at the city's outskirts. So in the afternoon I removed the luggage from the bike and headed down a local gravel road. This was my first time riding on sand, which made for good preparation for what was awaiting me in Mongolia. The tire treads on my motocross bike were fit perfectly for the sandy terrain. I didn't start off gradually (which would have let me get used to the new terrain); instead I just dug in, pushing the gas to the floor and headed up the steep incline. But after weaving a bit, I ingloriously came to a halt about halfway up the hill. I couldn't go forward or backward. By swaying some I managed to get the rear tire out of the hole it had dug. Then I slowly turned the bike around and went back down the hill. It was interesting, but I obviously needed more practice. I continued on the flat ground and sort of figured out how to ride on sandy terrain. However, the chain housing had almost fallen off. It was hanging on by just one loose screw. I didn't have a spare one, but I did have time to get a new screw.

I parked at a big shopping centre that surely had what I needed. A few parking spots away I noticed a parked KTM 990 Adventure. The bike's owner approached me and asked, "Need help?" when he noticed me squatting and measuring the screw size and housing. We went to the shopping centre together and looked for a part that would do the job. All we could find was something similar but a little too long. The guy suggested we go to his place and shorten the screw in his garage. Once there, we mounted the housing and tightened it. It was as good as new! And better than new! I thanked the kind guy and left.

VANCOUVER

I headed for the city of Vancouver, my last stop in Canada. Actually, it was the starting point for the beginning of the next part of my journey. I cruised, without rushing, as I got closer to the coast, a bit surprised by the dry, almost half-desert landscape of interior British Columbia. Irrigation pipes ran alongside the road, for kilometres at a time. The farms here would have never succeeded if it weren't for these pipes. You could see the difference between the places where the water reached and those where it didn't. I had organized accommodation at the home of the President of the Canadian-Croatian Congress, Mr. Ivan Curman. I just had to phone him when I got to Vancouver. The address of the Croatian Cultural Centre was already in the GPS's memory, but I didn't turn it on yet.

Riding in the big city at sundown felt good, so I let the roads lead the way. Darkness fell, and I stopped for a moment only to realize I had reached the Croatian Cultural Centre, on Commercial Drive. I wanted to turn the motorcycle around, so I went down a dark alley and turned at about the halfway point. Two days later I found out that I had turned the bike around right in front of a service station owned by Ivan Curman.

His son, Kristofer, called me on the cellphone and tried to give me their address by spelling it out. Thinking that I understood, I typed the letters into the GPS as he dictated them. But that street didn't exist. I tried calling the number that Kristofer had called from, but he didn't answer. So there I was, sitting on the sidewalk, staring at my motorcycle and wondering what to do next. I tried to recall the letters that I had heard and was convinced were part of the street name. Since I didn't have any

Bear Glacier.

LEFT: Always at a crossroads

paper, I wrote the letters on the pannier and with the help of the GPS, found some possible combinations. Then, while squinting and straining my eyes, I stared into the little screen and eliminated the streets that I was sure weren't what I was looking for. Only one street remained. I read it aloud, and exclaimed, "That's it! That's what I heard!"

I started the motor and got going. It took me about ten minutes to reach the large house and knock on the front door. They took me in as if I was a member of their family, and I spent some very pleasant days in Vancouver. Social gatherings for Croatian-Canadians are held on weekends in Richmond (a suburb of Vancouver). I felt at home there. I noticed our emigrants are managing quite well, are well respected, and—what I especially appreciate—they highly respect and love their homeland. Some were surprised to see a motorcycle with a licence plate from Šibenik in Vancouver.

I phoned Tim and Cory a day before they were supposed to come to Vancouver. We agreed to meet in front of the Simply Computing store on West Broadway, at noon. The following day, I prepared my motorcycle for the next phase of my journey. I needed to change the chain and brakes, in addition to the most basic and necessary maintenance of changing the oil and filters.

A little before noon, I parked the motorcycle in front of the Apple store. Twelve o'clock passed, and the guys were still not there. For a while I sat and stared at laptops with the recognizable bitten apple before that became too boring, so I went back to the street to see if I could see two BMWs approaching. Soon after, two vehicles showed up from the right. First to show was the large GS that Tim was riding. I couldn't believe how loaded his bike was. In addition to panniers, he had transport bags: one big one in the middle and two big ones on the sides. Cory had plastic saddlebags and a 150-litre transport bag on top of them. Both also had tank bags in the front. I couldn't figure what they had packed. They parked next to my Tenere. Next to their loaded bikes, my Tenere looked a little unsightly. We entered the store and printed the documentation we needed for transporting our bikes. The motorcycles were going to be transported by cargo plane to Seoul, and then by truck to the city of Sokcho, where we would catch the ferry to Zarubino, in Russia.

In the meantime, a police officer had noticed that I hadn't paid for parking. I saw him through the window, but didn't heed him until Cory mentioned he was writing a ticket for one of us. We ran out to say that we were just leaving. He answered us with a question, asking where this brown Yamaha was from. Since he couldn't seem to figure it out from simply staring at the licence plate, he just skipped it and went on to the next motorcycle. Tim was the only one to get a ticket, and it ended up in the trash can right away. When we reached the airport, we looked for the cargo terminal.

We had notified Air Canada in advance, so, once at the check-in counter, we presented our documents and papers, and were let in. Right away, our motorcycles were put on the vehicle weighing scales. My Tenere, with all its equipment and empty fuel tank, weighed 273 kg. I saved a few kilos since the oil and sprays for the bike I had bought did not pass the customs check. They are prohibited in cargo plane transport. We paid and waited for the receipts. One of the clerks took the "Dangerous Goods" form, and corrected it in front of us. We couldn't figure out what was going on, but he probably knew what he was doing.

The whole process took three hours. Instead of packing the motorcycles in crates, we simply left them in the airport parking lot, hoping everything would turn out all right.

THE FAR EAST
(16/7–27/7/2009)
By bus 250 km,
by ferry 500 km,
by motorcycle
1 200 km

ACROSS THE PACIFIC TOWARDS THE LAND OF THE RISING SUN

The last day in Canada was definitely interesting. In the morning, after saying goodbye to the family who had hosted me in Vancouver, I went to the hotel where Tim and Cory were staying. Before I even entered their room, I heard the phone in their room ringing. Someone from Air Canada Cargo was calling to say that some complications had arisen with our motorcycle transport. The manager from the morning shift had noticed that one of the documents had been altered. The conversation was tense. I watched Tim, and could see he was angry. But I knew the problem would be solved. In just three hours we had a flight to Tokyo and then to Seoul! So we got in a taxi and rushed to the cargo terminal! Tim and Cory jumped out of the taxi and sprinted to the office we'd been in just the day before.

I stayed to "watch" the taxi, since it was our only mode of transport. I waited and waited. Every few minutes the taxi driver would say something in English with a heavy accent, and I would answer, "Yes, yes," even though I didn't really understand him and was trying to avoid communication so I could stay focused on Tim and Cory. Every so often I tried to see what the guys were doing. They managed to fix the situation, but the motorcycles would be sent a day later, which meant they might arrive late for loading onto the ferry for Russia. We were short on time to get to the airport. And on top of all that, we had to wait for a guy named Brad, who worked at the Apple store in Vancouver, to meet us at the airport, since Tim had forgotten forgot his cellphone at the store. We checked in and passed through security, then rushed to the gate that led to the flight for Tokyo.

As we sat waiting to board, together with all the other passengers, we heard that our flight was going to be delayed. Four hours more than expected. We weren't going to make it onto the connecting flight to Seoul. But, it didn't matter anyhow. What mattered was how the five seats next to mine in the waiting area were empty, so I could lie down and rest. I used part of the time to walk around the airport and look for something to eat. Air Canada gave us ten-dollar coupons. I used mine for food, since I had been fasting all day (that is, I hadn't eaten a bite). Then I returned to the five seats. But the seats were taken, so I sat on the floor and watched the clock, waiting to board.

Joining us in this waiting game was Michelle, a friendly girl travelling to Thailand. Waiting became easier while talking to her. After a while, my eyes became heavy, so I shut them. I was resting, but ready to spring up in a flash. A soothing lady's voice woke me, saying it was time to board. There, enough of Canada for now. Maybe there'll be more to say later if I remember anything interesting!

I remember the hours spent crossing the Pacific Ocean because of the uncomfortable seat on the plane. During one part of the trip, I could feel the knee of the passenger behind me on my lower back. I even watched a movie from beginning to end and listened to some music.

We landed in Japan at midnight. Air Canada paid for hotel accommodations. The next day we were to fly to Seoul. Michelle joined us, and we ate a quick dinner, then went for a walk in town. Actually, we were in Narita, which is, as we learned from the locals, a two-hour ride from Tokyo. While walking around town, we met a few British tourists who invited us to join them in a karaoke bar. The steps leading to the bar were only wide enough for us to go up one by one, in single file.

I opened the door to the bar, and as I entered, a cloud of cigarette smoke engulfed me. Mainly foreigners were seated at the tables and low-backed couches. We sat at a table in the middle of the room. The door leading into the bathroom from the bar was half the width of standard doors, and the only way to enter was to walk in sideways while bending down since the door was the height of my shoulders.

Tim was trying to convince Cory and me to order a song and sing. Cory gave in, but Michelle and I refused. He pulled my arm, trying to get me up, but to no avail. They decided to sing a song by AC-DC. I said I had never heard of that band because back home I listened to only local bands. I was laughing so hard it was starting to hurt. My stomach muscles got a great workout from my laughing—better than going to the gym. All my muscles were sore. Since it was already late and we had a plane to catch at six o'clock the next morning, we went back to the hotel. More tired than The Beatles singing their song "I'm so tired," I was half-asleep when I entered the hotel room. I slumped on the bed, and continued sleeping.

SOUTH KOREA

A little before six o'clock, the alarm on my cellphone rang. I glanced out the window. It was a bleak dawn. The bus soon arrived and we went to the airport. We were flying Korean Air, if I remember right. After landing in Seoul, we were examined for signs of the Swine Flu virus. They took our temperatures. At a currency exchange counter, I exchanged one hundred dollars for Korean money. Tim realized he was missing something. This time, after he had changed money, he couldn't find his passport. He checked all his pockets and backpack, and, no, it didn't just hop out. He headed back towards the plane, with the obvious intention of searching it, but then he came back. In the end, his passport was in his rear pants pocket.

We took a taxi to the hotel. Nearby was a war museum, so after taking some pictures in front of it, we entered and walked around for about two hours, examining the exhibits of weapons and watching short documentaries about the war between North Korea and South Korea. After we had had enough of the monotonous exhibits, we left the museum. Black clouds were sneaking up above us in the sky, waiting for the moment to surprise us. And they did. Never in my life had I experienced such rain. The thick, heavy drops were pouring so forcefully that within just a few seconds, I was soaking wet. A river was already flowing down the street in front of the museum. There we were in the midst of a monsoon, and we barely had time to run to shelter at a bus stop. Cars were bumper to bumper in a traffic jam, and some drivers were even turning their engines off altogether.

Already pretty hungry and wet, we somehow managed to pry our way through to a restaurant. Hurrah for restaurants! People were seated with their legs crossed on the floor around low tables, which did not look very practical for us long-legged westerners, so we sat where we could fit our legs under the table. I say we sat; actually, we stretched our legs out under the table, and looked at the menu. I couldn't find anything that suited me. This restaurant mainly served beef and pork, which I avoid, so like Tim, I ordered a portion of rice, while Cory took the beef.

We said goodbye to Michelle, since she was staying on in Seoul. Her plan was to stay a few days before continuing on to Thailand. She would spend the next three months in Thailand, training in Thai boxing. We met with Wendy, who was in charge of transport documentation, and did the paperwork for our motorcycles. Since there is a law in South Korea that prohibits motorcycles on highways, and the only way to get from Seoul to Sokcho is via highway, she arranged for our motorcycles to be transported to Sokcho by truck. We were to take a bus. Wendy met us at the bus stop, and waited with us until we got on. The rocking of the bus lulled me to sleep. I awoke when we stopped at a large parking lot at about the halfway mark of our trip. We stopped for a ten-minute break, so I went to buy some water while my friends went to get a bite to eat. The parking lot was full of people and vehicles; much more crowded than any rest area back home in Croatia. This looked like the place to stop for all hungry and thirsty travellers. I returned to the bus with all the others, but my co-travellers were nowhere to be seen. Just sitting in the bus and waiting for them seemed dumb, so I went out to look for them. I pushed through the river of people and looked in the store, the restaurant, around the kiosk, and then went towards the parking lot, but I didn't see them anywhere. I repeated this tour, pushing my way through the crowds. I didn't want the bus to leave without them. Figuring they had returned to the bus by some other route, I went back. When I climbed onto the bus, there they were in their seats. The driver yelled something. Obviously he was yelling at me, but I didn't understand him anyway. I had messed up the schedule, causing a delay of a whole four minutes.

We continued towards the coast. The rain started falling again, and then the sky cleared as we approached Sokcho.

CLOUDY SOKCHO

The city where we were to sleep and stay for a while seemed empty. Though there wasn't anyone around, there were hotels in abundance. We chose a cheaper one and took a room. We were really excited about our bikes' arrival. With the help of a forklift and workers from the storage house where we were to store our bikes, we lifted the motorcycles out of the truck and lowered them onto the ground. Then we pushed them to

ABOVE: The team in Vladivostok.
LEFT: This is how fish is dried in Korea.
BELOW: Road markings in Japan.

the storage house. All we needed to do was pump the tires, connect the batteries, and pour some fuel in the tanks. I did all that while Tim and Cory took care of additional preparations for Russia. All day they worked on setting up the communication systems we were to use while on the road. While working on the motorcycles, we noticed that the right fog light on the big GS was missing, and the light protector on the little GS was bent. One of the turn lights on my motorcycle was slightly damaged. It appeared that someone had been bothered by the sight of these great motorcycles, set for a journey.

The next day started bright and early, since we had a lot of paperwork to do. We went to the harbour, where we did the paperwork, paid the fees and were given the tickets for the ferry. On one of the forms, my name had been written as Petar Hrvatsko Rikić, as if *Hrvatsko* was my middle name. Actually, it's my nationality. *Hrvatsko* literally means "Croatian." This mistake on the form probably occurred because of the way the Croatian passport is configured: On the identification page, the line for nationality is located just underneath that for the name, so it looks like it could be a middle name.

We had some interesting fun trying to exchange currency. At the bank, each paper bill needed to be scanned through a machine before being accepted for exchange. Trying to get the dollars that I had kept all wrinkled in my wallet to flip through the apparatus drove me crazy. It seemed to go on forever.

After filling out all the forms and exchanging our money, we finally slumped on some chairs and relaxed until the time came to board the ferry. A clerk called us forward to load our motorcycles onto the ferry. I pushed mine aboard since the fuel tank was empty.

When I had no more strength left, about halfway up the ramp, one of the workers helped me push. I followed the hand gestures of the people motioning where the motorcycle needed to be set, and tried to push it forward. But, while I was trying to push it forward, two workers were pulling it backwards. When we realized this wasn't working, we made a deal about where to place it. And then once again: I pushed forward, they pulled backward. Obviously we were having trouble understanding each other, and were stuck in a comical situation. In the end I let the "qualified persons" take over, but only under my watchful eye.

We locked the motorcycles together and got ready to embark. All the passengers were lined up, ready to board, and we were in the line for a ticket check. But then the official who had processed our paperwork for the motorcycles appeared and said that a problem had arisen: "Check the email right away!"

The email was from Wendy. Some of the paperwork wasn't complete, so the motorcycles could not leave South Korea. Just a few minutes earlier we had been standing in line, patiently waiting to have our tickets and passports checked. Where'd this come from all of a sudden? We ran towards the ferry! Towards the motorcycles! I jumped over a locked fence and ran up the ramp onto the ferry, then began untying the motorcycle. Tim and Cory were breathless. They rode their bikes back to the warehouse, while I pushed mine. This situation wouldn't have occurred if it hadn't been for that unforgettable moment with the cargo company in Vancouver. The next ferry was scheduled in two days time, and luckily, our tickets were valid for the next trip. We went to look for another hotel, this time somewhere closer to the port. I wasn't happy about the fact that I had to pay for two more nights in a hotel, since I was watching every penny, but other options just didn't exist. While going down one street, I noticed how most people here sell and make a living from one industry. We counted about fifteen shops that sold the same thing: fish and fish products.

The key to the hotel room was the size of a tomahawk, and didn't fit in my pocket. So each time I left the room, I'd either hold it in my hand or leave it sticking out of my pocket. For the next two days, we walked along the rocky beaches, watched movies, and searched the Web for information about Russia, the paperwork required to enter the country, travel routes, etc. One evening, Tim prepared dinner: rice with a ready-made sauce. He cooked enough rice to feed the entire army. Our preparations were still underway for Russia. The preparation consisted of learning the language, or actually, learning words I didn't know, as well as the Cyrillic alphabet. It took me three days to learn to read Cyrillic, which I thought would come in handy, since we were going to spend a lot of time in Russia.

THE FERRY TO RUSSIA

The day we were to embark, we noticed another motorcycle in the storage house, which was also being loaded onto the ferry. It was a Yamaha XT660R ridden by Terry, from the United Kingdom.

Terry was really interesting, and talked about his plans to cross a demanding stretch in Siberia. Since I was accustomed to listening to Canadian English, it was unusual for me to hear his British accent.

We got on board and tied the motorcycles again. This time everything was ready, since we had no intention to stay another day in South Korea. The ferry embarked a few hours later than planned. All night long, we sailed towards Russia. The route avoided North Korea. Every so often, I would go out onto the deck because I wasn't used to such big waves rocking the boat. Just as the sun began rising, we arrived in Zarubino.

ZARUBINO: ALL ROADS LEAD TO SIBERIA

I got off the ferry and noticed tiny droplets of water stuck to my skin. Wearing just a short-sleeved shirt, I realized I'd need to dress more warmly here. Russia's easternmost region, just like Korea, is susceptible to monsoons. We unloaded the motorcycles and rode over huge puddles to the office, where we needed to take care of more paperwork. They checked our passports, dogs sniffed our stuff, and we were given the OK to move on to the next phase. We filled out some basic forms and successfully finished the forms.

We thought we were done; all we needed to do was to start the motorcycles and head over to another building for phase three. I sat on my motorcycle and started up, then noticed that the big GS didn't want to start up. Tim thought it was just the battery, and he was right. We charged the battery and moved on to the third phase, since phase two of the paperwork was just preparation for the customs officers.

We needed to exchange money for some Russian rubles, since dollars weren't very useful here. One note for those of you travelling to Russia: watch out for the year each bill is printed in. Bills printed before 2002 are worthless; Russians don't accept them. Eventually our little three-member team used those old bills to return debts among each other, passing worthless bills from hand to hand.

TOP: The motorcycles reached Korea.
ABOVE: Boarding the ferry to Russia.
RIGHT: Zarubino: welcome to customs.

TOP: First day and first borscht in Russia.
LEFT: Rules!
ABOVE: Riding in the rain with gloves on makes my fingers change colour.

After changing money, we spent the next three hours sitting or walking from room to room, waiting for the paperwork to be finished. Some may feel this is all unnecessary, but obviously, Russian administration remains a greatly valued means of work, carried over from times past. The estimated half-hour we were told this would take stretched out to three hours. We suspected it would take about that long too. Who knows, maybe people in this, the largest country on the rotating globe, feel that their land is so huge so they measure time differently? Maybe? Actually, why rush or improve systems when "we've got all the time in the world," and the old half-divine bureaucracy has already proven itself to be "adequate and efficient"?

My first chance to try out my Russian language came while here, in Zarubino. Before leaving Korea, I had studied a little by reading my Russian dictionary. This first effort didn't go too well, but it was worth something. My buddies didn't know any words in Russian except "hello" and "goodbye." I tried figuring out what the locals were saying, but I still had a lot of homework to do.

Happy to finally have all the papers in our hands, we got going, proudly counting the mileage on Russian ground. We stopped after about three hundred metres to tank up at a gas station. It took us about half an hour to figure out how to get the fuel flowing, and how to get the old babushka up from her seat in the bunker-like cement house to show us how Russian fuel pumps work.

First we needed to pay, and then fill. We succeeded in getting just a few quarts each, since the pump kept stalling. Somehow, we managed. It started to rain, and we continued our journey to Vladivostok.

At the first intersection, we stopped, because none of us knew where to go next. My knowledge of the Cyrillic alphabet wasn't enough to read the sign in front of us. I imagined a map of the world in my head, and our position on it, and then decided to turn right. It turned out to be the right decision. We rode along a worn asphalt road until we reached much more demanding terrain: gravel, with pothole upon pothole and a combination of mud and water. Not bad for the first day in Russia. This was definitely great preparation for what awaited us along all the roads we would travel in the near future. We released some air from the tires in order to adjust to the off-road riding. Vehicles going in the other direction blinked their lights at us in greeting.

Wanting food, we stopped to eat some chocolate, but the kind and friendly Russian soldiers that we had met along the way and immediately befriended, insisted we eat something cooked in a restaurant across the street. So I ate borscht for the first time in my life.

It's a soup made primarily from beetroots, often served with sour cream. Although I had always felt some sort of aversion towards that kind of food, the kindness and hospitality of these people helped me enjoy this warm stew.

Further along towards Vladivostok, other than the first few stretches of gravel, the road was better. For our first day in Russia, our experiences with the locals were very positive, and we were satisfied.

VLADIVOSTOK

By late evening, we reached Vladivostok. This city, with a population of half a million, is situated in the Peter the Great Gulf, the largest gulf of the Sea of Japan. It was founded as a military outpost by Russia, after the Russian expansion across Siberia east to the Sea of Japan. Vladivostok is also the last stop on the Trans-Siberian Railway. We found a hotel for the night. Our co-traveller, Terry, contacted a local motorcycle club called Iron Angels. Club members let us keep the motorcycles in their covered garage. In the garage next to ours were some sports motorcycles covered under sheets. I am really curious to know how anyone in this city could have such a motorcycle, since the roads are so bad. It would be much more practical to ride an Enduro.

Andrej, one of the members of the Iron Angels, took us for a ride in his jeep. Since Japan is so close by, the witty Russians often buy vehicles with steering wheels on the right side of the car, which makes driving on the right side of the street risky. It was interesting to see my Canadian friends in shock, since they were so used to strict traffic laws and mutual tolerance. Of course there are laws in Russia, but *Russians* live in Russia, which means the laws are interpreted accordingly and the driving style is completely different. No one stops at cross walks. In general, people ignore the speed limit, and overtake other cars despite a solid median. This was normal behaviour.

We saw and experienced numerous other similar situations. This wasn't new to me, but to my Canadian friends, it was.

We went by jeep to a friend of Andrej's to download and install some maps on my friends' GPSs. I could have installed the maps myself, but I thought it wasn't necessary since we knew which way we were going, and that was all we needed to know when riding across this corner of the world, where there are hardly any roads at all. In the afternoon we met with Alex and his wife, whom we had contacted through Couchsurfing. We decided to stay at their apartment. After going for a walk with them and getting acquainted, we reached the building they lived in.

The building looked as if it was in the last phase of wear and destruction. According to Alex, it was only about twenty-five years old. The stairway inside looked as if someone had passed with a hammer or mallet before we had come. They lived in a small one-room apartment. We realized we were going to sleep on the floor in the same room as our hosts. OK, we didn't have a problem with that. Except for the fact that with them in that apartment lived their pet, named Cat, who actually *was* a cat. Since Tim was allergic to cats, it would be too risky for him to sleep here. The people that we had met when parking the motorcycles in the motorcycle club's garage came to mind, and Tim phoned them. He made arrangements to sleep at their place, at the other end of Vladivostok. Cory and I would be in one apartment, Tim across the city, and our motorcycles somewhere else. None of us knew who was where, but with such hospitable hosts, it didn't even matter. Cory and I had the opportunity to try some *kvas*, which is a drink made from bread. I didn't like it, but somehow managed to drink a full glass and convince my host that he didn't have to pour refills. Tim's friendly hosts insisted he sleep in their bed while they slept on the floor in another room. If someone were to judge Russians just by the way they are portrayed in Hollywood films, you would be left with the completely wrong impression.

WHERE THE MONSOON PASSES

In the morning, we met once again in front of the garage where we had left our motorcycles. We got spray lubricant, said goodbye to the great people who had taken us in, and continued on our way towards Khabarovsk. The light rain that had been falling since early morning was now getting heavier. The name of this region sounded like it was in Croatian, *Primorski Kraj*. I had talked with Alex, in Vladivostok, and he had said that it had been cloudy for weeks, and that this weather would last until the monsoon got "tired." So it rained and rained, every day for the entire week. We rode through rain for hours and hours towards Khabarovsk. The vegetation was thick and green, which didn't surprise me, considering it was the rainy season. Villages in between the larger cities were few and scattered, so we had trouble finding accommodation. My fingers turned purple, since I was riding for hours with wet gloves on. Already pretty hungry and soaking wet, we found an abandoned building and parked our bikes inside. We cooked a warm meal on the gas cooker. It was food for our souls and bodies.

It's a great feeling to be able to take wet clothes off after having spent a day riding in the rain. It's even better when that is followed by a warm meal. But, there's nothing like putting those same clothes back on, afterwards, while they're still dripping wet. The sound is special: each step we took was like walking in boots through a bog, and when we started to ride, the air circulating through our wet clothes kept us cool.

We continued, following the road to Khabarovsk. After a while we turned, entering a village in search of a hotel. The soldiers we met along the way and befriended took us to the door of a hotel. We thought about staying here and drying our clothes, but we couldn't find any cover for our motorcycles, so, while still in our wet clothes, we decided to keep riding.

The daylight had "turned off" and the night had come. Bugs stuck to my visor blocked my vision so well that I could hardly see anything at all. We became part of a queue and went with the flow. Tim, who was riding ahead of me, began looking for a place to stop. He was fed up with it all and suggested we look for a spot to camp by the side of the road. But since it had been raining all day, there were mud 'n puddles to our heart's content! I didn't feel like setting up a tent on ground like this. We were tired, but I recommended we keep going. Cory agreed. So, although the rain just kept on falling, and we still had about 250 km to Khabarovsk, we continued riding. We'd manage somehow.

Luckily, we came across a village that had a gas station and a hotel with a garage. We took care of the motorcycles. Under such conditions, none of us cared what the price was, for we had been on the road, freezing cold and wet, for the past twelve hours. The hotel had just a few rooms available. We took one room with three beds, took showers, laid out our clothes and boots to dry, and hit the sack.

We made a deal not to ride by night anymore; that is, to be better organized, since night driving demands higher concentration and there is a greater risk of accidents. After breakfast, we continued on our way to Khabarovsk. The sky cleared up and we had a chance to ride in some dry weather. This was great, because our clothes finally dried out. Not even the heater working all night had been enough to dry them.

I'll never forget the primitive gas station where we refuelled. I was first, and while I was tanking up, Cory and Tim were riding in circles around me to avoid attacks by the swarms of mosquitoes. That proved to be an effective method of defense, since these little buzzing buggers are exceptionally annoying and persistent.

As we neared Khabarovsk, we came across some good asphalt roads, as well as the need for our first small repair. Cory noticed that a screw holding the pannier rack on Tim's motorcycle had broken. The whole right side was tilted, and the pannier and the transport bag were about to slide off. We stopped by the side of the road and used some short bungee cord that I always carried with my equipment, and secured the pannier to the frame. We noticed one more screw was loose, so we tightened it.

I noticed Cory was not doing "very well" with his jumbo 150-litre bag. He had overdone it, obviously! When going on long rides, it's better to place as little weight in the panniers or saddlebags as possible, to avoid breaking or bending the frame. In panniers, it's good to keep mainly light stuff, such as clothes, sneakers, a laptop or toiletry bag, while in the transport bags on the seat behind, it's good to keep spare parts, tools and all the other heavy stuff. I always make sure the heavy loads are as near the centre of the bike as possible in order to lessen the damage done by the vibrations that occur while riding on rough terrain.

SIBERIA
(28/7–7/8/2009)
4 300 km

KHABAROVSK

> Where there's no fear,
> there's no need for bravery.
>
> —P.R.

The city of Khabarovsk, the capital of the Khabarovsk Region, is situated in a swampy region by the Amur River on the Chinese border. By then we were accustomed to the local driving habits. While riding down the main street, we saw a large shopping centre. Tim and I went to search for some food while Cory stayed to watch the bikes. That was his job anyhow, since he was a bouncer. In the frozen food section, I noticed a container of ice cream with CCCP (which stands for USSR in the Cyrillic alphabet) written on it. I wondered if that container was left over from a long-ago era? Either the ice cream was that old or they liked to joke on their own account, which was highly likely. I noticed that joking around is the most popular form of recreation in Russia; people prefer to be spontaneous instead of following rules and regulations.

Cory and I picked up some ice cream and then moved on to the other part of the store. Compared to the day before, the weather was completely different. Yesterday we were riding through rain, and today it was so hot that we had to splash ourselves with water. We all knew that we needed to find a place to sleep that night, so we called up a guy named Alex, from the local motorcycle club called the Iron Tigers, but no one answered the phone.

We returned to the main road and kept going. To the left I noticed a bikers' café. I was riding last in line, so I sped up and told the guys to follow me. We stopped in front of the café and began a conversation with Elena, the owner of the café. Just then someone called Tim on the cellphone. We figured it was Alex, whom we had called just a few minutes ago. Since Tim didn't understand a word, he just hung up. Elena helped by phoning her husband. He said he'd be there in a minute. Turns out her husband's name was Alex and he was a biker. Hmm . . . ? Tim took his cellphone out and showed Elena the number from the last call. "Oh yeah, that's my husband!" she said.

In a city of about 800 000 people, we had managed to run into exactly the person we were looking for. After we had a drink in the café, Alex showed up on his motorcycle. Next to the café was a shop specializing in tire repair and replacement, so for a great price we changed the tires on the bikes. Though the tires I had were still good, I mounted some Metzeler Karoo tires and prepared the bike for the upcoming terrain.

I hadn't expected such a lively and nice city in faraway Siberia. The guys from the motorcycle club, Iron Tigers, really went out of their way for us. I could tell they were proud of their city and respected it. With such great company in Khabarovsk, we stayed a day longer than planned. Actually, we had two unforgettable days there. Who'd wanna leave? This used to be a place where people were sent to work camps, in exile. But as far as I could see, everything is OK now. Obviously, things have changed in faraway Siberia. Actually, it's not far away, because, obviously, I am here too, I thought. Now, something else is far away.

From what I could see, a great number of the sacred buildings in the city seemed relatively new or renewed. That surely showed that people cared about this place. Also, not only is Khabarovsk a beautiful city, it's a city with beautiful women. You can't not notice! I began thinking about how I could stay here for a while. Maybe until the end of summer? But our technician, Cory, brought me back to reality. He had gotten rid of his huge transport bag and got two new ones that were more ball-shaped, so they were almost impossible to strap onto the motorcycle. Besides the unusual shape for motorcycle gear, the stuff packed inside was almost poking its way out to who knows where. Maybe it didn't want to be a part of the adventure anymore? Who knows? I couldn't help it anymore; I started choking with laughter. Cory was a bit offended, but what could I say?

We would have loved to stay, but it was time to leave for the Chita Region. Police controls were stationed at all entrances and exits to the city, and as we left Khabarovsk, we were stopped for the first time. They quickly checked our papers then let us go. I'm sure they weren't really that zealous or keenly devoted to the job, and had stopped us out of curiosity only to see where we were coming from and where we were headed.

After leaving Khabarovsk, the further we went, the more forests we crossed. Long stretches of roads were gravel combined with scattered sections of asphalt. I noticed the next leg of muddy gravel looked like it was being prepared for asphalt, however, so I figured my biker-adventure across the Far East would soon turn into a tourist ride. It was interesting how sparse the signage was on the roads, especially where roadwork was underway. Imagine riding at about 100 kmph on asphalt and then, without warning, you suddenly dig into deep gravel and have to manoeuvre like crazy to keep balance and not fall. We began driving more carefully and watching out for such situations.

After a whole day on the road, we reached a little village. A guy on a motorcycle showed us where we could find a hotel for truckers. The price was OK, but the conditions were unimaginable. I couldn't fit on the bed; not even if I lay diagonally across it. There was no shower, and the outhouse was infested with what seemed like every type of insect in this region, so we decided to sleep in our tents. At least they were cleaner and we'd be saving money.

We moved on and after about half an hour, started looking for a spot to set up camp. To protect our privacy, and to avoid interrupting the daily life of the locals, we always looked for camping spots away from the main roads. Depending on the terrain, at times we had to hike further than we'd hoped, which just added to the experience. We turned off the road, entering a forest trail, and then realized we were sinking deeper and deeper in mud.

"I think it'd be better to turn around and go to the other side of the street." I said. So we somehow managed to get ourselves out of the muddy trail that obviously hadn't been in use for a long while, and headed for some high grass. Suddenly my front tire got jammed in a hole that had been waiting just for me for who knows how long. I fell off my bike onto the left side. Since the terrain was just getting worse the further we went, we decided to set up camp where I had fallen. We stomped on the grass to flatten it so we could set up the tents. I won't describe the number of insects again, but maybe it would be good to write about how some

TOP: Moscow – Vladivostok.
ABOVE: Boardwalk along the river Amur in Khabarovsk.

Khabarovsk.

parts of the motorcycles seemed to attract the bugs and were completely covered with flies, wasps, grasshoppers and mosquitoes. One swarm was attacking the remains of their insect relatives, which were stuck to the bikes, while a greater swarm was attacking us. Thousands of them were crawling and flying towards us. Insect repellent was useless. Neither Autan nor any other similar substance could help.

The high humidity was also unbearable. Nothing unusual for this part of the world, though. Sticky from sweat, dust and the remains of various pests, we dove into our tents. Since we were in the habitat of the Siberian tiger, I began thinking about them. I knew there weren't many left, and was wondering whether they would survive, and for how long, if they do?

DAY 2

We planned to get going as early as possible, but in the end, we woke up at about eleven o'clock. So we packed up our tents in a hurry and tried to start the motorcycles. I turned the motorcycle around, manoeuvred some, and prepared for takeoff. The Calgary Cowboys, instead of riding towards the sunset, rode into the high grass in search of a good place to turn around.

A motorcycle sounded stuck, so I ran to the source of the noise. I followed the noise and descended down a valley, only to see Cory trying to get his bike out of a bog. At the same time, I felt myself sinking. A swamp! That explained all the insects and who knows what more in this area. Good thing, at least, that Tim didn't go further into the field where the bog was hiding. We removed all of the luggage from Cory's bike. It was stuck deep in the mud, so we had to pull, push, carry, huff and puff. We carried the bike over the toughest part. This process lasted almost an hour. I think it would be good next time to check out the terrain in advance.

I often rode last in the group, since that suited me. That way, I didn't have to look over my shoulder or in the rear-view mirror. During what was the early phase of my Canadian friends' journey, equipment would fall from their motorcycles at times, especially from Tim's. Spare fuel canisters, water bottles, even a pineapple. The best was when his spare helmet visors fell out. I nearly ran over them because I didn't want to risk manoeuvring along the stretch of gravel and falling.

I turned to Cory with a quizzical expression on my face.

"That's Tim, he doesn't have time to bother with minor details." he said with a smile, while shrugging his shoulders and raising a brow. We laughed together.

In addition to this, my co-travellers often needed to stop by the side of the road. They were constantly making adjustments to their motorcycles, it seemed. In the beginning, I was bothered by the way Cory always shrugged his shoulders. But then I got used to it. After all, we were a team and we were riding together. We worked together and helped each other out, joking and fooling around without getting angry. So why was I bothered by behaviour that differed from mine? Should everyone think and act the way I do so that I could be satisfied? They probably noticed faults in me, too. Some of the things I did probably seemed strange to them, and I'm sure I'll hear about that when they read this part of the book. Maybe tolerance was a lesson that I needed to work on while spending time with these guys. So I decided to free myself of expectations and be more patient in my approach.

There wasn't much traffic in this part of southern Siberia, partly because there weren't many settlements here and partly because of the economic crisis. We expected to see trucks transporting Japanese cars, but not that many passed by. There weren't any problems with fuel. For the Tenere, one filling was enough to cross 450 km, and there were gas stations every hundred kilometres.

Rain accompanied us part of the way, which made riding on these dirt roads demanding, but that suited me. We started looking for a place to set up camp earlier than usual, after our experience from the day before, and found a spot that was perfect for us muddy motorcyclists: a lake with a sandy beach and some cheerful Siberians taking a swim. We "dug" our bikes into the sand and set up our tents some fifteen feet from the lake, then took advantage of the opportunity to wash ourselves and our clothes. A light campfire was crackling by the shore. I love campfires in the wilderness because of the special atmosphere that they create. The fire—actually, the smoke—protected us from unwanted flying pests. As darkness fell, there were more and more insects and fewer and fewer people. We hung our clothes up to dry on a makeshift clothesline we fashioned by stretching a rope between bikes. Each time one of us needed to get out of the tent and go to the lake, however, we had to step over the clothesline. Since I had a feeling that someone would trip over the line and fling the clothes onto the sand, I washed only one shirt.

DAY 3

We woke at nine in the morning. I found my shirt hanging on the makeshift clothesline the way I had left it the night before, but with lots of grains of sand sparkling on it. Of course, that had been Tim. We got ready and returned to the main road. Tim stopped, wanting to put on his sunglasses, since the strong sun was shining in our eyes, but he just couldn't find them anywhere, so we went back to the campsite. All three of us searched, but with no luck. We looked everywhere, but to no avail. Maybe he had lost them somewhere else? Who knows. But, it didn't matter. He'd buy new ones. We went back to the main road and continued riding.

After about five hundred metres, we reached an intersection. There, we turned left, even though it seemed to me that we should have gone straight. The left turn seemed like a shortcut. But I didn't regret it. I was actually glad we turned left, because now we were riding down the absolute worst terrain ever. Yesterday's rain had added to all the existing puddles and transformed this road into a stretch of mud. Tim took off and sped around a corner. I lost sight of him. Cory was behind me, following my speed. We reached a plain, and in the distance I could see Tim's bike lying on the ground, and Tim with his hands in the air. The huge muddy puddle that was the reason for his fall was near him. Tim had fallen when he had tried to circumvent it, so I aimed at its deepest spot, in the centre. Maybe that wasn't advisable, but I got going. The motorcycle dove deep enough so that about a third of the panniers were in the mud and it stirred up the sticky, thick liquid as the wheels turned. I made it through. Both the motorcycle and its driver had earned a new,

LEFT: The team in Khabarovsk.
BELOW LEFT: Preparations underway for the joys of Siberia.
OPPOSITE TOP: First campsite in Siberia,

earthy colour. Cory also aimed at the centre of the puddle, but he somehow lost balance. Luckily I was fast, and captured it all with my camera. We were muddy, but we didn't care. Obviously we had been expecting something like this.

The temperamental Siberian sky was starting to frown upon us and heavy cloud cover was approaching. A stretch of freshly set asphalt appeared ahead on the road, so we sped along, riding the rain-wave. Then the asphalt ended. Soon after, so did the rain. We reached a gas station, which was being serviced. While we waited for them to finish, we did our daily push-ups. We did push-ups almost every time we stopped. Tim even began keeping a record of how many sets we had done, and how many push-ups we had done per set, per day. Within a few minutes, the gas station was ready for use, so we put off our push-ups competition for some other time.

With our tanks full, we continued. The gravel road, which later turned into some bad asphalt, was to blame for our first improvised motorcycle maintenance. Our bikes were shaking so much because of the large potholes that the rear suspension on Cory's bike tightened until the horizontal rod of the luggage rack was pressing on the rear tire. One of the bolts on a tire had also almost fallen out. Obviously we needed a welder, but that day we weren't going to reach any villages.

Our *putešestvija* (which means "journey" in Russian) was becoming more and more defined by the taiga: vast stretches of thick, unfathomable Siberian woodlands, the greatest forest in the world. Many parts of it have been cut down, and the taiga has suffered from other tampering, but for now it's holding. Hopefully the taiga won't be doomed and fall victim to the changes people inflict. No one who's aware of the taiga's significance would wish its doom.

Time to look for a campsite. We saw a path that led us far enough from the main road and set up our tents atop a grassy hill. I grabbed my axe and went to gather some wood for the campfire. Twigs and branches cracked and snapped under my feet. I walked a few steps from the tents and looked around.

The taiga was surrounding us and taking care of us unconditionally;

offering its gifts to us: comfortable accommodation and wood for the fire. These woodlands are brimming with life and are home to big Siberian brown bears. We heard that these bears are really curious, so in order to avoid, um, unwanted encounters, we kept all our food and everything that smelled like food far from our tents, just in case. The cackling fire warmed our faces for a while, and then we crawled into our tents to sleep. I relaxed and listened to the wind play with the leaves and branches in the trees. A few times I thought I could hear something walking around. Then I'd turn "nature's music" off, hold my breath, and try to locate where the sound was coming from.

All was fine.

Just one of the guys snoring.

DAY 4

The early morning light woke us. First, we thought about the repair work we needed to do, then, about how to adjust the pannier rack so that it wouldn't damage the tire anymore. We arrived at a village and found a welder, but it just so happened that on this day his welding machine wasn't working. He gave us directions to another welder in the village, and we left to find him. The building we eventually found ourselves in front of looked abandoned, but people lived in such conditions here. Inside the brick house, a man was working on some iron pipes that were lying on the earthen floor. Cory managed to explain what he needed using mimicry and hand movements, without saying a word. The welder recognized this opportunity to earn an extra buck, which Cory "specially" paid. I don't know how much, but by the expression on Cory's face, it was too much.

Tim snapped some photos of our welder with his camera. The man reacted explosively. He began shouting loudly at Tim and insisted he erase the pictures. The situation was becoming uncomfortable. Actually, when I think about it, the man was right, but he could have reacted more calmly. Who were we to come into his life uninvited and without even asking? Knowing my friend and co-traveller, Tim, and how considerate he is of others and knowing his good intentions, it was obvious that this was all just a misunderstanding. But that could happen, also. It would be good to be more aware of these potential situations and be able to avoid possible misunderstandings, since some people don't want to be part of someone's motif, album or comment, and that's their right.

It would be good to just start from ourselves. People should try to imagine themselves as a photograph in some magazine followed by some caption. We should ask ourselves, how would we feel?

Tiny droplets of water were flying all around and sticking like magnets to my helmet's visor. Dust was lifting from the ground and mixing with the water on the visor, creating a sticky mass. I would wipe away this mixture from my visor with a few swipes of my glove, but soon a new layer would form. Cory was riding with an open visor and sunglasses, so his whole face was covered with a thick layer of dust. We stopped by an improvised booth with items for sale. Besides potato chips, the booth contained an impressive array of cigarettes and a few bowls of instant soup I remembered seeing in South Korea. We ate some chips and went on. As we rode further towards the west, the dark clouds disappeared.

The sun was shyly beginning to reveal itself and we slowly began removing layers of clothing. Soon we came across yet another situation involving Cory's motorcycle. We turned off the main road and stopped by a river, realizing the chain on Cory's bike had broken. This didn't worry us, at first though, since Cory had a spare chain and links. But, there's always someone in a group who seems to liven things up by doing everything differently. When you buy a new motorcycle and new chain to go with it because you are going on a trip around the world, check to make sure if the sales clerks have given you the proper size chain. It turned out, the chain and links did not fit the sprocket. We had two options: either wait for a truck to come along that could transport Cory's motorcycle or try to solve this problem ourselves. I went by bike to the main road and waited for a vehicle to come along. Cory and Tim stayed under a bridge trying to fix the chain.

Soon, a motorcycle appeared on the horizon. Obviously we had been destined to meet. A cloud of dust trailed behind it. Who knew how long the motorcycle had been trying to outrun this cloud, but it followed closely behind, not letting go. The biker, a guy named Max, stopped. By

LEFT: Grocery store by the desert road.
BELOW: Tim's tire needs help.

ABOVE: Max, the master mechanic, comes to the rescue.
RIGHT: Cory and Max, talking "man to man."

the look on his face, our presence was clearly baffling to him. His dust cloud instantaneously engulfed us before it began settling upon us as an additional layer.

"*Čto slučilos?*" Max asked, which means, "What happened?" in Russian. Max is probably a shortened version of the popular Russian name, Maksim.

"*Avarija,*" I mustered the Russian word for accident.

With a combination of Russian-Croatian-English, I explained the situation we were in. Max went under the bridge to see what the guys were trying to do. I remained sitting on the railing, thinking about ways to get the motorcycle to Chita. Trucks passed, but all were coming from Chita and not going towards it.

It was so hot that I took my bandana, soaked it in water, and tied it over my head. In the meantime, Max got to work. He tried to fix the chain. Improvisation, the mother of creativity, usually takes longer than a simple replacement with an original part. But Max gave it his best shot, and with a hammer and a piece of wood, he succeeded in combining the old chain, the new chain and the unsuitable connector into one working whole. Way to go! "Better than the original!" as my friend, Anton, would say.

Because of the situation with the chain, we knew we weren't going to make it to Chita that day. Max suggested we follow him, since he knew of a hotel we could sleep in. Without further thought, we got on our bikes and followed. He led us to a village that was about five or six kilometres from the main road. My engine stalled right as we exited the main road. The others did not notice, so while waiting for someone to come back, I tried to figure out what had happened. Why wasn't the engine starting for me? A few minutes later, Cory came back. Right away, he suggested that the contact with the battery had loosened. I removed the seat and saw how the positive end of the connecter was really loose. I tightened it with a screwdriver, put the saddle back on, and, with Cory, joined the rest of the group. It's interesting how Cory is the best mechanic in the group; he really is a professional, yet his bike needed the most repairs.

The dirt road suddenly ended and asphalt followed. The village ahead seemed isolated, as if time had stopped. Unaccustomed to visits from such weirdos like us, people ran into the street and began clapping. The people that lived here had never had a chance to see in-person the vehicles we were riding and the clothes we were wearing. Soon it felt like we were in some sort of a parade. A rush of discomfort overcame me. For a moment, I saw myself as a rich Westerner with a lot of opportunities in comparison to these people here.

We reached the hotel, which, according to Tim's description of it in his travelogue, looked as if it would crumble to ruins during the night. After parking the motorcycles in the garage, we took what we needed and climbed up some creaky steps to the reception. There we paid for two rooms in advance. Cory and Max in one room, Tim and me in the other. As soon as we opened the door I could see that the beds were just old couches with one side removed, barely allowing enough space to stretch our legs. Since we could already sense each other's, um, scents, a good scrubbing was a necessity. But showering turned out to be a special experience. Just like with all other showers, we could regulate the water temperature, but with this shower, we could only choose between "ice age" and "crematorium." In between did not exist. Actually, there was lukewarm water, but then the pressure was too low, so while showering I felt as if I had to wring out each drop of water I needed. This experience was further enriched by the locals, who would walk into the bathroom—since the lock did not work—and go about their business as if no one else was there.

That's probably normal, right?

After showering, we went to the restaurant, disco club and café. All in one. Since the electricity had gone out, and only a limited number of lights were working—thanks to a diesel generator—we ordered in the half-dark: chicken with potatoes. The meals came quickly, and soon afterwards, they turned some more lights off so that people could dance. They pumped up the volume and turned the disco lights on. I somehow managed to cut a piece of meat for myself in the dark. What entered my mouth definitely was not chicken. It surely was something else, and I definitely could not eat it. Cory managed to eat just one piece, while Tim decided to just skip this meal. My hunger disappeared after trying the food. So I went up to brush my teeth and hit the sack. Thoughts about the history of this nation crossed my mind. Lax Slavic organization, Ivan the Terrible, Peter the Great, the Siberian Cossacks, the October Revolution, Rasputin, comrades Lenin and Stalin, the Gulag, perestroika. My legs were hanging off the end of the couch, but I got a good night's rest.

CHITA

I often mention rain, so I'll mention it again. In addition to all the gear we put on in the morning, we got our rain gear on, too. Since all roads lead to Chita, that's where we were heading. The gloves that I had weren't meant for such conditions, so just like all the times before, they got soaking wet in the rain and my hands, inside them, turned a purplish blue.

Soaking wet, we sped through gravel, mud, and stretches of asphalt. We reached a gas station and filled the tanks. The "fuel pump" consisted of one huge cistern with a tube. There wasn't any roof or shelter, so we all tried to fill our fuel tanks without letting any rainwater in. A few drops did make their way in, nevertheless. While there, we pumped the rear tire of the big GS. It had been gradually deflating the whole time. The landscape had changed and now reminded me of photographs I had seen of Mongolia, before my trip.

A few kilometres before we reached Chita, Max left the group and headed for a village where he was going to spend the night. We stopped by the side of the road to study the *Lonely Planet Russia* travel guide, reading the map of Chita and looking for a hotel. I took note of the approximate location of a hotel and we reached it with the help of some locals we met along the way who gave us directions. Cory, the bouncer, stayed to watch the motorcycles while Tim and I went to the front desk in the hotel to reserve a room. When we came back out, Cory was busy tending to a dynamic and intrigued crowd who were questioning him about our journey. He was answering their questions, all the while watching our stuff. Cory and I went to dinner, while Tim checked what was up on the Internet, since we hadn't had access for the past few days. The restaurant that the receptionist at the hotel had recommended was crowded. Hungry as wolves, we stood by the door.

A wedding celebration was underway in the hall. We stood at the entrance to the hall. All eyes were on us, and ours were on them. Now what? Let's get going. Where there's a will, there's a way, so with some effort, we got a table and ordered some food. Really, anything can happen in such a short period of time. Yesterday, we were eating in a hotel restaurant where I would recommend not even tasting the food, and here we were dining at a wedding celebration. I don't remember what I ordered, but soon I received caviar, rice, apple juice and vodka. I stuffed myself with all sorts of food, then sat for a while and watched the cheerful Russian bride and groom and their guests. My friends went a step further and mingled with the guests. They liked the spontaneity of these people. In the meantime, I retreated to the hotel room and went to sleep.

We decided to take a break from driving for a day and went to search for spare chain links for Cory's motorcycle. Max came to Chita, so we asked him where we could find the needed motorcycle parts. He called some numbers, while standing next to us, and then told us a car would be there in about ten minutes to take us to a store that supposedly stocked the chain links. A guy named Aleksandar, driving an old jeep, came for us. I went with Cory to search for the part. He took us to the way we had gone the day before, out of town and towards a warehouse. Inside, trucks and motorcycles taken apart and in pieces were lying in piles. The chain that Aleksandar brought forth in a plastic bag and put on the floor was definitely too wide for Cory's bike. Apparently there was some misunderstanding.

Just by looking at Aleksander and Max, I could tell they weren't happy with Cory's refusal to buy the chain and links. They returned us to the hotel, then left. We tried to understand Max's words when he repeated, several times, that we should have taken the chain. Obviously we didn't understand. Maybe he was even capable of installing that inadequate chain, but Cory wasn't satisfied with that solution. I could see Max was angry. However, later on when we were saying our goodbyes in front of the hotel, 'ol Max came by and said to keep in touch by email. He even said he was sorry he couldn't continue travelling with us. We went for a walk in downtown Chita. This city, with about 300 000 inhabitants, is the centre of the region that carries the same name.

We approached a motorcyclist and asked if he knew where we could buy a chain. He gave us directions. The "motorcycle shop" we entered was well-stocked with spare parts for all kinds of agricultural machinery, as well as for motorcycles, but not for the kinds we were riding. So we asked the same motorcyclist for additional instructions. After we explained the situation, he said to follow him. We rode behind him to a garage, where, he told us, a friend of his might have just what we needed. All we could find were used chains, but we thought we could remove the links from them.

However, despite all our efforts, we could not convince the seller of these used parts to sell them to us for an acceptable price, so we left without the links. I spent the last evening in Chita mainly staring at the monitor of my laptop typing up material for this book.

ON THE WAY TO ULAN UDE: DAY 1

Someone on Motori.hr, in the section about my journey, wrote about how a guy named Doug was riding a chopper eastward, also around the world. Just at that moment, he was somewhere near Chita. We met about 190 km west of Chita, stopping at the side of the road.

Doug had invested a lot of effort adjusting his chopper for the trip. Nevertheless, it definitely wasn't my vehicle of choice for longer journeys. Although, obviously, there are people who enjoy riding such motorcycles. Just a few centimetres separated the leather saddlebags from the ground. I wondered how Doug would cross the stretch from Chita to Khabarovsk, which wasn't that difficult, but with those saddlebags, it could be. Doug said he'd cross that leg by train. I took a closer look at his motorcycle and noticed how one of his saddlebags had motorcycle club emblems on it. Such stickers didn't usually interest me, but this time? It was nice to see the logos MK Kumovi, from Virovitica, and MK Alka, from Špišić Bukovica, so I asked Doug where he had been. I found out he had passed through Koprivnica, where I am from. That was neat to hear. A very interesting guy! We kept in touch.

BELOW: My fellow travellers and friends on the journey across Siberia, Mongolia, and Kazakhstan: Tim and Cory.
OPPOSITE TOP: Camouflage attempt.
OPPOSITE BOTTOM RIGHT: Doug, the legendary chopper rider.

Since we had a late start from Chita, we looked for a spot to set up camp after going just a few kilometres. We turned off the road and entered the forest. There, the gravel road worsened and became more demanding. Frequent obstacles in the form of water got us to think about returning to the main road and finding a better spot. I almost laid the bike down several times. Slippery terrain along with luggage loaded on the motorcycle is definitely a good recipe for sliding to the ground. Tim, with the heaviest motorcycle, succeeded in falling several times, but since he wasn't going fast, nothing was damaged. Collecting mileage, turning our heads left and right in order to see if we could find a spot to camp, we reached a small village and stopped at a gas station. Once again, we had a chance to see a wedding. A white Lada was ceremoniously decorated for the occasion. We met the bride, the groom, the maid of honour and the best man. I'm sure we would have gotten acquainted with all the others attending the wedding, but they weren't there at the station.

We found a camping spot a few hundred metres from the main road. The sun was hanging low. There was just enough time to lay down the mats for our sleeping bags and get some wood for the fire. We then checked Tim's tire to see from where the air was escaping. Twice a day, we had to pump the rear tire. After spraying it with a mixture of shower gel foam and water, we spun it and saw how the whole length of the entire middle section of the tire was full of tiny holes. Tires with inner tubes are definitely better than those without them.

DAY 2

In the morning, after a good night's rest, we got going westward, towards Ulan Ude. Rolling steppes and a sunny day truly are something beautiful to experience while travelling by motorcycle. Though we had been planning on reaching Ulan Ude earlier in order to spend the rest of the day there, we didn't. Instead, we spent several hours in the village before Ulan Ude, solving another problem with Cory's motorcycle. Apparently, his motorcycle (BMW F800 GS) had a faulty connection with the battery, which he hadn't replaced before the journey, even though it had been recommended he do so. That day, I got a headache for the first time in my life and I know why. We were working on fixing the bike and the sun was shining directly above our heads for hours.

I went to a nearby store and bought water to wet my bandana and put on my head. Right away I felt better. In the meantime, some local biking enthusiasts gathered around our motorcycles. They looked like a great bunch of people that might know where to get a new battery.

The store that sold batteries was about one hundred metres from where we were standing. Tim and I went to buy the battery, while Cory waited. We bought the only one that was the right size without thinking twice. I missed out on the actual installation of the new battery, since my craving for ice cream was stronger. At the store across the street where I had bought water earlier, I got some ice cream, water and gum. The store clerk put everything in a bag, and then calculated on an abacus how much I needed to pay. I was a bit surprised to see an abacus still in use. While the ice cream was melting from the heat, which was also heating my black motorcycle outfit, I helped my friends as much as I could, but I wasn't much of a mechanic. However, while spending time with them, I was slowly learning the ropes.

It took a while to connect the new battery with the word "East" spelled out in large Cyrillic letters on it. I had no idea why, but obviously something was not fitting right. I also noticed how a tank bag was missing from Cory's motorcycle. I don't know when it had disappeared; I hadn't noticed until then. Instead of a specialized Touratech tank bag, he had to buy a children's backpack with Sponge Bob on it. In the end, he didn't even use it. After we fixed Cory's motorcycle, we got going towards Ulan Ude.

ULAN UDE

After the usual huge sign with the city's name on it, we entered the capital city of the Republic of Buryatia, Ulan Ude. The Buryats are an indigenous Siberian population who live in the region around Lake Baikal and partly in Mongolia.

For several days now, we hadn't had Internet access, so we circumvented several hostels in the city that did not offer this service.

RIGHT: **Good morning.**

ABOVE: The taiga.
LEFT: Repairing
the battery in a
village in Siberia.

While riding, I noticed a sign for Irkutsk—this was the road we'd have to take for Baikal. Near the city's centre, we finally found a decent place to settle for the next two days. Before entering Mongolia, it would be good to prepare the motorcycles and get them ready for further riding. Somehow, despite the reception clerk's poor English, and my Russian, which was not yet good enough to express what we needed, we got directions to the large store that sold oil for the motorcycles.

Large public squares, which we were already accustomed to, are a typical feature of Russian cities. Of course, these squares come with the mandatory statue of Lenin, or the statue of just his head, as was the case here. Apparently, this one was the largest. Throughout its history, Russia has been subjected to authoritarian rulers: for a long period as an empire, and then later, as a result of communism. One characteristic of such systems is the rise of personality cults created by the rulers. This statue was just more proof of that.

The city where we were currently marks the start of the road that leads to the east side of the deepest and richest freshwater lake in the world, Lake Baikal. It is also where the Trans-Siberian railway and the roads to Mongolia separate.

The bad weather forecast for the area leading to Baikal and the good forecast for Mongolia got us thinking about whether or not to visit the lake at all. I wanted to see it, though, rain or shine. Not even snowfall, rain or any other kind of storm should stop us. Since we were already so close to the lake, it would be good to go visit it. And maybe we could go for a swim? Though reluctant, Tim and Cory saw my determination, and so we decided to go.

We crossed the river Selenga, which begins in Mongolia and pours into the Baikal *Ozero* (which means, "lake" in Russian). Expecting the heaviest rainstorm, we were wearing complete rain gear. Out of curiosity, the police stopped us at the city limits. These kinds of cops are cool. They didn't ask us for our documents. Instead, they just asked where we were from and where were going. I wasn't in the mood for repeating the story, so I let the Canadians communicate with the Russians. They understood each other, though I have no idea in what language. Since the weather conditions were worsening, the police put their raincoats on, and we got going. Though I had already experienced riding during a rainfall, the drops that were hitting us now surpassed all my expectations. Fog formed in front of us. The sky was pouring rain so heavily, that I was soaking wet after only a minute. Great tides of water flowed down the road and filled a nearby stream. Large puddles on the damaged road surprised me each time I'd cross one. Riding fast, I would run into a deep puddle, and the water would throw my legs back. From then on, I always made sure to anchor my feet better when crossing such puddles. The rain gradually decreased in intensity, and then stopped. And then we stopped.

Once again, the team was questioning whether or not to keep going. I wanted to continue. Seeing my determination, my buddies decided to continue driving towards the lake. As we rode further, we were once again honoured with a new wave of heavy showers.

We hid in a gas station and asked for the nearest *gostinjica* (which means, "hotel" in Russian). "About one hundred kilometres from where you are," was the answer.

LAKE BAIKAL

Along this one hundred-kilometre stretch of road, we occasionally had views of the lake. I had been expecting to be able to see the lake the whole time, but in this southeastern part of the *ozera*, because of the forest, only passengers on the Trans-Siberian railway had the best view, then the foresters, and then all the others who wander the roads of Siberia.

We almost sped past the sign for the hotel, in Cyrillic. By then, even my Canadian buddies had memorized the shapes of the letters. We got off the main road and travelled down gravel towards the forest, then crossed a stream and reached a tourist complex, hidden between the lake and the thick forest. As soon as we arrived, we became the main attraction for curious tourists and locals, Russians and Buryats. Tim went to look for a hotel that would suit our needs. A safe place to park the motorcycles, plus water and electricity were all we needed.

I took out my video camera and started filming Cory's interaction with the Russians. I understood every word. It was funny how Cory tried

CLOCKWISE FROM ABOVE:
Lake Baikal.
Comrade Lenin in Ulan Ude.
Welcome.
On the way to Ulan Ude.

to understand them, but in the end got everything wrong. That made him angry for a moment, so in the end I answered the questions, explaining what the Russians had asked and what he had actually answered. Cory got confused trying to figure out what they were saying.

He was waving his hands, shrugging his shoulders, and looking to me.

Tim returned with a bright smile on his face. He had found good accommodation with an acceptable price. We started the motorcycles and parked further down. Right away, we hung our stuff up to dry and almost flooded the place, since everything was dripping wet. After showering, we went with our new friends to the lake. There, we got a campfire going and enjoyed its light and warmth. I noticed that people gathered around a fire, especially when out in the open, are more relaxed and spontaneous, more ready to enjoy each other's company. As if the warmth and light brings them back to their primordial selves and relaxes learned patterns of behaviour that have been imposed by others. Someone mentioned swimming, but we put that off for some other time. We were offered and enjoyed some very delicious dried omul fish. This indigenous fish is a specialty in this area around the great lake. I noticed quite a number of visitors, more than I had expected.

We returned to the hotel to get some sleep. The next day, we took pictures of the lake. Though we were there in the summertime, when the winds blow, it gets pretty cold. What is it like, then, in the winter? Everything is covered in ice, and the lake's surface serves as a road for trucks. I could just imagine the surrounding woods decorated with a silver shine and the smoke lifting from fires that mean life to these people. What do these people do during the long winters? They drill holes at the lake and fish, gather around fires and drink warm drinks. They have enough time to think about everything, and about themselves, which is really good.

Though some of the Siberian people have accepted Russian influences, and thus Christianity, a great number are of the indigenous population have revived their shamanic tradition after the end of repression from the communist regime.

Our clothes were dry, so we could continue with our journey back towards Ulan Ude, since the road to Mongolia leads through the city. Once at Ulan Ude, we spent the night in a hotel. Tomorrow we'd head for Mongolia!

A lot of Russian soldiers waved at us along the road to Mongolia. There were quite a lot of them that day for most of the way. At the border, we did not know which way to go. We obviously hadn't understood the directions given to us by a man we had met along the way. We noticed some huge Mongolian flags flapping in the wind in one direction. Even though we had begun to head in the opposite direction, we soon realized our mistake and headed back. A herd of cattle was blocking our way, so we had to wait for the cows to pass. These gents and ladies did not seem in a hurry to move, so we started honking. That sent them running in a stampede down the valley.

MONGOLIA
(7/8–21/8/2009)
2 600 km

Three foreigners from the north rode into the land of the great Genghis Khan. Hah, were the Khan still alive today, these three foreigners would still be at the border of his kingdom, exiting Japan, and wouldn't be greeted by a bunch of unorganized officials whom you have to seek out only so that each one of them can stamp your paperwork. They would receive only one stamp, and it would be of value, just like when it was of value to Marco Polo. Maybe they would even send an entourage to accompany these foreigners? But, now? These are new times now.

There wasn't much of a line at the border; just a few cars in front of us. We were given some forms to fill out, so we focused on the paperwork. We were sharing the only pen we had, when we suddenly heard a heavy crash. My motorcycle had fallen over. I knew it was risky to balance it with the kickstand on flat ground, but I hadn't expected it to topple over. Nothing was damaged; I just had to be more careful while waiting my turn for the documentation check. Things went smoothly at the Russian side of the border. We were done quickly, so we continued towards Mongolia.

The Mongolian side was a bit more interesting. One of the border police knew some English, so we quickly filled out the new forms, which were in Cyrillic. Some more officials needed to stamp them. However, as I said earlier, we are no longer living in the era of the Khan, so first, these officials needed to be found. Of course, they weren't at their desks. Instead, they were standing outside the building, taking care of their share of the job of affixing multiple stamps on travellers' paperwork. We needed to wait even longer for some of them. But, they proved to be courteous and considerate, and later on, they wanted to take pictures with us. So we got that done and continued towards the Mongolian Gateway, a giant metal arch marking the entrance to Mongolia, where our passports, as well as our other papers, were checked once more.

Soon, after rounding the first curve in the road, I noticed that Tim's tire was almost completely flat. I didn't even get a chance to react before it went ahead and "slipped" off the rim. We stopped to fix the tire just as it started raining again. I had always thought of Mongolia as a dry region, but then again, we were just getting going. Already accustomed to wearing wet clothing, we didn't pay much attention to the weather and got to work. We tied the tire to the rim, and with a lot of effort and skill, managed to pump it up. Though we had been planning on camping for the night, because of the rain, we decided to look for a hotel. We headed to the first settlement marked on the map, which was called Suhbatar. Our first hotel in Mongolia, with a price of three dollars per person, was definitely something we should have come across more often on this journey. True, it did not have Internet, nor warm water, nor much of a choice of meals. And true, the beds were too small and the rain was seeping in. But even so, all we needed was a roof over our heads and a garage for the motorcycles.

We prepared our own food for dinner, and then went to sleep. After years of sleeping in all kinds of conditions and surroundings, I had no trouble falling asleep right away. Cory and Tim, however, spent hours staring at the ceiling, listening to some Mongols in the hotel who yelled all night long.

In the morning, the view of the gloomy weather outside the window killed our mood for riding to Mongolia's capital. Nevertheless, we decided it was best we get started. We packed our stuff, and then ran from the hotel to the garage in order to avoid the rain. After mounting everything on the bikes, we got going, all the while wiping raindrops from our helmet visors. We hadn't had breakfast yet, so hunger forced us to stop by the side of the road and grab a bite in a hurry. While eating our snack, we admired the scenery. Rolling steppes spreading to the horizon, and maybe even beyond. In the distance stood a *ger*, an easily transportable dome-shaped dwelling used by nomadic people across a great part of Asia. In Russia and Kazakhstan, they are known as *yurts*. A vehicle began moving away from the ger and slowly approached us, all the while rocking as it went along the rolling steppe. Some curious and benevolent guys got out of the car to meet us. We tried to exchange a word or two with the company. All of us were doing our best, and laughing, but we were getting nowhere with the conversation. So we said goodbye to our Mongolian friends, and got going after we had filled our bellies. The clouds were already getting bored with us, so, to our joy, they decided to depart.

The road we were following, which connected Ulaanbaatar with Russia, served as the route for the import of most goods to Mongolia, so it was kept in good condition. Because of the wet conditions, we drove carefully. Nevertheless, after taking a left curve, I could see Cory losing control of his bike just a few metres ahead of me. He swung to the left side of the road and separated from the motorcycle as he fell. After skidding along the asphalt, he luckily ended up in some high grass. At the same time, the motorcycle flipped in the air and crashed to the ground, luckily, far from Cory! I stopped my motorcycle and ran to Cory. He got up quickly and said he felt all right. Fortunately for us, no one was coming from the opposite direction. Otherwise they would have crashed into his motorcycle. The high grass helped cushion our friend's fall, as well as his bike's. When I saw his motorcycle doing a somersault in the air, I thought we were going to need a good mechanic in order to continue our journey.

Not even noticing that the two of us weren't behind him anymore, Tim rode onward, listening to music. We could soon hear him rushing back towards us. The three of us lifted the motorcycle. Other than some cracks on the plastic, fender, dashboard and rear-view mirror, there was no serious damage done. We had just a few more hours of riding to go before Ulaanbaatar. The parts we needed in order to repair the bike could be easily found in town, so we picked up the bits that had fallen off and continued on our way. Cory drove first so that he could ride at a speed that suited him. I noticed his steering was not centred, but it'd hold.

We trusted the road to lead the way, and soon it led us up a hill. From the top, we could see a valley and the city, below.

ULAANBAATAR

We stopped in front of a sign for the city of Ulaanbaatar to take some pictures. I took my laptop out to look at the map of the city and to find the address for the hostel where we were planning to stay. The hostel was run by my father's friend, Zaya, and went by the same name. After taking note of its approximate location, I led the way. We entered the city, crossed some train tracks, and passed several hotels and hostels.

We had trouble finding the hostel. We rode in circles, asking passersby where we were and where Zaya Hostel was, but we just couldn't find it. When we reached the State Department building (in a shopping centre), I asked a beautiful Mongolian girl where the hostel was located. She pointed in the direction we needed to go. While the two of us were still talking, I could see Tim and Cory starting up their motorcycles and shouting: "Follow us!"

Not sure what was happening, I hit the gas and rushed after them. We pushed our way through the crowd and stopped in front of a restaurant called Marco Polo. Cory and Tim then told me how some men had tried to rob them. Two guys had approached Cory and tried to grab stuff from his motorcycle. He managed to pull away and hit the gas.

Already a bit nervous because we hadn't yet found the hostel, we turned onto Peace Avenue, which was blocked. The road was all dug up. There were no cars, just confused pedestrians staring at us dusty travellers searching for accommodation. Cory then saw the sign: Zaya Hostel. But then came the question: How to get to the hostel when the road was a mess. Go around! Like some lab mice racing through a labyrinth, we rode across backyards, up banks, and dipped under overhanging tree branches. The locals followed us with their stares. We reached the hostel! The motorcycles were given some parking space in a garage and we entered the building. We spent the remainder of the day resting and planning our next moves.

The two most important things were getting tools to fix Cory's motorcycle and getting myself a visa for Kazakhstan. Cory, the best mechanic on this team, said we needed a drill, some wire and glue. So we got in a taxi and headed for the so-called "Black Market," where used tools could be found. From my view in the passenger seat, I could see people staring at us. This didn't surprise me. The Black Market, despite what its name implies, was actually an open-air market with booths that sold all you'd ever need, including spare parts for the used cars that are driven here. Merchants here were selling everything from wolf skins to satellite antennas. It's hard to describe, but believe me, it was a special experience!

Some of the people were dressed in traditional clothing, including stiff horseman boots. A few merchants were even lying on top of the booths. Music was blaring, while the scents of deep-fried food shocked us. We passed through the area where people were selling car engines. It wouldn't have been anything strange to see two or three engines on the dusty street, but to see thirty of them! That was a surprise! Even better: all the engines were the same; the only difference was that some had less rust, others had more. Next to the engines was a pile of shock systems. The pile of shocks looked as if a dredger had just dumped them on the floor. All around were piles of alternators, wheels, switches, brakes, headlights, wipers.

We reached the spot where drills were sold. Cory caught sight of one large booth. The savvy merchant noticed us Westerners and wanted to adjust the prices accordingly, so Cory gave up on buying. However, each time Cory passed by the booth, the price would drop. So, finally, our master mechanic made a deal, and bought a drill. But that's not all! Can you imagine a drill that worked when it was bought, but then went on strike and refused to work afterwards? Imagine getting started repairing the motorcycle, and then the drill stops working. However, after being launched into the air and hitting the wall, magically, it started working again.

The city of Ulaanbaatar (which means, the "Red Hero," in Mongolian) is situated along the river Tul Gul, and is surrounded by four mountains. The city's centre is designed according to modern standards, yet is surrounded by a settlement of dome-shaped tents (gers) and simple shelters made from planks and logs.

This city was founded at a crossing of caravan routes, and developed greatly at the beginning of the twentieth century. Not long ago, in 2000, Ulaanbaatar experienced its greatest increase in population, when numerous nomads lost a great number of cattle after an exceptionally harsh winter. In hopes of finding a job—in hopes of anything—many nomads left their cattle behind and settled along the city's outskirts. Nowadays, at the edge of the city, and also often at the edge of survival, some of these once-free nomads still search for new possibilities.

This situation was probably further exacerbated by the government's lack of preparation. As in other parts of the world, it was more occupied with taking care of itself than with taking care of its people. The media also bears its share of the blame for this by portraying urban life as a "blessing."

Leaving the Black Market, I showed the taxi driver the tourist map of Ulaanbaatar, with the embassy in Kazakhstan marked on it. We drove to the other end of the city and reached the spot where the embassy used to be. It had been relocated. So we got in the car once again and drove to what should have been the embassy's new location! We looked for the embassy, asked around, walked around, and then finally saw the Kazakh flag waving in the wind. In addition to my passport, I had a letter of invitation from an agency in Almaty, so soon after I had spoken with the consul, I got the green light for the visa. I left my passport at the embassy, and was to pick it up the following day.

Meanwhile, Cory started repairing the motorcycle. He didn't want help and looked as if he was in the midst of some sacred ritual. First, he took apart the larger part of the fender, then spent hours meticulously putting the fragments of plastic together, gluing them in place, and then drilling holes in them in order to reinforce them up with wire. I really do admire him.

IN THE COMPANY OF GENGHIS KHAN

In the afternoon, I went for a walk and visited a museum, where I spent most of my time looking at the exhibits of dinosaur fossils found in the sand of the Gobi Desert. Then, I went to the Ulaanbaatar's main public square. Most public squares and parliament buildings in European cities are miniscule when compared to Suhbatar Square and the Mongolian Parliament Building. Obviously there is a certain symbolism involved, which is most evident when standing before the statue of the ruler of this, the greatest of empires.

There he sat—Genghis Khan, with his legs and arms spread wide apart, sitting on his horse with an upright posture, gazing firmly into the distance. He looked as if he was expecting delegates to arrive from

CLOCKWISE FROM LEFT:
Ready to meet the Great Khan.
At the Mongolian border.
Cory's fall.
The motorcycle after the fall.
Entering the capital city.

ABOVE: The "turtle boulder."
OPPOSITE: Ceremonial ovoo: a place for worship and for ensuring a safe journey.

all over the world, while at the same time, as if he was judging, judging life and the destiny of this world.

Temujin, which means the "Blue Wolf," or "Son of the Blue Sky," whom Mongols are very proud of, is a unique example of a leader and coordinator. Throughout history, his achievements have been unsurpassable.

While Alexander the Great and Napoleon led great and rich nations with complex systems and a well-organized and structured army, this nomad—leader of a small clan with just a few tents in the steppes— created the greatest national organization in history, from scratch. He introduced an efficient administrative system with clear laws, known as *Yasa*. He brought order and developed a system for the spreading of information. Of course, this was all to serve a military state, but the system did function well. It is said that he was very brutal towards those who did not recognize his government, although, in comparison to other rulers of that era, he was no harsher than most.

By applying a new, extremely efficient strategy, the Khan's well-organized and highly motivated horsemen travelled throughout the known world. Kingdoms fell, cities collapsed: Beijing, the central Asian centres of Bukhara and Samarkand, the whole of Persia, Baghdad and Mesopotamia. Japan was saved by a storm that sank Mongolian boats, but the Russians were defeated. Numerous times, the Chinese emporer sent strong armies forth to defend his empire. Nevertheless, he did not succeed. The Khan's horsemen made their way to Pakistan and Afghanistan across high, snow-covered peaks. In Europe, the Hungarian King, Bella, failed to defend his nation and fled to Dalmatia to save himself.

By destroying the central Asian empire, Genghis Khan opened channels for communication between the East and the West. Merchants and missionaries from a large part of the world could now travel safely and without restrictions. They spread new ideas, customs and traditions, many of which were then adopted by the local populations.

I'm not really interested in what the map of the world looked like in the Khan's mind. Neither am I supportive of the old-fashioned ways of Mongolian life, nor did I write this just so that this book could be a page or two longer. I was just trying to imagine and find the key to this nomad's success. How did this small group of people from the steppes succeed in attaining so much? What was their secret?

The museum I had visited on the way to the square came to mind, so I headed back there. There, I ought to be able to find some answers. I walked around a little, looked at the exhibits, tried to seem interested, and asked an older gentleman if he had some time to spare. He did not know much English, let alone Croatian, so he led me to Mrs. Ayuna. A very nice and inquisitive lady, she was pleased to see such a young guy with a list of questions in her area of expertise. The meeting turned into a friendly conversation and moved on to the topic of the country I am from. Our conversation confirmed what I had suspected: This capable and determined nomad, Genghis Khan, succeeded in conveying his feeling of power to his people. He awarded numerous titles and ranks, both according to merit and in advance—to be earned. He succeeded in convincing his people that they were important. They started to feel important and powerful! A Mongolian could not be a slave or a servant, and that was the prerequisite for such success!

So, with this strategy, Genghis Khan created an army of inspired and powerful individuals, and led them, in order to achieve his goal. This seems somewhat the opposite of what I see today, when the goal is to disorient the individual. People spend more and more time with psychologists and communicate through lawyers, allowing the media to focus their attention on trivial and shallow things. Poor choices are offered and a "freedom" that actually isn't. But how to find your own voice in all of that, and how to know what is really yours and not part of someone else's plan, the plan of some khan, or who knows who?

Is it easier to not ask anything, or to hear your own self?

"Ah, what am I thinking about and writing?"

"Actually, this is my book and I can write what I want to."

•   •   •

Early the next morning, a taxi pulled up in front of Zaya's hostel and out came a man with a familiar face: my father. He was delivering the equipment necessary for us to continue south across some very interesting yet demanding terrain—the Gobi Desert and the central Asian mountains, the Altai, then the Russian Altai region, and finally the semi-desert region of Kazakhstan.

A traveller himself, my father has in the past crossed many parts of this region in various ways, by jeep and by horseback. Along the way, he would find accommodation in nomads' tents, and once he almost froze to death during a snowstorm in the mountains of Saihan–Gurvan, in the southern Gobi.

Already accustomed to combining pleasure with business, instead of paying for the equipment to be sent (tires, chains, sprockets and other smaller pieces of equipment that we couldn't find here), my father bought a plane ticket. After a brief hello, he was already walking with me towards Gandan, the Buddhist monastery in the northeastern part of the city. It's a large complex that includes a Buddhist university and several colleges.

Since I hadn't had enough money for a small video camera before the start of this trip, my father brought one along with the other equipment. And while in the neighbourhood, he was planning on visiting some friends here.

Cory really put a lot of effort into it and finished repairing his motorcycle. He had accomplished the most he could, under the circumstances. Around noon, I took a taxi to the embassy and picked up my passport, which was all the wealthier for one more visa. We wandered around a little before we found the flag again. When I opened my passport, I saw that the visa was pasted on one of the pages and the text was handwritten with a ballpoint pen. I didn't know people still did that here.

The next day, my father and myself, along with Tim and Cory, took a trip to the mountain region of Ghorhki Terelj, which is northeast of Ulaanbaatar. Unlike the dry central and southern regions of Mongolia, this region is rich with fresh water sources.

Larch and birch tree forests in the lower regions create an unexpected landscape for Mongolia. To the great joy of wild and domestic animals, fields of grass abound.

Mountain passes in Mongolia, Tibet and parts of Nepal are places

RIGHT: **Our friend's ger.**
BELOW: **View from inside a ger.**

ABOVE: **Wild horses, takhi.**

for prayer, and are marked with *ovoo*, piles of stone with prayer flags and scarves. We reached one, on a ridge. As is customary, we walked in a circle around the temple in the direction following the sun's path, threw some stones onto the pile, and made a wish that was important to us. Nearby stood a man with an eagle, offering us a chance to take a photo with this king of the skies. We followed a river upstream and came across a cliff formation where nature, the master craftsman, had really exerted an effort while at his job. Several different shapes had been formed. For instance, one boulder was shaped like a huge turtle.

After climbing up the boulder, we sat and rested for a while, watching life around us. Several gers were scattered throughout the vicinity. Some voices could be heard. Children were having fun riding horses. I watched their carefree games, listened to their shouting, the horses galloping, and the children laughing—an idyllic scene. Along the rocky peaks, at the edge of the forest in the distance, was a temple. We set off to visit it and crossed a hanging bridge to the temple. The temple turned out to be much bigger than what it had seemed to be when we had seen it from the turtle boulder. Respecting the traditional practice, we walked a few ritual circles, spun prayer wheels and then entered the temple, which was filled with statues, ritual objects and mandalas on the walls.

Later on, we went to see a friend of my father's. Bajra lived with his family about 20 km upstream. After a heartwarming welcome, what else would we do in Mongolia, but go horseback riding? Tim decided to skip horseback riding and go for a swim in the river instead. We crossed the stream and continued through the forest of birch and larch trees, then reached the river, where we stopped to let the horses drink some water. The horses crossed the river and galloped across the steppes to a great cliff, then climbed up it. After the climb, we enjoyed the view from the top, while catching our breath, as well.

The *mor*, which is the name used by Mongols for this breed of horse, is a sturdy yet agile horse, with well-balanced behaviour and stamina. Such horses were used to transport the Mongolian army from the Pacific Ocean to the Adriatic Sea, crossing hundreds of kilometres a day. They are modest animals that don't need barns or care, and during the winter, they can endure extremes of –40°C, along with the harsh north wind. Though I had ridden astride my bike across almost half the globe, I was a little sore from the stiff saddle, and so was Cory.

A meal after the horseback ride was welcomed. The menu for the day was traditional food: buzz. This consisted of meat wrapped in noodles. Then, vodka. Here, vodka is poured in one glass; a big one! It is swallowed all at once, and then poured for the next guest, and so on, the glass passed around from person to person until there's no more left—which doesn't take too long. Since this was some sort of ritual, even though I didn't "train" in this discipline, I poured the shot down my throat, and then hollered: *"Manhtue!"* which means something like, "Cheers!" At least, that's how I had heard it being said. I was saved from drinking the second round when I noticed this ritual included a gesture that indicated when you didn't want to be offered any more: with my ring finger, I touched the elixir, then my forehead, before pointing it to the blue Mongolian sky.

We sat with the cheerful people gathered in the ger and talked. The whole time we were talking, I was looking around and studying the room. Quite an interesting dwelling. The ger, or yurt, as it is known in Russia and Siberia, is actually a half-domed tent with a light wooden frame and between five and six centimetres of wool insulation. Despite their humble appearance, these structures, which nomads call home throughout a great part of Asia, keep their inhabitants warm during the extreme weather typical of the Gobi Desert.

Instead of thinking up descriptions of these people's temperaments, I'll just quote the words of our host:

"Peter, we're always for "everything": to drink, to sing and to fight. But we also forgive easily and make peace with everyone."

I even had a chance to see this with my own eyes. Later on, a man joined us. His chest was wrapped in bandages for the aforementioned reasons. Also, one night, I'm not exactly sure which night it was, a loud banging on the door at Zaya's hostel woke us. Luckily, Zaya had not been skimpy when refurbishing the hostel, so while the door shook— everything was shaking—it didn't give in. We just looked at one another and then went to the entrance. On the other side of the threshold stood

RIGHT: **Crossing the sand**
BELOW: **. . . and across the steppes.**

a large, hefty man who had wanted to enter for who knows what reason. Cory had slightly overdone it and was holding our small axe, but the man decided to give up. Though acceptance of Buddhism has, for the most part, calmed the impulsive nature of these nomads, obviously, alcohol can, at times, cause an interesting situation. Anyway, it all ended OK.

EN ROUTE TO KARAKORUM

After having spent the past few days resting, we revved up the motorcycles out front of the Marco Polo restaurant. Though taking a break wasn't such a bad idea, it was time to get going. Our destination: Kharkhorin (Karakorum)—Mongolia's "old throne," the former seat of the Mongol Empire. We were already accustomed to the traffic congestion we wove through. Maybe my buddies weren't totally used to it yet, though, since they were slowing down and stopping for pedestrians at intersections. Right away, the cars behind us would start honking in a "what're you doing?" kind of way. Someone stopped for pedestrians! That didn't happen often, and probably won't happen again soon. Here, the vehicle is the law. The stronger and bigger it is, the more respect it receives.

As soon as we got out of the city, we reached the open roads. We accepted the local drivers' habits. Though this stretch of road was paved, we were eager for some dust and gravel, and went off-road to ride along-side the main road. Who cares for asphalt, we've got all we want of it back home. But, to make the party more fun, the chain on Cory's bike broke again. It had been holding together since Max had repaired it in Siberia. Some playing in the dust followed, and the new chain from Croatia was soon shining brightly on Cory's motorcycle. The quick delivery had proven to be a good decision.

We got going, but it seemed the weather had other plans for us.

The wind picked up and clouds were looming. In the distance, we could see an abandoned shed for livestock, so we headed for this meagre shelter. The half-open shed was on the southern side of a hill and was thus protected from the harsh north winds. It had a floor of dried sheep and goat dung. The shelter protected us from the rain and allowed us to prepare a warm meal.

In regions devoid of forests, such as the steppes in the semi-desert and desert regions of Asia, dung from sheep, goats, and larger animals, such as horses, camels and cattle is dried and used as fuel for fire. Actually, cattle provide almost all the necessities of life, here: milk, cheese and other dairy products, meat for food, wool and skins for clothes and shoes, and the aforementioned dung for heating and cooking. What's interesting is how that dried and compressed grass smells good when it burns. Besides the dairy products made from fermented mare's milk, a special process is used to prepare the well-known alcoholic drink, *airag*. This drink is believed to be medicinal, and maybe it is, but to me, its taste isn't that great.

The rain was trying to fall all night long, but when the sun rose, the sky cleared. This was the dawn of a beautiful sunny day, perfect for travelling and admiring the steppes.

TAKHI: WILD HORSE

We continued on our way and soon turned south. I drove about 20 kmph on dirt and sandy terrain; at times making my way through some pretty high grass. We were trying to catch a glimpse of a herd of wild horses, known here as *Takhi*.

In stories and descriptions, the famous Russian explorer and traveller, Nikolai Przewalski, introduced these animals to the West. He had encountered them around the year 1800, while travelling through Tibet with the intention of reaching Lhasa. In the West, this wild horse is known as Przewalski's horse. Though I wanted to see them, I was wondering how to go about doing so without imposing upon them? After a lot of searching and riding through the steppes and up the mountains, we almost gave up. But then we met a group of rangers who took care of this protected species, and they directed us over a hill towards a smaller herd.

Due to a lack of understanding, people have brought these animals to the brink of extinction. Just a small number remain today. But thanks to the special effort of a few people, these animals have survived. At the moment, there are over 200 here in the steppes, and a smaller number live along the edge of the Gobi towards Altai. The leader of the herd we saw

ABOVE: Three foreigners . . .
LEFT: . . . on their way . . .
BELOW: . . . to Karakorum.
OPPOSITE TOP: At the entrance to
Erdene Zuu, Karakorum.
OPPOSITE BOTTOM: Musicians per-
forming traditional Khumi music.

especially impressed me; the whole time it was watching over the behaviour of all the others. I enjoyed observing them while they roamed freely in their natural environment.

After watching the wild horses for a short while, we continued towards Kharkhorin. About an hour later, the ground beneath the tires became sandy and there were sand dunes all around. The motorcycles were digging into the sand and clouds of dust were forming. We fell a few times on the soft ground, but with no damage done. After a walk and a rest in the sand, we continued riding.

KHARKHORIN (KARAKORUM)

Other than some administrative buildings in the city's centre, this long-ago seat of the greatest kingdom in the world now consists mainly of cabins and gers spread throughout the valley. We passed by a huge specially decorated ger and parked in front of the temple, Erdene Zuu.

This impressive monastery, with hundreds of towers (posts), is a complex of temples built from materials taken from the remains of what was then the abandoned city of Karakorum. We looked around the museum on site, visited the temples, and walked to the central part of the old city. A team of archaeologists was working there.

While resting in the shade of the large turtle-shaped boulder, we watched people go about their daily chores in the temples' vicinity. The Mongols have mainly accepted the influence of Lamaism, or Tibetan Buddhism. Nowadays, after a stagnation of religious freedom while under the dominance and influence of the Soviet Union, traditions are being revived, as well as the cultural monuments and all other aspects of religious life.

The Kublai Khan transferred the kingdom's seat from this region of harsh climate to the conquered, wealthier and more comfortable region of Kanabalik, or, as it is known today, Beijing. My fellow European, Marco Polo, visited these parts during his travels. I tried to imagine what this had all once looked like. Horses and other animals grazing as they once had, and the rocks that now form a temple, and which were once a city. The descendants living here today wear clothing similar to that of their ancestors. Using my imagination, I removed some buildings from the scene around me, and I was there—in the past!

The nomads who perform traditional Khumi music prepared a little concert for us. Though I had already had an opportunity to listen to recordings of this kind of music, I got goosebumps from this experience. And from the surprise at what was happening before our eyes! These sounds probed to the heart of every cell in the body and touched the soul.

It's really complicated to convey the feelings that overcame me while listening. First, there were the vocals. Using only his voice, the singer created the effect of several other instruments accompanying him. I saw Cory trying to figure out where all the sounds were coming from. Several compositions followed that included other instruments and a very interesting dance.

In the end, the performance was concluded with a ritual round of vodka. Out of respect for the tradition, I took part in the first round, but declined the remainder of the rounds by using the gesture: ring finger, forehead, sky. It seemed that Cory participated in several rounds. Despite their offers for us to spend more time with them, we decided to continue on our journey the same day. To wish us good luck, our friends adorned our necks with blue silk scarves, known as *khadag*.

BEFORE THE STORM

On the way to Arvaikheer and the Gobi Desert, we decided to avoid the main road and take a scenic, smaller road instead, which turned out to be a great choice. This road rewarded us with a joyful ride and beautiful scenery. Sheer enjoyment for us, with room for riding like nowhere in the world—no walls or fences. How long will this last, without any fences, I don't know. Probably until the first Westerner shows up and offers money to build a concession stand? Here, for now, herds of horses, sheep, and goats graze unhindered, and the current law is, go where you want and settle where you want. The only condition is that you don't bother your neighbours. Yet with about 2.5-million people in these great expanses, most often there aren't any neighbours.

After a while on the road, we came across a ford we needed to cross.

At the site of Old Karakorum.

RIGHT: **Prayer mills** at the temple.

RIGHT: The storm is nearing.

I went first and felt the water filling my boots, then my pants getting soaked above the knee. I reached the other side, and since I was already wet, I crossed again. Tim followed. Something in the central part of his motorcycle started choking. He stopped. I ran into the stream and we somehow managed to push his motorcycle to dry ground. Cory crossed without difficulty. After several more tries, Tim succeeded in starting the engine. Water and white smoke spit out of the exhaust pipe. We continued on our way.

While resting and eating under the shade of our motorcycles in the steppes, we noticed heavy grey clouds building up and approaching from the northwest at unbelievable speed! What clouds, a storm! Saddle up and hit the gas! We were racing, but we could feel the storm was at our heels. The wind was swirling the dust in whirlwinds and lifting the vegetation. I noticed heavy sleet falling along the northern slope of the mountains. An interesting scene. In front of us, the sky was sunny and stable. Behind us, the sky had blackened as if it was night, and we were caught in between, trying to get to safety. Not sparing our motorcycles, we raced for the next hour. On the other side of the valley was some asphalt, so we crossed the stream again and headed in that direction. As soon as we reached the asphalt, we picked up the speed. After some 15 km, we saw a city ahead. What's interesting is how, after all that racing and rushing, the storm decided to change directions and circumvent Arvaikheer.

After a pretty dynamic day, accommodation, which included a shower and a cooked meal, was a true reward for this happy crowd.

ACROSS THE GOBI

Refreshed and cheerful, we got going once again. And my father, with a quick goodbye, left the group in order to carry out some of his own plans before heading for home. Knowing him, I thought he would just keep going.

Near Arvaikheer, we came across an impressive statue; a tribute to the sturdy Mongolian horse, the mor, known for its stamina. I have already described the nature of this humble and noble creature, so I'll just mention that while racing at a gallop, it can travel over twenty kilometres.

All Mongolians whom I had come across loved telling long stories about horses.

After a little over an hour of riding on mixed gravel and dirt roads towards Bayankhongor, the landscape began changing from steppe to desert. A small stream flowed nearby. We were going pretty fast, so I was surprised we even noticed it. I slowed down and crossed with ease where the water was deeper, but the ground more firm. Cory was coming relatively fast. Without slowing down much, he chose a shallower yet muddier spot to cross. He lost his balance. The motorcycle slipped and fell to the side. The fall looked pretty bad! I ran to him. Luckily, the mud had softened the fall. He stood up, and before I could reach him, he lifted the motorcycle from the water and mud by pushing it up with his back. We pushed the motorcycle out of the stream. Tim came along. Other than being wet and muddy, Cory felt OK. The motorcycle was also all right. We rested some before continuing the journey.

As we passed from the steppes to the Gobi Desert our journey was became even more interesting. I noticed solar cells on the roofs of some gers, as well as satellite antennas. This was nice to see, because in a way, with this evidence of modern technology the people were confirming their willingness to continue living where they were. Beyond the settlement, as in most places in Mongolia, there was enough room and choice of roads for us travellers to not have to worry about road congestion. However, the question of which road was the right one did come up. When that would happen, we'd always stop, examine the map, and then continue, sure about our choice of route. Sometimes, each of us would follow his own trail. Since the trails tended to diverge, we separated at times, and then waited for one another further down, before going on. And one thing's for sure, if there's a heaven for Enduro riders anywhere on this earth, then its name is Mongolia.

At Bayankhongor, we refuelled, bought some necessities, and then went on. We turned off the road towards the mountains in order to find a more sheltered spot to set up camp. We set up camp in a valley between three rocky peaks, which offered good protection from the wind, which had started blowing strongly. We set up the tents and Tim, the master chef,

. . . to sunset.

prepared an unbeatable meal. Invigorated after the warm meal, I climbed up a rocky incline not far from the tent. I listened to my footsteps as I walked. The dry and cool desert wind reminded me of how, even during the summer, it would be good to have a scarf or shawl. The Gobi is a cold desert, with more rocks than sand. It was formed from the Himalayas, which block the monsoons, so most of the humidity remains in India. Tibet, Ladak, Takla Makan and the Gobi depend more on the snowmelt from the mountain peaks for precipitation. Temperatures here range from –40°C in the winter to 45°C in the summer, which allows only the well-adapted to survive. Daily expansion and compression causes the rocks to crumble, and the wind carries the sand away, letting it settle where it pleases.

The sun was lowering behind the western desert horizon. City lights were shining in the east. Bayankhongor is actually an oasis surrounded by streams flowing with valuable water, which means life to these people. In some places there is more water, in others, there is less. But without it, there's no life. I recalled a text where a noble man warned about the balance in nature that we are responsible for because of our power.

How can you sell the sky, the air, the water?

The sun warmed our backs in the morning as we rushed down the sandy road, and clouds of dust trailed behind. Every now and then we'd meet a vehicle coming from the opposite direction and the clouds of dust would join together for a short period, then the vehicles would push out of the clouds and each would continue on its own way. No one is bothered by dust here; it is part of nature, part of our equipment and everything else.

We reached a gold-rich field, where miners were trying to find pieces of that yellow metal that someone once said is very valuable. I hope the efforts will be rewarded for these people, whose hopes lie in the earth that they dig. The way they work—under extremely strenuous conditions, in the direct sunlight, without protection, and using only primitive tools—shows how important the gold is to their livelihood. We wished the gold diggers luck and continued westward. More and more often, we were coming across wild two-humped Bactrian camels, grazing the prickly grass and bush. At times, they would even cross our path, so we would have to slow down until these ladies and gentlemen would decide to make way.

Oftentimes, they would raise their heads and watch us with their half-shut droopy eyes and long eyelashes. They were probably asking themselves what these odd creatures were doing in their sandy and dusty Eden; releasing smoke, making noise and speeding so much?

ACROSS THE RIVER

There was no shade, and the sun was burning in the desert. During our breaks, we'd rest in the shade of our bikes, pop a handful of raisins or dried cranberries into our mouths, drink some water, and then get going to the west once again.

Another ford lay ahead; this time, it was pretty wide. I went first, and somewhat carelessly charged straight across to the other side, without taking into consideration the water's current, which could push the motorcycle down. Though the water poured into my boots and I was soaking wet to the waist, I succeeded in crossing the river. Tim was next. He started at the same spot, but his motorcycle turned off halfway through. I jumped in to help, and with a lot of strain, we pushed the motorcycle across. Cory successfully crossed the river, and came over to where Tim and I were right away to help restart Tim's bike. We removed the spark plugs and air filter, and dried them. In the meantime, a group of local guys and curious kids gathered around us, all eager to help. Tim somehow managed to start the engine. We got going, but after a while, the GS started stuttering. A lot of white smoke started coming out of the exhaust pipe. I was hoping the motorcycle would just clean itself out, but soon after, we had to stop again and do some more repair work. The sun was blazing, and there we were, trying to unscrew the oil filter.

It was pretty "interesting," but after we poked at it with the screwdriver, we got the oil filter open. The next problem was to get enough oil. Tim and I had a total of three litres, but we needed three-and-a-half more. Sweaty and tired from the hot sun, we took our shirts off and sat in the shade of the motorcycles. Oil, where could we find that now?

A dog cautiously approached Cory and me. Or to be precise, the shadow of a dog. It was so emaciated; all its ribs were showing. With its tail between its legs and its back arched, it tottered as it walked. The dog was standing just a few steps from us and began circling us. Though it was acting a bit strange, and touching strange animals isn't something I'd recommend, it seemed hungry.

I opened a can of tuna and placed it on the ground, offering it to the dog. It hesitated a little, but when it sensed I meant it no harm, it came forward. The dog licked the can clean. Cory, who has two dogs of his own, joined us and started petting the dog. One more can of tuna, some water, and, reinvigorated, the dog lay down next to us. Now it looked like it had decided to be our dog!

While we sat, we saw a cloud of dust in the distance that seemed to be speeding towards us. The dust cloud stopped beside us, and the dustiest faces I had ever seen appeared. A thick layer of dust was covering these people's clothes, faces, hair, and everything else, except for their eyes. They looked as if they had been buried in sand and dust for days and had just unearthed themselves. They were a team from Scotland participating in the Mongol Rally. They were riding an unusually shaped make of motorcycle, which, among all the other things that were missing from it, had somewhere along the way lost a windshield. But they had enough oil for us all. Long live the dusty Scots! We would have managed somehow, but these guys came just at the right moment. They didn't linger, since a long ride to Ulaanbaatar awaited them. We said goodbye to our dog, who belonged to the local people, and continued across the desert towards the city of Altai. In the distance, the desert appeared to blend with the blue sky. The ground we were riding on was partly sandy and partly rocky. By now, I had improved my skills for riding on sand; weaving my way around sand dunes was starting to be truly enjoyable.

From what I could see in the distance, the trail we were following turned northward in a great arc. So I suggested to the guys we take a shortcut. We got going, but after maybe a kilometre, I realized why the road circumvented this part. Under the grass, the ground was full of holes and bumps that you don't see until you reach them. Our bikes' shock

BELOW: Gers in the desert: Satellite antennas and solar panels.
RIGHT: We're thirsty . . .
OPPOSITE BOTTOM: Our hungry dog.

systems were starting to suffer under the burden. Tim went back. Cory followed me some more, while looking for a way out. Since I had gone the furthest, I turned west, and, after some time and a lot of effort, made my way to the trail. We picked up speed again. The desert offered us numerous directions in which to go. Occasionally, Tim would fall on the sand; luckily, without consequence. We would help him lift the heavy motorcycle, and then continue riding.

CHILDREN OF THE DESERT

We came across a small settlement on a hilltop: a few gers and some humble houses. Since this place was probably a rest area for travellers, there was, in fact, one store. As soon as we stopped, a curious crowd of people, most of whom were children, surrounded us. They examined our motorcycles and equipment. Well, we fair-skinned foreigners were also a sight to see. The variety of merchandise in the store did not leave us much room for choice. No time was lost searching the aisles and shelves. You take what is offered, and that's it. Outside once again, a ball appeared from somewhere. Tim joined in the fun right away. It was cute to see him playing with the kids. Cory was laughing, while trying to communicate with the kids.

A few boys asked if we could sit them on the motorcycles. I was glad to oblige. They enjoyed the moment, probably imagining themselves riding. *I recalled a selfish thought of mine from when I was admiring these regions and wishing that modern roads never reach them. The adventure would then disappear. Actually, for us passersby, it is an adventure, while for these children, it isn't. Their adventure will begin when they start fulfilling their dreams.* Maybe this road will open new possibilities for them, but it would also bring them things they don't need anyway.

My thoughts were interrupted by a boy standing next to me. A special attraction were these boots of mine; they received a lot of attention in this part of the world. *Gutul* (which means "boots" in Mongolian) are worn every day, here, in winter and summer alike. But my shoes were a European size 48, and were probably the biggest seen since the time of Marco Polo. Oftentimes, young men would set their boots next to mine, in order to compare sizes, and then they would eye me, then my boots, then me again, and so on, for a while.

Since Mongolia is actually a plateau, the land has a gradual incline from Ulaanbaatar westward to this spot. So we didn't even notice how, by now, we were almost at an elevation of 2 000 metres above sea level, and still climbing. The sun was strong all by itself, and here, at the increased elevation, the sunrays radiated even more intensely. At these altitudes, the angle of the sun in the afternoon made riding even more difficult.

In the city of Altai, at 2 180 metres above sea level, I filled the tank and decided to test how the Tenere would manage with this much fuel for the next part of our journey. The main public square contained a statue with text engraved on it that I did not understand, as well as a large picture—an advertisement, actually—depicting Mongolian wrestling champions. Measuring some 15 metres long and about 3 metres high, this picture of about ten wrestlers, wearing special clothing, was by far the largest ad that I had seen in Mongolia. We bought some basic supplies and left the city.

After about half an hour, we entered hilly terrain once again. With only the sunset and silence accompanying us, we set up our tents for the night. I left the team and went for a walk up a nearby incline. Darkness had already engulfed our little fort. I could enjoy the last sunrays of the day from my seat on a pile of rocks atop a hill. When I took a better look, I could see that the rocks I was sitting on were actually the remains of a *chorten*. Chortens, or Tibetan *stupas*, are simple sacred constructions that are formed from piles of rocks, which in Buddhism, serve as three-dimensional symbols of the elements: earth, water, fire, and air. With just a few sweeps of my hands, I repaired the pile of rocks my own way. It'd hold until some eagle decided to use it as a watchtower, or until the next strong wind came along. I sat there for a while before returning to the tent.

THE JOURNEY TO HOVD

Part of the 450-km journey to Hovd proved to be a special test for us and for our vehicles. Riding on uneven terrain similar to bumpy roof tiles was strenuous for all the joints and connections in the motorcycles. And the rocky terrain next to the road didn't offer any possibilities for an easier

LEFT: Why the rush, you're making clouds of dust, noise, and releasing smoke . . . BELOW: Take a time out. OPPOSITE BOTTOM: . . . In a world without borders.

CLOCKWISE FROM RIGHT:
Gold diggers.
The bridges of Bayan Hongor.
Saying goodbye.
Good luck, big guy!

ride, either. After this exhausting stretch of road, we stopped in the desert for a bite to eat. No matter in which direction you looked, all you saw was the sky and desert blending at the horizon. We opened some canned food and ate while standing.

A familiar scent got me looking around. Unbelievable! Onions! Thin blades of onion were poking out of the sand. I pulled one out and tried it. A sea of onions in the desert! Cool! This was going to make for a great side dish with our tuna.

Vibrations from the bumpy terrain caused my front fender to crack where it joined the front wheel. Of course, this happened while I was riding.

I packed the fender in my luggage, planning to fix it later. When I started up once again, I noticed it was still hard to ride?! For a moment, I thought about how strange it was that simply removing a fender could make such a difference in the quality of the ride. Then, I noticed a nail stuck in my rear tire. There weren't many nails in these regions, but I had managed to find one.

The next few hours under the hot sun of the western Gobi strained the last drop of sweat from my body. Sweaty, sticky, and suntanned, my body was the perfect place for all the dust particles carried by the dry desert wind to settle. I removed the front wheel and began replacing the rubber tire. By then, the guys had returned and had joined me (they had been riding a few kilometres ahead of me). We mounted the new tire, however, just as I was about to get going, it started releasing air again. This had to be a joke! The new tire, which I had been carrying as a spare, already had two holes in it. The sun was blazing, and I felt how my lips were chapped. Though I couldn't see myself, I *could* see the dried and worn faces of my Canadian friends. We repeated the whole repair process. After double-checking the tire—in the hot sun with no shade—we didn't waste energy on words and just got going.

To top it all off, we were down to our last drops of water in our bottles. Since the sun was still shining high in the sky, we still had many hours of riding across the rocks, sand and numerous mirages ahead of us. Obviously, the Gobi Desert gets bored from time to time, and decides to

Shopping in the desert.

Games in the sun.

play with us. It knows all its visitors, their intentions, and why they are crossing it. I could just feel this, and believed that the Gobi would take care of everything. And that's how it went. There, under the shade of a prickly bush, we noticed a cool stream. The icy cap of the mountain's peak in the distance was melting under the summer sun, causing streams of water to flow down it. A thin, cool and clear stream of water trickled down the valley. After we refreshed ourselves, we filled our bottles with drinking water. And as a compensation prize for having had to "play around" with the tire tubes, the sky presented us with a unique spectacle: in the distance, the red ball was about to descend behind the peaks of the distant Altai Mountains. We decided to ride westward some more. About an hour later, tired from the dynamic events of the day, we set up our tents in the sand and hit the sack.

In the morning, as usual, first I shook out my boots, to make sure no little visitors were stuck inside. We folded our dusty tents in a hurry, filled our stomachs, checked our bikes and then got going. While riding, we enjoyed the view of the Western Gobi, as well as the mirages in the distance that were a result of the heat. Until then, I had thought mirages couldn't be seen too often. But here, they were a normal occurrence. Mirages even appeared in different shades of colour, depending on the hue of the surrounding environment.

We reached a caravan. I slowed down. It was interesting to see the camels and horses loaded with all the belongings of these people, going somewhere. Some people were riding horses, while others were herding cattle. Dogs were trying to assist with the cattle, while children waved at us from their comfortable seats astride two-humped camels. I'm sure they know the song about *Timee*, the Mongolian camel, I thought. This was a song I had heard earlier, and it seemed like a popular children's song in this region.

Earlier, children eagerly told us about a camel, which, at times, did not allow her baby camel to suckle. After playing the *morin khuur*, a Mongolian bowed stringed instrument, and singing certain notes, the camel would relax, shed some tears, and then let the baby suckle. Music is obviously just a vibration that resonates with the mother camel and relaxes

LEFT: Leave at least a little . . .
BELOW: . . . and then a stream, after all.

BELOW: Service station in the desert.

her. Everything else just falls into place afterwards, as with people. Each of us has our own vibration we resonate with; it gets us in synch.

Here, distances are measured in kilometres, by the hundreds. Every now and then, we would come across a ger surrounded by a herd of livestock. This livestock supplies the nomads with almost everything they need for life. Just like their masters, these camels, horses, sheep and goats, are well-adjusted to the harsh climate and scarce resources. They share this vast land with wolves, desert foxes, eagles and falcons, which seem to live in great numbers here.

Meeting such people is always interesting to me, and gets me thinking. The nomads here have become one with the desert, and live here isolated from social contacts, almost all alone. Yet, they don't seem lonely. They are surrounded by sand, rocks, the occasional spiky bush, and the great expanse of the blue sky that looks as if you could just touch it if you stretched out your hand a little. Connected with nature and with themselves, to us, they appear to live a humble, yet satisfied, life. I noticed that as soon as guests would arrive, the hosts would serve a cup of tea, as well as anything else that was available. Accommodation was easy to find, as well as assistance, whenever needed. At any moment, they were ready to drop whatever they were doing and focus on the needs of others. And, if necessary, they would spend the whole day, or as long as it took, to help finish a task. Adults watched over all children as they would their own, and all responsibilities were shared. And for these curious—and oftentimes, barefooted—kids, we always had a sweet or an apple to offer. Although there weren't many stores in this region, whenever we'd come across one we'd stock up, also taking some fresh fruit and treats for local children. To some of these children, our apples were the first they had ever tasted.

Since the nomads' past is an important part of their identity, it is present in the stories and songs of today. People there live their lives in the here-and-now. Nevertheless, their famous past is ever-present and plays an important role in their lives. The three traditional disciplines they enjoy, and often compete in among themselves, are: horseback riding, archery and wrestling. I wouldn't say these are sports; they are more like life skills. A traditional competition, known as *Nadaam*, is held every year throughout the country. *Nadaam* means "game," and during Nadaam, skill, strength and speed are measured. All participants are respected, but the most skilful are respected the most.

A dark spot in the distance seemed to be advancing. As we neared it, the spot grew in size until we could recognize it: a car that had broken down. We stopped and learned that the man driving the car was expecting other assistance to arrive soon. Someone had already passed by earlier and was going to send help. But, who knew when that would be? We left him two bottles of water and some food. He appreciated the gesture, thanked us, and we continued going west.

As we approached the mountains, the roads occasionally led us through canyons. Shadows were stretching out and parts of the road were in the shade. *Har Us Nuur* (which means "Black Water Lake" in Mongolian), a large lake to the north, attracted our attention. Just a few metres deep and overgrown with reeds, rushes and other water vegetation, this national park is home to numerous marsh birds, such as those we had often seen fly past us. Soon the road led us up an incline.

At the ridge, we came across a large sign marking the entrance to the city of Hovd. To the east, we saw a large ovoo. This pyramidal pile of rocks with a blue *hatag* flag atop it, situated on quite an impressive spot some hundred metres from the road, is a place where travellers stop to pray for a safe trip. From this vantage point, looking down at the city in the valley surrounded by mountains, I felt as if we were entering a kingdom from long ago. We circled the ovoo, walking, as is customary, took some pictures, and then began our descent towards this unknown kingdom. I tanked up at a gas station and was glad to see that we had reached the city, since I had only four decilitres of fuel remaining, meaning I had had exactly enough in my tank for the distance between Altai and Hovd.

Satisfied, we set off to look for a hotel. Finally, a shower! Now we needed to fill our stomachs and recharge the laptop batteries, maybe even check emails. But our hopes didn't last long, because the electricity went out in the city. This happened more often than not in these regions. So I could forget the warm shower. I just freshened up with a bottle of water.

At the entrance to Hovd.

Next we went for a candlelit dinner at a restaurant that ran by the saying: "You can order whatever you want, and we'll bring you whatever we've got, and you'll be satisfied." Whatever it was, it was delicious. Even Tim tried to grab some of my rice.

In the morning, we heard that the electricity had come back around three in the morning, but by that time, I was deep asleep. While checking out of the hotel, I enjoyed a show put on by the nice lady at the reception desk and Tim, as they tried to combine elements of western practicality and the rules of this lost kingdom. In order to compensate for his dissatisfaction for not having had running water, electricity, and thus a warm meal and shower, Tim tried to bargain his way down to a lower price for the rooms. Dead serious, he deliberately put fewer pieces of Mongolian currency, *tögrögs*, on the counter, underpaying. The black-haired lady took the money, counted it, and then, with a straight face, placed it back on the counter near Tim. He found himself in a slightly awkward situation. Cory and I just stood to the side and watched, smiling, while the black-haired receptionist coldly ignored Tim. Since Tim is one of those people with a soft nature, he judged this battle was futile. So, he added the remaining amount of money to the pile, smiled, and we left.

THE ALTAI MOUNTAINS

We left Hovd and headed for Olgi. Outside the city, the road disappeared between the distant mountains. At first, the road was good enough for us to ride at 100 kmph. But, as expected, the road, or better said—the path—worsened as we went. So, we gradually had to slow down.

With clouds overhanging and us climbing to higher elevations, it was getting colder and colder. We rode slowly, following a mountain river. Since we had been travelling together for quite a while, our mealtimes were well coordinated, and the rumbling of our stomachs reminded us it was time to eat. In search of a spot for us to eat and rest, my co-travellers were on the lookout for access to the riverbank. We turned off the road and crossed some rocky terrain in order to get to the river. Listening to the river hum as it flowed, and seeing the snow-covered peaks around us, we could tell we had reached the Altai Mountains.

CLOCKWISE FROM RIGHT:
After the fall.
At a crossing.
Desert onions.

I could see some people and livestock in the distance. Tim was already putting the water on to boil, while Cory prepared the packages of dehydrated food. Here was the perfect spot for camping. Smells of the food cooking spread from the pot. Sunshine managed to make its way through the clouds, warming us up. After just a few bites of cooked food, we felt even better. We were eating in silence, each absorbed in his own thoughts, when a man wearing a hat approached us.

Short and stout, the man with the hat walked towards us holding a stick in his left hand and carrying a worn out rucksack on his back. When we came face to face, he offered some cheese. I accepted, and ate a piece. Cory and Tim kindly declined. Like numerous others before him, our new friend noticed the map in my tank bag. Since he seemed pretty interested in it, I took it out for him to have a better look. He showed me a valley that was not too far away, and then pointed at my motorcycle. I understood what this was about. He wanted me to give him a ride, in order to shorten his mileage on foot. Maybe he wanted to take us in as guests. For a while, now, I had been thinking about installing firmer shocks, since the ones I had were too weak for my overloaded motorcycle on this kind of terrain. I couldn't take him aboard because of the luggage. He simply had nowhere to sit on my motorcycle. I explained that this was impossible. He took my rejection well, said goodbye, and continued his trek.

I watched him leaving in the direction we were headed, and thought about motorcycles I had seen in Asia. Almost all of them had been loaded to the maximum. In Mongolia, three persons comfortably fit on one motorcycle. If necessary, there was always enough room for one more person, and for a sheep, too. Not to mention how the cars were overloaded!

Feeling I hadn't done everything I could have, I felt bad. But then again, all that equipment loaded on my motorcycle . . .

We got going. This region demanded warmer clothing. Knowing I'd be snug in my warm sleeping bag at night, though, I didn't even feel the cold while riding. As we were enjoying the view of the great expanses and new horizons opening up before us, we noticed a motorcyclist approaching from the distance. Right away I supposed this was some local. We were nearing each other at great speeds, so I squinted and strained my eyes until I could see that the motorcycle was like ours. Surely some traveller, I thought. The Suzuki Strom stopped by the side of the road, as did we. The rider took his helmet off and greeted us in English. I don't know how, but I recognized he was Turkish.

"Hello. Where are you coming from?" Tim asked, while I checked out the California licence plate.

"Hello! I live in Los Angeles, but am coming from Turkey. I'm riding to Vladivostok. From there I'll fly back to California." Mohamed said.

"Interesting! We're circling the world and heading towards Europe." Tim answered, while I took advantage of the chance to snap some photos of the landscape.

Mohamed was travelling alone by motorcycle from the direction we were headed in, so Cory and Tim asked him about the road conditions awaiting us in the next few days.

That day, we planned to reach Olgiy and spend the night there, before heading for Russia in the morning. In this land without fences, as I have said, and without bridges, as I would add, the landscape became increasingly vibrant with colours and variety. *Snow-capped peaks and glaciers nurture a special world of their own in these high Altai Mountains.*

This mountainous region is the home to the renowned eagle hunters, the Kazakhs, and is also the home of the rarely seen snow leopard.

A white mountain appeared before us, leaving us breathless with its grandeur. Then, we came upon a mountain lake and a stream to cross. This was one of those places where I would have loved to spend some more time. We took a break and admired the landscape before we got going down the dusty road to Olgiy.

Not long after we left the lakeside, we came across a group of locals trying to repair a motorcycle tire, so we stopped to offer assistance. I was glad to be able to help, and they were happy to see us, with our well-equipped motorcycles. Since he had a tire filled with tiny holes, Tim always kept his pump at arm's reach. Everything was great until we realized the pump's valve and the tire's valve weren't compatible. What bad

Altai – in the heart of Asia.

luck. Accustomed to scarcity in these regions, these guys would manage by improvisation somehow. So we went on our way, relaxed. There wasn't much left of the day, but we were stopping often to enjoy the unique scenery. We caught up with a truck driving in the same direction we were. Tim had overtaken it a while ago, and sped on. Next was Cory, then me. Another truck was coming from the opposite direction. It lifted a cloud of dust, making the right turn ahead of us a "mission impossible."

THE FALL

It just appeared in front of me! There was no time to react. I entered the curve at too great a speed and fell to the right. My bike slid on its side, and I slid part of the way with it. There was a lot of dust and pebbles flying all over the place! The spare tires, which had been tied down, flew off the motorcycle and to the side. While I was still falling and sliding, I noticed Cory also lying on the ground. The dust slowly settled, and we saw how the two of us, along with our motorcycles, were lying on the sand between some large rocks, on the same curve in the road! We each called out to one another, "Are you all right?"

"Yes!" we both answered. Not understanding how this could have happened at all, I quickly got up. Cory was having trouble getting up, so I ran over to him to help him and lift his bike. He seemed to have injured his ankle, but since he could move his toes, he figured no bones were broken, and it'd be OK. Just a little rest would be enough. I could feel that my right elbow was injured. The elbow pad in my jacket had slipped from its position while I was sliding. My jacket and my elbow were ripped. It was OK, though. None of our bones were broken. Seeing what had happened, Mongolians and Kazakhs astride horses hurried to us. Since Cory couldn't walk, I asked one of the locals to help lift my bike.

After lifting it, we saw that no major damage had been done; just some scratches on the gas tank and plastic parts. We pushed the motorcycle over to where Cory was. I put the kickstand down and noticed that the panniers on Cory's bike, as well as the racks, were bent. His motorcycle was better off than mine, though, and, little by little, I started to repair the damage. Soon, piles of stuff surrounded me on the ground, since I had to empty the panniers in order to fix them. The front right turn signal was also damaged. I was angry this had happened at all, but there was no going back in time.

I let the locals straighten out the panniers with the small axe, a task they completed eagerly. What was most interesting of all was the fact that an hour had already passed since the fall, and there was no sign of Tim. We hoped he was all right and would come soon, since he had obviously continued, not seeing that we had fallen. After about an hour-and-a-half, Tim arrived, clearly fraught with worry.

His eyes were all red, but he was happy to see us. I had never seen him like that before. I was glad he found us, because I could just imagine what thoughts had come to mind while he was looking for us.

"I kept riding and stopped after a curve. I lay down on the ground and waited for you guys to pass so I could film you. Then I realized you weren't coming, so I turned around and started coming back. No one along the way had seen you. The further I went, the more worried I became. I rode forty kilometres," Tim said.

It was OK; at least we now knew where each of us was. We straightened the panniers on my bike, while the Mongolians finished straightening my aluminum cases. After we cleaned and bandaged my wounded elbow, Cory limped over to his bike, and we got going slowly towards the city. Night was already falling. Back in Russia, we had agreed we wouldn't ride by night, but this was an exceptional circumstance. We needed to reach the city. I rode first, swallowing dust from a truck in front of me.

Riding on gravel by night was strenuous, especially since the load on the back end of my bike made the headlight point too high in the air, so visibility was poor. Also, the steering was off-centre after the fall, so I had to be especially careful while riding. I crossed over to a path that ran parallel to the road, and that's how I got rid of the truck. This was the only way. My buddies followed, though occasionally, I stopped to wait for them. In the distance I could see a few lights shining, meaning we had a little further to go. We went down towards the city, and reached a paved road.

Right away, we searched for a hotel. After the accident, a comfortable rest would do us good. However, the hotel we came across did not have any vacancies. Not even one room was available, but we were told about a ger-camp nearby. Sure! We agreed. As long as we had some sort of accommodation so we could have something to eat and drink. We headed out of town in the direction that the hotel receptionist had suggested. After going down a gravel road, we saw some lights. But, the lights were coming from the other side of the river, and the river was too deep to cross. (I should note that only light that was, in fact, shining, was just one light bulb in the distance, and a transmitter in town, blinking a faint red hue.)

We reached some sandy ground and struggled as we rode across the fine sand. My motorcycle swung off balance, and I fell. So we decided to camp right there. We'd had enough for the day. We had no idea what was around us, but that didn't matter, anyhow. We were done. While preparing the tent, Tim noticed that his pegs were missing. I probably would have laughed at the situation, but I was in no laughing mood. All I wanted to do was drink some water and rest. Cory took the water filter and went to the river. But he returned with no "catch," since the water was too muddy and smelled strange. We shared the precious four decilitres of water that we had. Even our food supplies were running low. Luckily, Cory had two cans of tuna. Totally tired, thirsty and sweaty, Cory and I went into our tents while Tim just lay on the ground and covered himself with what remained of his tent.

The sun rising above the horizon woke us. Actually, Tim helped also, since he couldn't sleep any more. Good thing, since we needed to reach the Russian border as early as possible. On weekends the border is closed, and we reached it on a Friday. I got out of the tent and noticed we had camped in a beautiful spot. But, we packed up and got going. These were our last kilometres across the Mongolian Altai. It was too bad we had to go, but I was looking forward to reaching the Russian part. After about one hundred kilometres, we reached the Mongolian side of the border. Tim and Cory bought water and changed money at a booth before the border, while I kept watch over the motorcycles. When they came back, I went in to the booth to buy some Russian rubles.

As soon as I entered, I found myself in a living room. Several people were seated. I let them know I wanted to buy rubles, and placed one hundred dollars on the table. They made an offer, which I refused. That was probably a test, since I thought a dollar was worth more than three thousand rubles. Their next offer was better, so I accepted. While putting the money in my pocket, I remembered how I had a lot of Mongolian coins to get rid of. Once again, I did not like their offer. They had offered me a box of cookies that had already faded in the sun. I had a good laugh, and left.

I drank some water, replenishing the lost liquids in my body, and gave a sign to the guys that we could get going to Russia. Amazingly, we filled out the papers on the Mongolian side with surprising speed. They put stamps in our passports and did the paperwork for the motorcycles. After chatting with the Mongolian officials, we were told we'd reach the Russian side during lunch break. They opened the gate, opening the way to Russia. We entered no man's land, a thirty-kilometre stretch of land between the two countries.

ABOVE: **Across the river and towards the Altai.**

OPPOSITE MIDDLE: **Let's give it a try...**

Chorten.

ONCE AGAIN IN RUSSIA
(21/8–29/8/2009)
1 200 km

THE RUSSIAN ALTAI

At the Russian border, we spent the next half-hour sunbathing. When a rainstorm came pouring down, we leaned against the wall of the border control building. After a few minutes, a man came out to "wash" our motorcycles. He took a hose and wet mainly the tires and rims. Apparently the Russians didn't want Mongolian dust from our motorcycles. This service cost us two dollars. Now with the receipt, we could move on to the next stage of the procedure. Once again, we had to fill out the same forms for passage back in to Russia. I already knew by heart what to write on each line. One more stamp in my passport next to my Russian visa, and time to move on.

The whole procedure for crossing the border lasted longer than I had expected. Most of the time had been spent sitting on a chair or shifting to and fro, so at least we were saving our energy for what was to come next.

When we got going, the rain was falling with less intensity. Nevertheless, since it was still raining, and we had lost so much time crossing the border, we decided to look for accommodation for us and for our motorcycles. We rode to the first village we came to and stopped at the first store we laid eyes on to buy some food and supplies. At the counter, I asked the cashier lady where we could sleep. She pointed to a wooden house right near the store. As I crossed the front yard, two cows that were grazing outside the house froze when they saw me, and followed my every move with their stares. In order to enter the old wooden house, I had to jump over a puddle, and then bend down, since the doorway was low. After a forceful push, I opened the door and found myself inside. I shouted a few times, but no one answered. To my left was a door, so I opened it and saw a man sleeping on a worn out bed. He woke after I thumped with my boots on the floor several times.

The man was obviously drunk, which, in these regions, is more or less a "normal state." He eyed me in shock as I stood nearby. Maybe that was because the doorframe was low, so it hid part of my face.

"I heard you offer room to sleep! Do you have enough room for three bikers?" I asked loudly, while watching his gestures.

"Of course! Wait till I get up. You can sleep in a ger outside the house." He answered.

"Let's first see what kind of a ger it is," I said.

It was clean on the inside, and neat on the outside. The Kazakh ger, or yurt, is more elaborately furnished than the Mongolian one. Great! I thought. I called the guys over and showed them where we could sleep. They agreed right away, and began taking their wet gear off. Sergej shared the ger with us, and slept on the only bed. We slept on the floor, which is the traditional nomad bed anyway.

Our plan was to get to Barnaul, where some motorcycle parts we had ordered from Croatia were expected to arrive in four to five days' time. After that, we would head for Kazakhstan. The parts we had ordered included everything we needed for the remaining stretch of our journey: tires for Tim and Cory's bikes, a spare chain, oil filters, a new rear-view mirror for Cory's bike, a thermostat for my bike and a few other important items.

Several times while on this journey, my motorcycle had overheated, making the coolant overflow. That was why Cory and Tim suggested I order a new thermostat, which would help regulate the temperature.

Since the motorcycle parts were a few days late in arriving, I suggested we spend some time in a cabin in the mountains that we had come across about 300 km before Barnaul. The acceptable price and great location of this cabin in the woods was just beckoning to us to stop for a rest. It had a large living room, kitchen, four bedrooms upstairs, a sauna, and gym.

This place couldn't be better, and we had enough time to service the motorcycles. We fixed the fender on my bike that had cracked back in Mongolia, straightened out the bent central stand on Cory's bike, and checked everything else. In the evening, we had a barbeque and relaxed, not doing anything at all. And that was good, just not for too long.

In the eighteenth century, During Russia's expansion across Siberia all the way to the Sea of Japan, Russia conquered this part of the Altai. Today, the indigenous population of Altai numbers about seventy thousand. Though partially assimilated, they maintain their autonomous

CLOCKWISE FROM RIGHT:
Barnaul.
Wooden house where we went for some relaxation and to repair our motorcycles.
Crossing the Russian Altai.
Detail from a yurt in the Altai.

status. Like most central-Asian nations, the Altai, including the Tuvans and the Yakuts in the north, belong to the Turkic linguistic group.

Tim loved the Russian sauna, known as a *banya*. He liked it so much that he asked the owner how it worked and asked to see the blueprints so that he could make one for himself in Calgary. I can endure the cold better than the heat, and don't care much for saunas or any other places where I can't breathe, and where I have to put up with heat and steam, but they convinced me to try it. So I went in, and then regretted having done so. It was so hot that I couldn't see a thing. My nose was burning. I covered my face with my hands and fled straight out. I'll relax my own way, by doing nothing.

By the time I was feeling back to normal after the sauna, the sun was already setting. Nevertheless, I went out for a walk. Two local dogs that I had fed earlier, with the remains of a cookie from my pocket, noticed me and joined me. Soon, the first stars appeared in the sky. Very easily, I noticed the one star that I sort of consider my own.

· · ·

When I was ten years old, I went with my father to Bosnia to visit the great-grandfather I was named after. I had always considered him very important from the stories I had often heard before meeting him. Though he had finished only a few years of elementary school, he kept an atlas at his bedside. He was interested in other cultures and lands. Despite his years, he was always doing something, and after a hard day's work, he'd drink his shot of whiskey, *rakia*. One day while I was visiting, after his evening ritual, he took me for a walk by the river. While walking, he talked about our family's history. He was proud of our history, and was especially proud of us youngsters, and he believed in a promising future for us. Each of us was important to him, and he wanted us to stay together and keep in touch. I took this conversation seriously and carefully listened to his every word. I was wondering why he was saying all of this to me, but I figured he probably felt like doing so and that he knew why. At the end of our conversation, he showed me a star in the sky, and said:

"Petar, see that star?"

"I see it." I said.

"Eh, good. I said this to your father, too. Remember it. When you're somewhere far away, look at it. I often look at it, too. It keeps us together, no matter where we are."

. . .

After spending three days in this paradise, it was time to go. Since rain always knew when we needed to hit the road, it accompanied us all the way to Biysk. We stopped only to get some water, and then continued towards Barnaul.

Situated along the banks of the river Ob, Barnaul is the administrative centre of the Altai Region. Just about 200 km from Novosibirsk, this is the only city in Siberia with a population of one million. I had been planning to visit Novosibirsk, since Yamaha had a service centre there. But after I met Tim and Cory, the route changed. So, the parts that I had been planning to buy in Novosibirsk were going to arrive in Barnaul, together with the other parts we had ordered from Croatia.

BARNAUL

As soon as we reached Barnaul, we started looking for a place to sleep. And we sure did a lot of searching. We would follow a main road, hoping to reach some sort of hotel, and each time, we would end up in some suburb. For some reason, we just could not figure which way to go, and we could not see any hotels anywhere. We asked passersby for directions to a hotel. I let Tim do the talking, and, actually, I was amazed at how well he managed with his Russian. Tim found out which direction we needed to go. Cory and I followed. While riding, I felt something scraping somewhere around the rear tire. At first, I thought it was the chain, but when I turned around for a glimpse, I could see that it wasn't. Just a few more kilometres, then we're there, I thought.

But what could it be? We parked behind the hotel. The wheel bearing. Nothing serious. Good thing I had some spare ones, so I wouldn't have to buy any here. It would be too complicated to try and find any that fit. Since we were going to stay here for two days, there was enough time to take care of this, so I put my stuff in the room and went with Cory and Tim to look for a post office. To ease themselves of the stuff that they had no need for while en route across Siberia and Mongolia, Tim and Cory had sent part of their luggage by post from Khabarovsk to Barnaul.

So now it was time to see how the Russian postal service worked. The main post office was in the city's centre. With my somewhat better knowledge of Russian, I helped my friends collect their stuff. They didn't have any sort of receipt to present at the post office. We just said we were expecting a package from Khabarovsk. As if the postal workers knew we would be coming that day, the package was set just behind the counter, waiting for us. Tim and Cory were happy to see the tires and the pile of dehydrated food that they had sent from the heart of Siberia just a month earlier.

In the morning, Cory and I went to change the ball bearing in my bike. We removed the tire and tried to get the bearing out. After a few strikes, we got it out, but we also broke the sprocket. The sprocket had already been partially damaged from when the chain broke, back in Canada. Obviously, we were going to have to find someone to do some welding.

Behind the hotel, where we were working on the bikes, some workers were building a new house. We were interesting to them, so they kept coming up to us. Noticing we had damaged one of the parts, they offered to take us to a motorcycle centre. Great! We sat in the truck and headed for the moto centre.

From the outside, Moto Centar—that was the store's name—looked like a huge container. But inside, it was a regular workshop in a typical Russian state of creative mess. Piles of dismantled motorcycles, parts and tools decorated the floor. And, as in most workshops, the inevitable calendars with pictures of naked women decorated the walls. I showed a repairman the damaged piece, and, right away, he knew what to do. He'd weld the piece and we could come the next day to pick it up. We went back to the hotel with the worker who had taken us there. People here were really friendly and willing to help. We went to look for a store that sold motor oil. We were still waiting for the final package to arrive from Khabarovsk. In it were, among other things, filters.

The package arrived the following day. Even though we were complete strangers to her, Julija, who worked at the post office, helped us a lot, and took care of customs. Tim was especially happy to see new tires for his motorcycle. He would no longer have to inflate his tire twice a day. Cory and I wanted to change the tire. Since we had time, we decided to do it manually. It was already too late when we realized that it would have been easier to mount the new tire if we had first lubricated the part between the tire and the rim.

While we were changing the tire, Tim watched a movie on TV in his room. He came out just in time to help fix the motorcycle. He had wanted to change the tires at a repair shop, but Cory had convinced him to change them manually. Tim rolled up his sleeves, got to work, and was all sweat after the first five minutes. I admit: we were also all wet, since there was no shade anywhere. We rode Cory's motorcycle to pick up the welded sprocket.

When I saw what the repairman had done, I said, "That's it! Just like new!" I was really satisfied with what I saw. By the time I returned to the hotel, the tires were mounted on Tim's motorcycle. All that was left to do was inflate the tires. While we were at it, we changed the oil. We didn't know where to dispense of the old oil. So I took two trash bags, put one in the other, and poured the oil in. A few larger drops splashed on my pants. Good thing they were black, so the spots were hardly visible. After we emptied the tank, I screwed the cap back on so that I could pour the new oil in. But, obviously, I still hadn't developed a fine touch for screwing! I managed to screw the cap on so tightly, that it broke. The cap fell to the ground, while the body of the screw remained inside the tank. I told Cory what had happened, and he suggested we tape the screw so that it wouldn't fall into the engine from the bike's vibrations.

But then he remembered that he had a magnet with him, so he tried to remove the screw with it. While Cory took care of that business, I took the old tires and threw them in the container. I wasn't even gone two minutes, and Cory was waving at me with the piece of screw in his hand. I was glad he succeeded, though just taping it would have been enough, since this was the last oil change of the journey. The next oil change would be in Croatia.

TOWARDS KAZAKHSTAN

The serviced motorcycles with new tires were ready for new challenges. We got a late start that morning, so it was questionable whether we would make it to the border in time, or would have to set up camp somewhere along the way. But that didn't matter anyway, since we weren't in a hurry to get anywhere. We rode without stopping towards the border, and stopped only to refuel. Every now and then, other motorcyclists would pass by. They were probably heading for some bikers' gathering, I thought, and guessed right. A group that was refuelling alongside us when we had stopped asked if we would join them.

Maybe part of me did want to go, but I was more for continuing the journey. So, we voted. Cory definitely wanted to go to the gathering, but getting there would require a 50-km detour from our planned route. Tim agreed with me. We knew we wouldn't reach the border in time if we went. My reason for not wanting to go was simple: I hadn't slept well the night before and wasn't in the mood for socializing. I'd rather sleep in peace in some field with the mosquitoes. And that's how it went. Some 10 km from the border, we turned into a field, got off the road, set up our tents, and cooked some food. Right away, we were surrounded by swarms of persistent mosquitoes. They were fighting amongst themselves to get through our clothes to our skin. We couldn't take it for long. We finished our dinner and dove into our tents. I fell asleep just moments later.

A ruckus woke me in the morning. As I opened my eyes, I saw that the sun was just appearing, and the world was just beginning a new rotation. So, I rubbed my eyes, and looked for a drink. When I poked my head out of the tent, I saw what was happening. Cory was putting his tent away. Nothing was clear to me. I got out of the tent and went to take a leak by a tree. The guys were almost ready to get going.

"We couldn't wake you, so we just started packing. Maybe that'd wake you." Cory said.

"You could have shaken my tent, I'd sure hear that," I answered.

So, it happened after all! I was usually up and ready to go before Tim and Cory, and would then wait or help out. This time, however, I put my helmet on started the engine while still a bit drowsy.

We reached the main road again and headed for the border. A few cars were already forming a queue, so we split lanes in order to be first in line. The border was not open yet, since these fine sirs started working at ten o'clock. Luckily, there was a mini store nearby, so we got ice cream for breakfast and some water. For the next hour, we sat, or lay, on the asphalt, waiting for the officials to come. A bus approached us. From a distance, it looked like a tourist bus, but when it came nearer, I realized it was transporting the officials, who were coming to work. I glanced at my watch and saw that they had come a few minutes early. Good thing that the bus didn't burst a tire on the way here, or we would have really waited a long time. The bus stopped right next to our motorcycles. People came out dressed in green uniforms. They looked more like generals than border officials.

The Russian side of the border was soon open, so we filled out the same forms that we had filled out a few days earlier, when crossing from Mongolia into Russia. In addition to correcting mistakes we had made while filling out the forms, we had to open our luggage and show the border officials what we were carrying. So far, we always managed to pass without receiving any "special treatment."

Already used to bureaucracy in this country, the surprising efficiency of their procedure, this time, shocked us. I almost felt as if they had forgotten something. Actually, who knows, maybe someone had informed them that they should get rid of us as soon as possible? Whatever, the answer will be this journey's secret!

KAZAKHSTAN
(29/8/–11/9/2009)
4 500 km

Sharing goodness multiplies goodness.

—Anonymous

We reached the booth where we were to hand over our passports. The visa that I had obtained in Mongolia was just a sticker in my passport, and it was filled out by hand. Obviously, that was enough. Though I knew we could communicate in Russian in Kazakhstan, the border officials insisted on communicating as much as possible in their own language. Not even I understood what the officials were saying. I know the Kazakh language is related to Turkish, but all I know in Turkish is *burek, sarma, baklava* (traditional food from Turkey popular throughout the regions where the Ottoman Empire once ruled). Whenever one of the officials would say something, the three of us would just turn to each other and shrug our shoulders. We'd finish with a wave of hands while eyeing the one speaking. And that's how we invented the winning combination for communication. We repeated this act at every counter and quickly flew past each with ease. Since there weren't many people wanting to cross the border, we soon found ourselves on the other side, in Kazakhstan.

We crossed the border to the Kazakh side on the August 29, 2009, or the year 1430, if we refer to the Islamic calendar, which is used here. The border officials probably made a deal with the elements to rid our tires of the Russian dust, because rain accompanied us all the way to Semipalatinsk, about 40 km beyond the border. I wasn't complaining. For a consolation prize, we were given the opportunity to photograph a double rainbow. And not only that: I kept part of the treasured Russian dust deep in my lungs, so I feel it even now, while writing this. Cory just sped past us, so he probably didn't even notice the double rainbow. It didn't matter. He'd see it in the pictures after the trip.

We decided to sleep in Semi. There, we found a hotel situated beside a traffic roundabout along the main road, and took one room for the three of us. One of us slept on the bed, the other, on the couch, and the third, on the floor. While we were taking our stuff into the hotel, someone noticed my Croatian licence plate on the motorcycle and approached me.

"How's the fish in Croatia?" The man spoke in Russian.

"Excuse me?" I asked, thinking either I didn't hear well or he wasn't talking to me.

"How's the fish in Croatia?" he repeated.

"To me it's great. I eat fish often."

"How much does a kilogram of fish cost?" he asked another question.

"I have no idea." I answered with an uninterested tone of voice.

"I'd like to start a business there like the one I have here," he replied proudly.

"All right. Enjoy! I have no idea how much a kilogram of fish costs." I really could not recall at that moment.

"Nothing, then. But, how are the roads there? Are they wide?" he proudly asked, since he was driving a Hummer.

"Yeah, they're wide enough for us motorcyclists," I answered with a joke.

He laughed and continued shooting question after question. I just said goodbye and left. Though I would have gladly answered all his questions, he was starting to get on my nerves. Perseverance is the key to success, so I believed he'd make it with his business.

In the evening, we went to the store to buy something for dinner: rice, tuna, a pineapple, onions. While Tim prepared the meal, Cory and I changed the thermostat in my motorcycle. I didn't even know where to start looking for the thermostat, yet, to Cory, this was just another routine task. First, he removed the housing, and explained how the whole system worked. Soon, he was done. I took the bike for a test ride, and then let the engine run for a while. There it went again! Overheating. "Looks like it's the sensor," Cory said.

We improvised, or, more precisely, Cory "The Pro" connected the ventilator to the switch. So, during slower rides across town, or whenever necessary, I could just turn it on. It worked; the motorcycle didn't overheat anymore.

. . .

With the disappearance of the CCCP (USSR) from the world scene, Kazakhstan, the land of free riders (*Kazakh* literally means "free rider"), with about fifteen million people, gained independence. These nomads once lived in the expanse of steppes and deserts from the Caspian Sea to the Altai. But, with the rise of democracy in the Soviet Union, a great number of herdsmen abandoned this traditional way of life.

Political systems, especially those of more recent times, don't really like nomads. They are constantly picking up and going somewhere else, with no regard for borders, making it difficult for institutions and authorities to send bills. And when they do receive bills, they aren't eager to pay them. Of course, nomads are reluctant to allow themselves to be watched. So, disharmony ensues. Nomads prefer the sky as the roof above their heads, while the authorities would prefer to be the "All-Seeing Eye" in that sky.

. . .

We continued south towards the city that was once Kazakhstan's capital, Almaty. Astana was proclaimed the capital city of Kazhakstan because of its geographic position, which enabled more balanced development and layout of the population in the city than the former capital Almaty, which is on the border with Kyrgyzstan. The road we were following was one of those you need to be ready to take on. It was paved, and, if you were to stand in the middle of the road and look into the distance, you'd think it was a good road. That's what we had thought. However, huge potholes with deep, sharp drops were hiding all over the place, waiting to swallow their next victims.

Kazakhs were familiar with the road conditions, and drove accordingly. They sped along in their clunkers and wove around the potholes, as if riding slalom. We also got the hang of it. I was under the impression that the Kazakhs didn't really care about what was going to happen. They overtook others without leaving any space between, entering and exiting their lanes with sharp turns and a slamming of the brakes. They didn't even try to return to their lane. That's why we sometimes pulled to the right and travelled alongside the road for a while before getting back on that wonderful pavement. We avoided several accidents by a hair.

Here's one example. We were riding along a flat stretch towards an incline with a right curve. Cory was avoiding potholes, but remained in his lane. A car came from the opposite direction and crossed over into our lane. Cory reacted at the last moment and narrowly avoided a frontal crash. Had he not succeeded, he would not have come out in good shape. That was really close! When we stopped at a gas station, we talked about the close encounter. We concluded that we definitely needed to drive more carefully.

While refuelling, I noticed an officer in his police car, a Russian Lada Niva, waiting, in hiding, to prey on passing vehicles. There was a fork in the road about one hundred metres from the police Lada. At the fork was a sign indicating which direction we needed to go to get to Almaty, and how many kilometres remained. Since it seemed that I hardly ever took my camera out of my tank bag, I reached for it, now, because I wanted to take a picture of this sign. After I filled my tank, I rode slowly forward and stopped by the sign. Cory and Tim were still refuelling. As I was about to take my camera out, someone honked. Surely it's the police, I thought. And yes, it was! They were honking and waving for me to come closer. I closed the bag and got back on the saddle. Curious about what they were going to say, I headed towards the officers. They asked me where I was from and where I was headed, and asked about my motorcycle and gear. Because of their neighbours to the north, and because of times past, most people in Kazakhstan understand Russian. My Russian was improving, so this interrogation soon turned into a comfortable conversation. But while talking with the police officers, I noticed the two cowboys speeding past us without even turning their heads. As if they didn't see me? I watched them as they continued down the road. Not even the police officers could figure out why they had not stopped!? They've also got interesting motorcycles! We talked some more, then I left to catch up with the guys.

Late in the afternoon. The sun was already low, creating longer shadows. According to our map, Lake Balkhash was to our left. Rivers flowing from their sources in the mountains along the border with Kyrgyzstan pour into this large lake, which is over 300 km long. A swim would feel good, but the day was coming to an end. We had crossed some 500 km that day,

TOP: Dusk in the steppes.
ABOVE: Tea house.

ABOVE: As long as it still does the job.
RIGHT: I'll consider changing jobs.

and it was now time to look for a camping spot. There was lots of room everywhere, but we were looking for some shelter. There was not even a tree in sight, just grassy steppes and plains spreading to who knows where? We turned off the road and went down the earthy-sandy terrain towards some high grass in the distance. The grass was getting higher as we went.

When we reached a spot that seemed far enough from the road, we began setting up the tents. Thinking no one would bother us here, we were surprised to see a red Lada appear from nowhere. As it passed, we noticed that there was only a driver, and no passengers, in the car. Who'd pass by here at this time of day? Go figure. We continued cooking dinner. The car returned. As it passed by us, we heard the screeching of brakes. A man came out of the car, smiling and carrying a watermelon as a welcome gift. He stayed for a short while, then said goodbye and left the same way he had come. His gesture was greatly appreciated. People here are very friendly and somewhat curious. The watermelon was refreshing, but the mosquitoes did their best to make sure we did not stay out for too long before retreating into our tents.

Then, the battle followed: An army of buzzing mosquitoes against me in my tent. I lay on my back and waited. With a clap of my hands, I'd smash a bloodthirsty pest. And just when I'd think I had gotten rid of them all, I'd hear more. My neighbours were also "hunting" mosquitoes in their tents. Whenever we'd hear some banging from a tent, we'd all start laughing aloud. I rested my head on my jacket, which I had rolled into a pillow, but it just didn't do the trick. It looked like I'd have to get myself a pillow towards the end of my journey.

When I peeked out of the tent the next morning, I saw that this playground known as our Earth had decided to keep spinning around the sun. Happy to be given this new day, I crawled out of the tent and took care of morning business. We stuffed some food down our throats, started the engines, and got going. The landscape reminded us of central Mongolia. Endless steppes stretched into the expanse, with the wind brushing the grass so that it appeared to flow like ocean waves. Hardly any vehicles passed us, which was good. There were fewer chances someone would suddenly swerve into our lane. Even the roads were in better shape. All we had to watch out for were the cows that often crossed from one side of the road to the other.

We reached a village and stopped for a break. Around us were simple houses with white walls and brightly painted window frames. I'm not sure about the meaning of these decorations. I went to buy ice cream in the store. Like in Mongolia, there was no choice, so no dilemma. The ice cream in this village was great: cheap and edible.

As we neared Almaty, or Alma Ati, as it was once known, the traffic picked up. Or in other words, the traffic was once again dangerous. The bad road turned into a better one, and soon led to a highway. I noticed that road signs and speed limits were almost non-existent. Grass lined the highway and served as a protective fence. Most people drove moderately. But oftentimes, an old Mercedes with a lot of spoilers, sporty additions, and loud music, would rush by, as if trying to beat the world speeding record. Other cars would also overtake us even if there were oncoming vehicles in the opposite lane, since we were on motorcycles and could easily move to the side, maybe even leave the road completely. It didn't matter to them.

Lake Kapchagay caught our attention. Sharing the same thought, and without saying a word, we turned towards the lake. We took our clothes off in a hurry and jumped in. Refreshment, then back on the road. I slowed down a few times to take pictures of the landscape. Then I'd get back on the saddle and rush to catch up with the guys. They'd wait for me by the side of the road and continue when I would come nearer.

ALMATY

At the entrance to the city, a line of trees provided shade and made for a great rest area. Hurrah for the trees! Which got me thinking, how many trees would be needed to line the streets of the world? This wouldn't take much effort, and yet the benefits would be numerous: positive effects on the climate, oxygen, shade, fruits for birds and animals, and later, wood for heating. Since I've got dictator-like tendencies, were I ever to rule, planting trees would definitely be the main focus of my citizens. All couples would have to plant a dozen, no, two dozen trees before getting married! Or maybe even more!

RIGHT: Land of the watermelons.

ABOVE: Tim's case decided to take a break.

We suddenly came across a colourful chaos of anything and everything. The open-air market at the city's entrance was situated more *on* the road than around it. Booths with fruits and vegetables and numerous other goods were all over the place. We had to really concentrate and watch the people around us closely in order to predict when someone might start crossing the street in front of us, usually without looking both ways.

What a strange location for a market! People all over the place, like ants. But we were on a highway! This highway-market had no protective fencing, and there were crowds of people bustling around. We drove cautiously and had to slam on the brakes several times. It seemed, though, that the people were accustomed to this kind of situation.

We entered the city and found ourselves in the middle of gridlock. Or, to put it gently, more chaos. Ahead of us was a huge queue of vehicles. Though we made our way past some of the cars, our panniers, carrying everything we needed for this long journey, were just too wide for us to weave among the cars. I had nothing against the rain that was falling, though it would have been better had it decided to fall somewhere else. Say, for a change, in Atakama, the Gobi, or the Kalahari. It was drizzling, and dust was lifting into the air. This combination of drizzle and lifting dust was sticking to our motorcycles, to us, and to our visors. So in order to see anything at all, we rode with our visors raised.

We were looking for accommodation, but couldn't find any. Hoping to see a sign, any sign, we looked everywhere. Only when we began riding on the sidewalk could we shorten the time spent in the queue. We finally reached an intersection, and a hotel appeared before us. Somewhat tired from the events of this day, we communicated with each other by simply waving our hands. We agreed to stay at this hotel.

Behind the hotel was a 24-hour car wash, so we parked our bikes there. With the carwash there, at least the motorcycles would be kept under a close watch. Of course, that was one of the main prerequisites for any accommodation in town. A hotel means nothing if there's no guarantee that the bikes are going to be safe. After checking in, we put our stuff away, took showers, and then made plans for the next phase of our journey. Since Tim is of Ukrainian descent, from the start of this journey, the Canadians had been planning on travelling through Ukraine. I wanted to go further north, towards Norway, and then across Sweden, Denmark, and Germany.

But since our journey was taking longer than planned, travelling more northward would be more complicated because of the cold. It would also be more demanding financially. I thought about changing my plans and travelling through Ukraine, then crossing Hungary and Serbia to reach Croatia. However in order to enter Ukraine, I needed a visa. That could be taken care of the next day at the Ukrainian consulate.

Another task awaiting us the next day was registration for Kazakh visas. While filling out immigration forms at the border, we were told we had to register at the immigration office within five days of entrance to the country. So it seemed we'd be taking care of paperwork all day.

We went to the supermarket. The variety and choice left us speechless. We were expecting something out of the movie, *Borat*, but not this! Who'd think such a seemingly benign movie could cause us to develop such stereotypes about a region or people? I spent the evening on the Internet reading local web portals to see what was going on in my homeland. There wasn't much going on, so, late in the evening, I went to sleep.

* * *

I don't know why, but before falling asleep, thoughts crossed my mind about explorations often celebrated as geographic discoveries. This guy discovered that, that guy discovered this. If you look at it one way, if, throughout history, the willingness to reach out and communicate between neighbours had been stronger than the desire to discover the unknown, then these great achievements would not have occurred. Yes, we would be without discoveries. In a way, people went to discover what could have perhaps been more easily found out, if only they had had more trust and had asked their neighbours.

If, in Constantinople, known as the bridge of the world, they wanted to know who was living across the Danube, or the Altai, they could have asked the Turkish nations of Central Asia. These people must have surely

BELOW: A scene from the half-desert.

BELOW: **At a gas station.**

known who their northern neighbours, and all their other neighbours, were. Those over Altai, neighbours of the aforementioned Turks, Eastern Turks, and Mongolian tribes, would have communicated with the Burjaati and the peoples of Siberia. And these people would have communicated with their neighbours, the Chukotka, who communicated with relatives in what is now Alaska, who knew who was in what is now Canada. These people surely knew who their southern neighbours were, etc., all the way to Tierra del Fuego.

To New Zealand and the Easter Islands, and to the other ends of the New World, people sailed in primitive sailboats, without gadgets, such as compasses, or they came by foot. And then later, someone else came along and "re-discovered" these people and regions that maybe didn't want to be discovered, and raised a flag in the name of some country.

Who were these people who were already there? To some explorers, the evident raison d'être of some of these places was just so that they could be discovered. It is OK to prove that the South Pole exists, to discover the source of the Nile, the Equator, and to mark where they are, but for everything else that comes along with it, a bit more effort and trust is needed. *Yes, but then we would be making some totally different discoveries.*

. . .

A telephone ringing woke us in the morning.

With almost incomprehensible English, the receptionist told us that someone was waiting for us in the lobby. Who needed us here? Confused and still unkempt, we got out of bed and went down to the lobby. We hadn't even washed up. A guy from France, named Fred, had seen our motorcycles and had asked the receptionist whose they were. He was sitting on the couch looking at our motorcycles out the window.

"Hey! I'm Petar. Where are you travelling to?"

"I'm Fred. I'm from France and used to work in China. Right now I'm touring by motorcycle to Israel, where I got a new job," he answered.

"Where are you staying at?" I asked curiously.

"In a cheap hotel just two kilometres from where you are."

"Great. We could go there, too," I turned around to look at my friends, and they nodded.

Right away, we went up to our rooms to get our stuff and went back down with our hands full. We checked out and packed everything back on the bikes, even though some of the stuff would be unpacked once again in just a few minutes. We then admired the surroundings and watched the traffic, while waiting for Fred to get his motorcycle.

Breaking every possible rule except speeding and drunk driving, Fred arrived on his bike. He was riding a 250 cc Yamaha that he had bought in China. That was logical, since crossing China by motorcycle is too complicated if you don't meet the authorities' special prerequisites.

We followed him to the hotel, weaving in and out of traffic. Fred didn't have panniers mounted, so he squeezed between cars more easily. We were riding down one of the most important roads in Almaty when Fred stopped all of a sudden. By the way his motorcycle was facing, I could tell he intended to turn left, even though there was a double full line. I didn't have a problem with that; it was just that the traffic was heavy and cars were constantly speeding by. We waited for a while, as close to the faded double line as we could, until the first opportunity came. The vehicles behind us were honking louder than a big brass band.

When the coast was clear, we jammed on the gas and rushed across the street into the hotel parking lot. We parked as close to the entrance as possible, and began transferring all our stuff to the hotel. We registered. My room was on the top floor. At first glance, the elevator did not look reliable. I took the stairs and climbed to the eighth floor. The first thing I did when I entered the room was look out the window to check on my motorcycle. It was important for me to be able to check on my bike at any moment, to make sure no one borrowed it, planning to never return it.

Tim's room was on the floor beneath mine, so I went to see him. When I got there, he was pacing, with his back hunched forward. His hand was pressing against his lower back. He turned to me with this serious expression on his face. I tried to help him straighten up. His spine cracked a few times, and by the look on his face, I could tell it was getting more painful.

"Nothing, then. I'll lie on the floor and you walk on my back so that the bones in my spine settle back in place." I wasn't sure that was such a good idea, since I weighed ninety kilograms. But he insisted, so I got on his back. Something cracked once again. I stepped to the side and asked, "Is that better now?"

He said, "Oh, now it's even worse!" He somehow managed to get up and lie on the bed. Sure that he'd get better, I let him rest. After an hour or two of rest, luckily, he was in a much better state.

It was already time to take care of our visa registrations. When I mentioned this to Fred, he grimaced, as if he had bit into a lemon. He hadn't realized this was required, so he came along. We locked the doors and went down to the lobby. Some took the elevator, while one guy remained faithful to the stairs. This time, we decided to leave the motorcycles and take a "taxi." Why the quotation marks? Because in this land, there are people whose profession it is to drive a taxi, and there are people who act as if they are taxi drivers. Actually, if someone has a car and wants to earn some extra money, he just stops and charges less than an official taxi.

A jeep stopped by us. We squeezed in and shouted where to go. For the next twenty minutes, we rode in the jeep and admired the city as we went. Though Islam is the main religion in Kazakhstan, I noticed women out in public not wearing the hijab, as in Europe.

At the Ukrainian embassy, they rejected me because I didn't have a letter of invitation. We reached the immigration office just in time. A lot of people had come for the same reason. All we needed was one stamp in our passports, nothing more. But when the man in charge, the one running this entire office, saw us, he obviously recognized an opportunity to make some extra money. We needed to fill out some forms, which turned out to be almost impossible, since we had no idea what was written on them. To our surprise and relief, a lady happened to show up from nowhere who knew just what we needed to do in order to finish registering.

Why did we have to register in the first place? We could have done that back at the border. None of this made any sense. Cory and Tim paid the fee, while I was hesitant. Exhausted by the bureaucracy, in the end, I paid too. I think they took about twenty dollars from each of us, for no reason.

Then, we waited in line, shifting our weight from one leg to the next and staring around the room. Every ten minutes, the "Lord of the Stamps and Human Destinies" would move to another counter. A crowd of people followed. Even we shifted to the next queue. I left the line to escape the crowded and stuffy room, and stood by the entrance. At least I was breathing some fresh air.

When I saw my reflection in the window, I noticed that my hair was all ruffled. To be practical, I usually cut my hair short. But at this point, I had been on the road for the past four months without a haircut.

Every minute, someone would leave with a stamp in their passport. Believing our passports were also ready, I'd reluctantly trudge back inside every so often. But then I'd see Cory, and just by the look on his face, I'd know we weren't done waiting yet. You could probably guess that our passports were the last ones to receive the green stamp. So, after a day spent in the waiting room at the immigration office, we had officially and proudly gotten our visas registered.

Pretty tired from so much waiting, we hailed a taxi and returned to the hotel. Then, each retreated to his own den. Our plan had been to go to the city's centre in the evening. But, according to what the guys told me, they couldn't wake me, so they left without me. I believe them. That waiting had exhausted me. I slept until the following morning, and was the last to wake!

I opened my eyes and looked out the window at the motorcycles. The sky was cloudy, so I couldn't guess the time. Cory was already down there getting his bike ready to go. Maybe it was already noon, I thought. I grabbed my stuff in a hurry, jumped into my boots, and fled out of the room. After checking out, I ran to the parking lot. It had been raining until just moments before, and the rain was starting to fall again. That was why no one had awakened me.

I organized my belongings in the panniers and yellow transport bag, put the luggage in its place, and tied everything down with bungee cord. I was ready to go. I noticed the rear brake pads were completely worn out.

Good thing there was a Yamaha store in this city; it should have what I needed. We said goodbye to Fred and went on our way on this gloomy and rainy day.

I remembered the directions Fred had given us to get to the Yamaha store, and started following them. We went down one of the main streets. I went first and followed the signs and street names, stopping at all intersections. After just a few kilometres, my visor was so filthy that I could see nothing through it; it was just a bother. So, I decided to ride without it.

The modern and well-stocked Yamaha store had the brake pads I needed, and with the money saved from the discount, I could even get them installed. We also got a map of Kazakhstan, which we really needed, since we hadn't installed a map in our GPSs.

SOUTHERN KAZAKHSTAN

The main road in Almaty led to Bishkek, the capital of Kyrgyzstan. But we weren't allowed across the border there, so we took the secondary road along the border to the city of Shu. Since the guys hadn't slept enough because of their night tour, and since it was going to rain, we agreed to set up camp at the first sheltered spot we found.

Finding a leeward spot was not going to be easy, since there weren't very many of them. We rode a few kilometres away from the road, and nestled under a tree alongside the riverbank. After putting up the tent, I went to look for some dry twigs and branches to light a campfire. Finding wood in a place with few trees was a tough assignment, even for my experienced eyes. But the odds here were better than in the desert. I gathered wood along the southern slope of the mountain.

Tim did the preparations for dinner and started the fire. Cory and I changed the brake pads. Theoretically, I knew what needed to be done, but with Cory here, I had no reason to worry. He showed me everything and explained it all. I was going to have to learn a lot more about mechanics before going on any future journeys.

The campfire was cackling lightly, warming us while we ate our meals and enjoyed the silence. Nearby was Kyrgyzstan. We would have liked to visit that mountainous country, but we did not have visas.

BELOW: I don't know
which road is "better"...

Surely we could try to get visas in Almaty, but that would be too complicated, since my visa for Kazakhstan was limited to one entry and exit. It was getting colder and darker. We fed the fire with twigs and it returned the favour by warming us and giving us some light. Since we were in a half-desert region at the foot of a mountain, I was expecting a cold morning. I remembered Tim had a sleeping bag to spare. Mine was too light for these conditions. While preparing for the journey, I had chosen gear that took up as little room as possible and had misjudged how cold it could get here. I'd manage, as I have numerous times, by using my jacket, pants, and other gear to cover myself. But after a while, that gets tiring.

The dawn, or *sabah*, as it is known here, awoke me with frost just as the first rays of sunlight appeared. I lay for a while more until I heard some noises. When I peeked out of the tent, I saw we were surrounded by a herd of sheep. The shepherd on horseback stood a little further away, and behind him, in the distance, were the mountains of Kyrgyzstan. He noticed me watching him. I rubbed my eyes, put my boots on, and got out of the tent. The frost had created a special cold morning ambience. Though low, the sun was slowly starting to warm my black jacket. This was enough for me to feel comfortable.

The middle-aged Kazakh approached us and took a look at our tents. I said hello. He returned the greeting and continued examining our camp. I had noticed that when locals notice my map of their region, they can't take their eyes off it. The map of Kazakhstan was in the clear pocket of the tank bag on my bike. I took it out and let him study it. We exchanged a few words while he read the map.

"Nice horse," I tried to say in Russian.

"And a good one!" the Kazakh shepherd also answered in Russian.

"How old is it?" I asked

"Four. Where are you going?" he asked.

"I'm going home, to Croatia. These two guys are going to Canada." I answered.

"Aaaa."

"How far is Shymkent?" I asked.

"Three hundred kilometres to Taraz and then one hundred and fifty to Shymkent."

He seemed happy we could understand each other.

Just then, Tim came out of his tent.

I could tell he was still sleepy just by the way he was dragging his feet. The conversation and the feeling that we were "surrounded" had awakened him. He shook hands with the shepherd and put some water on to boil for our breakfast. I took my camera out and shot some pictures of the landscape. After that, I waved to the shepherd with my camera, hoping he would give a nod of approval and let me take his picture. He just smiled and continued studying the map. Cory also awoke. I began packing my stuff so that I could put the tent away. The man thanked me and gave me the map. We ate breakfast, put everything away, and got going. It was good we got up so early; we had the whole day ahead of us. That's my favourite way to travel.

I remembered my journey to Nordkapp, when I'd wake at five o'clock in the morning, sometimes even earlier, just so I could reach the places I had marked on my map.

We got back on the road and continued towards Shymkent. After just a few kilometres, we reached a sign for the capital city of Kyrgyzstan, Bishkek. Just 24 km from this spot, but we didn't have visas. Too bad, but there's always next time. I usually make plans for future trips while travelling anyhow. I imagine that all travellers, while on their current trips, enjoy making plans for future journeys. We stopped at a gas station and filled the tanks, bought some Mentos candy, then continued on our way to Taraz and Shymkent.

Lots of watermelon and cantaloupe lined this stretch of road, enriching the landscape with their colours. There were so many of them that I could freely say, "This is the land of watermelons." The experience of eating, or should I say drinking, a watermelon, is vastly superior to that of drinking a questionable soft drink.

We were forced to stop several times along the way. The livestock here lived a fine life, without any restraints or fences, and at times would decide to cross the road. Sometimes, they even decided to lie on the road. If there wasn't enough room to go around them, we just honked, and they moved to allow us to continue on our way. I was relaxed, enjoying the ride across the planes and admiring the landscape. Ahead of us were the Moyynkum sand dunes, and to the south, the Kyrgyzstan Mountains.

We reached Taraz. Besides Almaty, Taraz is one of the fastest-growing cities in this country. Its level of development surprised me. We even managed to get lost. Obviously, we had missed a turn for the main road, I thought, since we just could not seem to get out of that city. It was time to read the map and ask a local, or in our case, forget the map and ask the first person we came across for directions. I stopped by a crowd at an intersection and asked for directions to Shymkent. They pointed which way to go, so we continued until we found the road for Shymkent.

While riding towards the mountain, Karatau, I noticed some police officers wearing unusually big police hats beyond a curve ahead. Police officers here probably wear such silly hats so that we could see them more easily, so I don't know how my co-travellers hadn't noticed them. But since we were going so fast, I didn't have time to warn them. The high grass was great for hiding the police vehicle. I released my hold of the gas throttle and hid behind a bus that Tim and Cory were just overtaking. And they got caught! One of the police officers waved for them to stop. They stopped, and so did I. The officers showed us their radar apparatus with a picture of Tim and Cory speeding. I wasn't in the picture, and so, was allowed to go, but didn't. I waited for Tim and Cory to pay the fee, which was obviously going to end up in the private pockets of these men in uniform. Tim and Cory didn't get a receipt. Why waste paper? The police took the money, and that was it. Since it was clear that there were cops in the area, we decided to ride slowly for awhile.

We kept to the speed limit for a while, but when that became too tiring, we increased the speed to one that suited us. After some 570 km, we reached Shymkent, and unanimously voted to find a hotel for the night. For the next several days, we'd have no choice but to camp outside, anyways. The hotel we found did not have Internet access. Darkness was falling as we spent the next hour at an Internet café not far from the hotel.

If we were to head south from Shymkent, we would soon reach Tashkent, in Uzbekistan, which would be good. Even while we were still in Almaty, we thought about that option: crossing Uzbekistan and Turkmenistan, then returning through Iran and Turkey.

However, getting a visa for Iran was pretty complicated for my friends with Canadian citizenship. We would have had to spend over ten days just taking care of the paperwork. So instead, we were crossing the Turan Plain along the valley of the river Syrdar'ya, and then continuing north-west towards the Aktobe Region.

We were beginning yet another day of our journey with a beautiful sunny morning. But soon, we were caught. Caught in violation. Police, once again. The warning from the previous day obviously had not been enough. I don't know much about the laws here, but the police back home aren't that good at camouflage. Two police cars and their drivers had hidden behind a thicket.

I suppose they had heard the motorcycles rumbling while we were overtaking a truck. But with the brush and overgrowth along the road-side, we hadn't even noticed them. Of course, once again, the standard little stop sign was waving at us. We pulled over to the side of the road.

"We could have done without this!" I said, expecting the usual treatment.

A plump officer with a face characteristic of this region asked for our drivers' licences. I noticed he understood some Russian, and was smil-ing, so I tried to take advantage of that. Once they had our licences, escaping them would not be easy. They could even try to blackmail us. One of the officers brought over a file folder and read out a list of laws that we had broken. I didn't know whether the folder he was hold-ing was even an official piece of material, or whether it was a special folder they used when they ran into foreigners, but the fees were high. These fees were high even when compared to European standards. We managed to make a deal, and after handing over two hundred dollars, we got going. Once again, we had thrown money away and had not been given a receipt. I hope, at least, that that money helped someone;

though it's more likely it ended up being spent in some local bar.

Still under the influence of this lesson, we tried to keep to the speed limit. That was bothersome, but we were aware that this was the only way to cross this region without having to pay even more. Several more patrol officers would have stopped us, had we been going faster. They hid behind hills, around curves, and waited in groves by the side of the road. That was kind of funny, but it was impossible to predict when one would show up.

Besides the police that waited like spiders for their next prey to show, in Kazakhstan, like in Russia, there were control points at every entrance and exit to larger villages and to all cities. We passed most of the control points without even stopping, but this time, they stopped me. Cory and Tim waited by the side of the road after successfully passing through, and watched as I turned the engine off and spoke with the officers. These guys were just curious. They wanted to see the motorcycle, where I was from, and see if I had any gift for them, either as money, or a souvenir from my homeland.

I was sorry I didn't have anything suitable. These police officers sure have it great, I thought. They have the authority to stop you, and once you stop, they can take a look at the motorcycle. Even start it up, hop on its saddle, honk, and rev it up. Imagine a police officer in Croatia, or anywhere in Canada, taking advantage of the opportunity to stop a car and take it for a "test spin," since he or she hadn't driven such a vehicle yet.

They asked me to call my friends over. I walked the ten steps and waved to Cory and Tim to come closer. They approached slowly and parked the motorcycles next to mine. The officers asked the same questions. But the language barrier got these guys communicating with their hands. Which wasn't bad at all. Cory and Tim did a great job communicating and tried to understand what was being said to them. The big hat, which was the trademark of the officers here, found its way onto my head. Tim also wanted to take a picture with the hat on, but he didn't look as good in it and was aware of that. Cory was surely "jealous" because he hadn't been accepted on to the police force back home.

But had he passed the test, and not been disappointed, then I'm sure he wouldn't have gone on this interesting journey. Instead, he'd maybe be eating donuts in a police car somewhere in Canada, when, all of a sudden, a motorcycle with a Croatian licence plate would speed across his zone before he noticed it. Who knows what he'd have thought then?

After this funny experience, we got back on our bikes and hit the road. We travelled through the city of Turkestan and then continued across the semi-desert. Nearby were some camels. These animals are perfectly adapted to living in such a barren landscape. Though all creatures are perfect just the way they are, these animals, which live in extreme conditions—without water, with so little food available—have a special fascination for me. They are so well adapted to the environment that they live in. They really are special to me. After glancing at us, the camels continued plucking out grass and thorny bushes.

Since the day was coming to an end, the urge to look for a spot to sleep arose in all of us. We turned off the road onto a sandy trail to look for a good spot. Dry and cracked ground marked with prints of various animals looked like a great place to camp.

We took out the tents and started preparing dinner. None of us had the slightest idea that some unusual worms were living in the tiny holes all around us. About a million holes and about two million worms. After a while, these little critters wanted to see who was trespassing, and started coming out of their holes. I wasn't much bothered by that; I just wanted to make sure that none got in my tent.

Aside from the worms, which were laying eggs wherever they could, this camp was in a beautiful spot. The sun was setting in one direction, while the moon was rising in the other. Wolves were howling, which was especially nice to hear. The sky was clear and the night, warm. To enhance the mood here in the open, we decided to light a campfire and gathered some dry branches, broken roots, and thick grass. While the fire crackled softly, we talked about what we had achieved so far. When people let go of their ties to one place, a feel for the nomadic way of life develops. This is a form of independence, but then again, it gets you thinking about what follows, about the next part of the journey. With these ideas awakening in us, we began talking about where we could go in the coming year. Maybe

Africa, I thought. My friends thought the same. "We will see." We'll see? I noticed Tim's look. I think he knew what I was thinking.

We got into our tents and shouted out to one another about what to do if those black crawlers came our way. I won't ever forget what Tim said: that he would sleep with his earphones on, so that if a worm got in his tent, it wouldn't lay eggs in his ears. We laughed. We could hear the wolves and other beasts going about their business outside the tents, rustling and calling out every so often.

My thoughts returned to coincidences in life. How many things needed to fall into place so that I could be, at this very moment, over here, in the desert of Central Asia, surrounded by a bunch of worms and listening to a pack of wolves howling? I thought about my decision to go on a journey, and everything in my life prior to that decision; about Cory's failing the test to gain acceptance into the police force, and his friendship with Tim, who is just the way he is. Because if he wasn't like that, then Tim wouldn't have been able to be convinced to travel, and everything else in their lives before that. What are the chance that our travel schedules, routes, and my getting to know Tim through Couchsurfing, all coincided, and a whole list of other details? *Are these all just coincidences, or part of something else?*

I'm glad we met. In some ways, we are different, but we are learning from each other more and more. These guys are cool, and I hope they think I am, too.

Morning. I opened my eyes and looked out of my tent. The guys were still sleeping. And better for them, so they wouldn't have to see what worms were infesting their tent. I put on my boots, which, after so many miles, still reminded me about how I would have been better off with a pair that measured a half size larger. I shook my tent to get rid of those curious worms. The howling had disappeared. Having heard the ruckus of me putting my tent away, Tim and Cory also got up. They grimaced, got rid of the worms, and slowly began putting their tents away. The water necessary for our dehydrated food was already on to boil.

I was satisfied with the tent that I had bought for the trip. It was big enough for me to keep all my equipment by my side while I slept. Setting it up and taking it down was simple. Once folded, this lightweight tent did not take up too much space on the motorcycle.

We devoured our breakfast, packed our stuff, and got going towards the main road to Aktobe. When we reached the asphalt, I noticed another larger colony of those same worms, inching their way across the street. Where were they going and what was their goal? Had I been at a distance, standing still and looking, the road would have looked like it was moving. We somehow wove our way out and continued our journey. Soon, we reached what had once been the fourth largest lake in the world. Lake Aral was once considered a sea. But as of the 1960s, its size has been reduced drastically. The lake has been drying up ever since water from the Amudar'ya and Sirdar'ya rivers has being redirected to the Soviet Union for irrigation.

The lake had, in fact, been reduced to one third of its original size, which caused water to evaporate more easily, causing the climate to change. The winters became colder and the summers, warmer. The land became infertile from the salt that surfaced. Today, as monuments to this ecological catastrophe, fishing boats remain stranded on the dry sand.

THE ROAD TO AKTOBE

The road was getting worse, but that did not bother us. No police officers were here, since there wasn't much need for them in this semi-desert. Besides, the roads were straight, and there was nowhere to hide. There weren't any trees or bushes; just some low brush, the rare prickly bush, and hardly any dry grass at all. Every now and then, the sand dunes would seem to be calling to me. I do love desert paradises, but experts warn that the trends in climate change are warming up. If something isn't done soon, this could become a true challenge for future generations.

We used a straight stretch of road for filming videos. We set up two cameras on the road; one facing the direction we were going in, the other pointing in the direction we were coming from. After going back some three hundred metres, we would turn around and speed past the cameras. Then one of us would go back to collect the cameras. The road conditions were getting worse, but our bikes were up to the challenge, since they

The road to Aktobe.

LEFT: Aktobe.

were built for such riding conditions. About one hundred kilometres before Aralsk, Cory felt he had had enough for the day. I would have rather continued riding, but leaving it for the next day did not bother me, either. This time, I won't describe the camp too much. We turned off the road, set up the tents, ate dinner, got a good night's rest, and then got going in the morning.

This was the day we were to reach Aktobe. At least, that was what we were planning. We continued from where we had left off the day before. As we went, the poor condition of the roads meant that they were everything *but* roads. Pothole to hole and pothole upon pothole. Deep potholes. The worst ones were those on the rare patches of asphalt. If we landed in some of these, getting out would be almost impossible. The edges were sharp, unlike holes in earthy surfaces, which have more gradual inclines. This road surprised us, but not significantly.

Similar to Mongolia, over here, there were dirt roads that ran parallel to the paved main roads. Oftentimes, these roads were curvier, but at least they didn't have as many large holes, so we took the secondary roads. After the asphalt in Kazakhstan, we were actually eager to travel on this terrain.

We were each having such a blast that we weren't even paying attention to where the others were at a given moment. That's how Cory crossed over to a road on the left side, Tim stayed on the main road, while I stayed on the road to the right. Not knowing ahead of time what kind of a road was awaiting him, Cory went down the secondary road, which gradually separated from the main road. Tim and I met up, but Cory was nowhere to be seen. We stopped, sat at a bridge, and waited to see if he would show up. The sun was burning hot. Looking into the distance where we had come from, no one could be seen. Ahead of us were an old couch and a few parked trucks. Who knew where Cory could be? After about twenty minutes of waiting and thinking, we became worried. Maybe he fell? Since Tim had a larger fuel tank, he went to search for Cory in the direction we had come from. I watched him as he disappeared behind a hill, riding in an upright position and looking carefully for any sign of Cory.

Thoughts kept coming to mind. What could have happened? A few trucks passed by at a snail's pace because of the poor terrain, covering my motorcycle and me in clouds of dust. A house in the distance caught my attention, so I got on the bike and headed towards it. Maybe Cory was waiting for us there. The further away I went from where Tim had started his search, the more I thought about how maybe I shouldn't have left. Tim and I had made a deal that I would wait at the bridge. But I continued, nevertheless. If I didn't find Cory there, I'd go back! I passed two trucks and reached a hilltop. From there, I could see Cory and his bike in the shade of the house, or actually, restaurant. He was waiting for us, and we were waiting for him. I explained the situation. He took out his walkie-talkie and tried to contact Tim, but could not get through. I thought about going back to tell Tim I had found Cory, but didn't. We waited a while, commenting on the situation. Then we heard the familiar sound of a motorcycle approaching. Tim was coming. He stopped when he reached us, obviously happy to see us, but also angry for not having found us earlier. I was partly to blame, since I hadn't returned to the bridge with the news that Cory was OK. This whole episode lasted at least two hours. We recapped the order of events once again, drank some water, and then got going.

The road, which looked more like a motocross track than a highway, continued another hundred kilometres. My bike was running on empty, and I began thinking about where to tank up. I had enough for about 50 km, maybe less, and we had over one hundred kilometres before the next gas station. However, since I always managed to find a solution, one way or the other, I wasn't worried. We'd think of something. Obviously it wasn't time for improvisation yet. Most homes in the next village were constructed from dried mud and straw. The straw served as some sort of binder. Apparently, one Kazakh in the village sold fuel. We found his house, which had blue window frames. Obviously he had a nose for business, and sensed the opportunity to earn some extra money. A cheerful man came out of the earthy-straw house, and confirmed that he had fuel for us.

Next to the house with the blue-trimmed windows was a grey container like the ones used for trans-oceanic transport. Hanging from the container was a blue board with a white "76" painted on it. You don't have to be a rocket scientist to figure out what this number meant. That was the fuel's octane number. Though it was more than half the regular price, we'd rather treat our bikes with a 93 octane. Right away, I said I'd buy 20 litres, to give the man a chance to earn some money. He brought over a few canisters of varying sizes and a funnel made from a roughly cut plastic bottle. This guy was a true professional; there was no way even a drop of fuel would spill. Cory had only one complaint: when the plastic funnel fell on the dusty ground. We rinsed it a little with water, blew on it, and then continued pouring. The Yamaha had 20 litres of fuel and room to spare. Tim was last to fill up. Since his motorcycle had an extremely large fuel tank, he had a good chance of reaching the next gas station without refuelling.

We thanked the vendor and he thanked us. A more relaxed ride across the desert followed, since we didn't have to think about how many more drops of fuel remained in the tanks. Here, we came across trucks that were older than me. Russian Kamaz trucks were showering us with dust. Large clouds of dust encompassed these trucks as they drove, limiting visibility, as well as our ability to overtake them. The best way to pass these Kamaz trucks was to stick to the paths alongside the main road. As a result of its weight and the constant vibrations, the right pannier fell off of Tim's bike.

I didn't see when the pannier fell off, but noticed something was wrong when I saw it leave a trail of stuff as it rolled away. I stopped by the side of the road and started rescuing as much as I could, before someone else could come along and run over it. The case was just bent in some parts, nothing the little axe we had couldn't fix. After a few good wallops, the metal was good as new. We remounted the panniers, threw all the stuff back in the case, and got going. Once again, we had to pass the same Kamaz trucks that we had passed earlier. I was choking in the dust, but I was sure that after so much exposure, my body had built some form of immunity to the dust.

We somehow passed the trucks and continued riding in standing positions. This upright position made handling the rough terrain easier. And while standing, we were able to see where a newly paved road started nearby. Brand new asphalt! Maybe even paved the day before. Only the signs were missing. If we could get ourselves on that road, we might even reach Aktobe the same day. But how could we cross over? Along the access roads were pits and mounds of fresh dirt, making them inaccessible to vehicles. Not even with motorcycles could we pass them. We stopped every now and then to look for access to the asphalt.

Maybe a motocross biker would have easily found a route to the paved road, but with our loaded bikes, we needed more time to find a more accessible and suitable path. And then I saw it. I turned right by a canal and with a "who-cares-what's-gonna-happen" shrug, I hit the gas and began climbing up a steep incline. Near the top, I climbed over an uneven mound of earth. We did it; my bike and I had reached the asphalt. In order to catch up with the guys, I sped up and then slowed down while honking as I neared them. They gaped in shock when they noticed me as I waved back. With hand gestures, they asked me how I had gotten there. Of course, right away I began looking around to see where they could climb up. And there it was. I stopped to show them the spot where they could cross. Tim and Cory slowed down, and made it! This passage wasn't the best one, but it was good enough. I helped them push their bikes, since they needed a boost. Then, with a speed of about 100 kmph, we had a chance to reach Aktobe in time.

Unfortunately after about five kilometres, we reached a mound of dirt that was impossible to cross. Since I had gotten us on this road, I felt it was my duty to find a way out. To the right was a steep drop to a ditch that led to some high grass. We needed to get down, and then climb back up. The incline was similar to that of a riverbank, except it was relatively steep for our heavy bikes. We went slowly down in first gear. My front tire pressed the high grass down as I went. Shortly after, I turned the motorcycle around and headed back uphill. Tim saw what I had done, and followed. Then Cory followed.

Up till then, we had been heading northwest. And now this road was leading us westward. Good thing our helmets had visors, which protected our eyes somewhat from the direct sunlight. They did not shade our eyes from the setting sun entirely, though, and in order to see, I had to ride

RIGHT: **Who knows how long it's been waiting for me . . .**

with my head lowered, which was straining my neck. After my neck muscles went numb, though, nothing mattered anymore. So I endured the uncomfortable position, ignored the stiff neck, and kept riding.

Unlike southern and central Kazakhstan, much more plentiful vegetation grew here, along the northern region near the Russian border. I recalled how my Canadian friends had been given strict advice: In no way should they take a shortcut from Aralsk to Aktobe. Apparently, there weren't many gas stations along this route, and the road was almost impassable. But then again, if that road existed on the map, then people had probably already travelled it. Next time, we would definitely take the shortcut. We reached Aktobe in the evening. Sunlight still reflected off the few clouds in the sky. After a quick search, we reached a hotel. Exhausted from the uncomfortable ride, we parked right in front of the entrance, which faced the sun, grabbed our stuff, checked in at the reception, and went to our rooms.

AKTOBE

Geographically, at the moment, I was near the fifty-seventh meridian. This meant I was just forty degrees from home base, my homeland. Hmm, if one degree is a little less than seventy kilometres, then that meant I had about 2 800 kilometres to go, the way the crow flies. According to time zone calculations of four minutes per degree, I had two-and-a-half hours to wait before the sun rose. It really is a small world after all.

Before the Mongols conquered Central Asia, the region we were crossing had rarely opened the door to communication between the East and West. Contacts were established in a highly controlled manner, exclusively for trading silk, spices and jewels. The Mongolians were the ones that opened opportunities for communication. Merchants and missionaries from all over started coming. The Pope sent the Franciscan monk, Giovanni of Piano Carpini, from Umbria to introduce Christianity to the Kahn and the Mongolian Kingdom. The Polo brothers set out on their first journey, and later, Marco joined them for the second journey. Ibn Battuta, from Fes, in Morocco, started out on his journey to Mecca, but then he turned off the path and spent practically the rest of his life travelling and writing about this great part of the world. In those days, people travelled slowly. Travellers were not in a hurry, and information was passed on mainly by word of mouth. Marco Polo spent twenty years travelling, and Ibn Battuta, almost his entire life.

In those times, wars started very easily and the wealth of a city or kingdom could easily become the motivation for an attack. For this reason, travellers were at times considered as possible spies, as well as possibly dangerous. Great threats often came from all sides, so wealthy cities protected themselves however they could, often by building city walls and great armies. Mobile nomadic nations in a way despised the stationary nations, but nevertheless wanted their wealth. By the nature of their way of life, nomads were constantly in a state of half-readiness for movement, were not tied to one place, could endure hardship and famine, and could easily pack their belongings on their horses and get going; basically they could withstand war-like conditions for longer periods, since this was their normal way of life. The nomads were great horsemen, and their horses provided them with all that they needed. They were known to attack unexpectedly, but the sedentary communities defended their homes, for that was all they had.

And that is how, throughout history, we have had examples of nomads conquering deep into settled regions. China, India, Mesopotamia, Europe. Most often these takeovers would not last long, but there were cases when entire nations would be forced to flee from the nomads (the Huns), or when new and permanent kingdoms were formed (the Turks).

And nowadays, now that most obstacles have disappeared, this whole world—the entire globe—can be circled by motorcycle or any other means of transportation fairly quickly. With the help of Google, we can easily, and without endangering anyone, peek into a neighbour's backyard, or count how many seals remain, along with koalas, deer, trees and bears, or see what people in Central Park are reading.

We can establish how this globe upon which we are all spinning is so full of possibilities, but also so tiny and fragile.

(Unedited and written in one breath)
(Writing from Astrakhan 12/09/2009)

The last time I wrote was five days ago. I have a lot to tell you since then. Because something unpredictable happened while crossing the last few kilometres of the huge country of Kazakhstan. I was riding just a few metres behind Cory. And because of the huge cloud of dust, it was already too late when I saw a pothole in the Kazakh road. That whole day we had been rushing because we had spent two nights in Aktobe and wanted to cover as many kilometres in one day as possible. And that's how I managed to hit two potholes. Everything would have been all right, had I not slightly changed directions.

I'm not sure if you can imagine it, but a thirty-centimetre-deep hole + my speed of sixty kmph = crash. A head dive. I slid for the next few meters on my head and left shoulder. The dust settled. By some miracle, there was not a scratch on my body. Not one scratch. But that's why the front part of my bike was damaged. The front fork was totally bent, including the discs, and the wheel that didn't have all the spokes it should have . . . Right away Cory and Tim noticed I had fallen, and came back to help me. They were surprised I hadn't broken any bones. Then it was my bike's turn to be checked. It needed to be taken out of the grass and back on the road. We tried to set it upright, but the rim started cracking. And then a jolly crew on a tractor arrived, and decided to help out. Since the bike was lying on its side, we just lifted it and carried it to the street where we set it on its side again. After a quick recap of the whole situation, we logically concluded that the motorcycle needed to be transported to a bigger city. Just at the right moment a truck arrived and pulled to the side near us. Two Kazakhs wanted to help. We loaded the bike on the mini truck. Next stop, Aktrau. Our ride wasn't going to Aktrau, so they left me and my motorcycle by a small settlement. Tim and Cory came a few moments later. What surprised me the most was how the two Kazakhs offered me

First let's take a picture . . .

. . . and then load the truck.

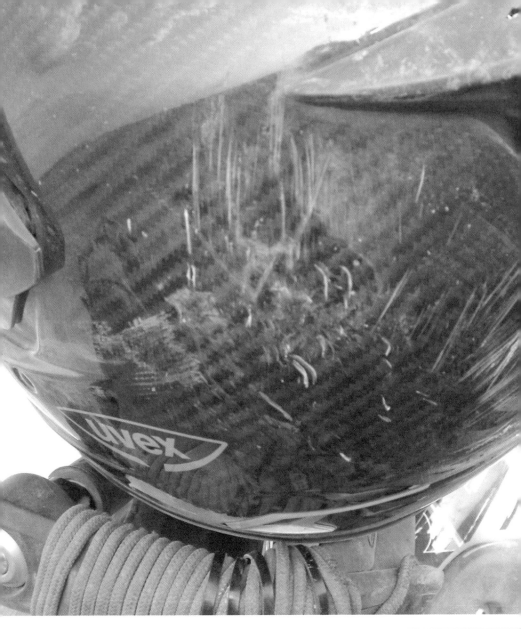

Kamaz – vodka.

money so I could buy something to eat since my bike wasn't fit to ride. I doubt coming across such good Samaritans in Europe would be that easy. Several more vehicles pulled over. Some people even tried to repair what obviously could not be repaired. Though they all had good intentions, I was getting tired of constantly explaining and recapping what had happened and what I was planning on doing.

Darkness was already falling.

I was tired, and couldn't think about the next step. All I wanted was to get the motorcycle to a larger settlement (that is, to a city). Cory kept watch while I lay beside my bike and Tim went to sleep across the street. At about two o'clock in the morning, some truck stopped about thirty feet from us. I was sleeping, so Cory went to ask where the driver was going. Then I awoke. Two Kazakhs were driving a Kamaz loaded with vodka and pulling a loaded trailer. Hundreds of boxes, with six one-litre bottles of vodka per box. We moved some rows of boxes forward to make room for the motorcycle. It barely fit, but we succeeded and got going. This truck was a twenty-five-year-old Kamaz! After two hours and less than 20 km (the Kamaz couldn't go any faster in Kazakhstan), we stopped by the side of the road to catch some sleep. Not in my lifetime did I think I'd sleep in a truck's trailer that was loaded with bottles of vodka.

The next morning we started the day with a shot of vodka. Excuse me. With a cup of warm tea, and then we got going on our adventure known as "The race to Atiran".

.   .   .

Since I had already done everything I could in this situation and could already smell myself and feel my stickiness, I did the only logical thing possible at that moment; I enjoyed my view of the scenery and of the Precaspian Basin. The dirt road led the way across the semi-desert and dry steppes. In this sparsely populated region, the few settlements with homes, built mainly of dried brick, blended perfectly with the landscape. But the experience wouldn't be complete without some background music. So, to top it all off, during the entire ride, we listened to endless repetitions of oriental ethno music from the only cassette available.

One song came as a special bonus in the repertoire: each time I heard "Freestyler" by Bomfunk MC's, I laughed unexpectedly. I had no idea how that song got there. What was even more interesting: The rhythm of the song was totally in synch with the way the clunky Kamaz was squeaking and bumping along because of the ruts in the road.

During the Soviet rule of Kazakhstan, citizens were discouraged from practising all religions, including Islam. Nowadays, after the end of this era of suppression, Islam has taken centre stage in people's lives. One thing that seemed strange to me is how alcohol is being transported, and probably consumed, in such great quantities. Kasim, the driver of the Kamaz, shed some light on this issue, explaining how old habits are still quite common. Our communication didn't go as smoothly as it may appear to have done when you read this. Since Kasim didn't know Russian that well, there was much more mimicry and communicating with hand gestures than with our mouths.

A thought came to mind about the differences between Eastern and Western approaches. In Western countries, organized services exist to assist when vehicles break down on the road or when accidents happen. Unlike in the West, the East functions more on the principle of solidarity, where citizens rely on one another to lend a helping hand. I believe the best solution would be a combination of both ways.

Because of these differences in approaches, most Westerners consider road travel through Eastern countries as a return to the past and as a direct encounter with relying on chance and passersby. But those improvisations are what make certain situations memorable.

While I was riding through Kazakhstan, my family back home was moving from Primošten, at the coast, to the continental part of Croatia. Friends were helping out with the job. This summer I was missing out on swimming and cliff diving, and I definitely was not enjoying the sunset and view from the best terrace in the world at Café Male Raduče.

The Report, Continued:

After about thirteen hours, we crossed some one hundred and forty kilometres and arrived in Atyrau. The man driving the truck loaded with my

Sunrise after the fall.

motorcycle entered a large parking lot for truckers. He said he was not going to go to Astrakhan (my destination of choice, since the chances of being able to repair my bike were greater in Russia than in Kazakhstan). So we transferred the motorcycle to a truck that would be "taking off" for Astrakhan at nine o'clock the next morning. Tim and Cory wanted to find a hotel so that they could rest while I stayed to sleep beside my motorcycle in the trailer. I didn't want to leave it alone in the trailer and go to a hotel, and knew that I would sleep better by my motorcycle's side. So that's how it ended up being. We agreed to get going for Russia at nine o'clock the next morning. I would ride in the Kamaz, and the guys would ride their bikes.

The next morning I woke up and opened my eyes. The motorcycle was still there. All I had to do was to wait for the whole team to gather so that we could get going. Everyone came on time and we had a brief meeting about our plans for the new day. Since the guys wanted to see some more sights in Kazakhstan, we agreed to separate for the day. Then just as we said our goodbyes, I waved to the driver that we could get going. And he answered that he wasn't even going to Astrakhan. But I had asked him that same question some sixteen times the day before! All sixteen times he said Astrakhan. I had no idea what this was all about. Why had I even loaded the bike on the truck if it wasn't going to Russia. I was angry, but I knew that that wasn't going to help me solve this problem. So I found another trucker willing to take my bike and me to Astrakhan. Once again we transferred the motorcycle from one truck to the other, and finally got going. The road to the border was in relatively good condition. Crossing the Kazakh side of the border was a piece of cake, but crossing the Russian side is always a special experience. Apparently the problem was in that the motorcycle wasn't allowed in Russia since there weren't any Yamaha shops in Astrakhan (despite the fact that I had contacted a Yamaha shop in advance and knew that the border officials were lying.)

I somehow managed to convince them that I'd solve everything quickly, which I was intending on doing anyhow. And then right while we were filling out the forms, the electricity went out. The computers stopped working, and all the information was deleted. Could it get any better?

After about thirty minutes the electricity returned. We filled every-thing out from the beginning, and finally entered Russia. I reached Astrakhan at about half-past eight. Though the Yamaha shop's working hours were till seven, they waited for me an hour and a half. Kudos to the Yamaha shop. They went out of their way to help me, and did all that they could. Most of my stuff is still in their salon. I left my bike at the salon and went to look for accommodation. The next morning, my buddies sent me a text message. "We're in Astrakhan!"

Great! I found them at the other end of the city. At one point, while on their way to Astrakhan, they had come across the Kazakhs going in the opposite direction (remember the truck full of vodka). Cory and Tim were really surprised to see them, and when they asked them where they had come from, they answered—Astrakhan. Go figure, they had gone to the very city that I had needed to go to. I was speechless. Why did we even transfer the bike from one truck to the other and had that compli-cation? We probably will never know the answer to that question. This was my last day with my Canadian friends. They couldn't stay to wait for my motorcycle to be repaired because then they wouldn't make it to Canada in time. In Calgary the snowfall could start as early as October, and it was already mid-September. At the beginning of my journey with the Canadians, Tim had said he would be honoured and happy to travel with me. I was honoured to have had the pleasure of travelling with the team from Canada!

I would wait for the bike parts from Croatia, then as soon as my motorcycle was repaired, I'd be hitting the saddle to continue my journey.

FROM THE VOLGA TO THE
CARPATHIAN MOUNTAINS
(11/9–4/10/2009)
3 200 km

ASTRAKHAN

After saying goodbye to my Canadian buddies, I felt, somehow, lonely for the first time during this journey. The guys had left, and my motorcycle was in the state that it was in, but what can you do other than keep on going. Through Couchsurfing, I somehow managed to find a place to sleep. A humble little room in a courtyard was going to be my home base for the next fifteen days.

These days were spent walking around and writing in my journal about my journey, since I had been neglecting that lately. By looking through the pictures and relying on my memory, I jotted notes down that were to become this book.

Astrakhan developed where the Silk Road and ancient tea route once crossed. At the moment, it seemed that the old part of town was waiting for better times to shine to its full potential. The new part of town, however, looked like it was trying to keep in step with the rhythm of the rest of the world.

The motorcycle parts that I was in need of had been sent from Croatia by way of a postal service known for speedy international deliveries. Still, I was faced with a situation that I usually try to avoid: waiting for others to do a job that is important to me, over which I have absolutely no influence.

Besides writing in my journal, I was wrestling with the folks in Russia who were in charge of the delivery of the package, verifying where it was at and when it would arrive. The package finally arrived in Russia and everything was going according to plan, especially the part where I had to pay. However, though they had claimed that there was an office in Astrakhan that could receive my package and deliver it within five or six days, the situation became so complicated that the parts, once they reached Moscow, had to be sent back to Zagreb. They gotta be kidding! I called the office in Zagreb, sent them emails, and called Moscow! One hundred complications! The guys in Moscow claimed that there was no one in Astrakhan able to receive the package so they got it ready to be returned to Zagreb. And the guys in Zagreb claimed that they had done their best, but there was nothing more they could do. I called, got angry, called again, but that didn't help. One of the managers at the Yamaha service centre, Mujib, of Indian descent, also tried to get things going. Time was passing, everything was paid, and no one was responsible for anything. It even got to the point where I started expressing myself harshly.

After a few days of effort, hassle and waiting, by some miracle, the wheels started turning. In Moscow, the manager in charge sent the package to Astrakhan, even though it needed to pass customs in Krasnodar. I had obviously underestimated just how incapable delivery services and Russian administration could be. Something worth thinking about! I was already thinking about how to get to Krasnodar. Probably by train? But what I still couldn't understand, something I had been asking myself this whole time, was what in the world was that post office doing right near the Yamaha service centre?

In this vast expanse of land, cities are sparse and far between. As I was told at the train station, any distance that's less than 1000 km is a joke, and by train, I'd probably need two days to reach Krasnodar. So I decided to make some more phone calls and try once again to arrange delivery in Astrakhan. Just the trip to Krasnodar and back would take too long and cost too much. Who'd have thought that a phone call to Zagreb and a harsh tone could be so effective? The urgent enquiry was sent to Moscow, and a response was expected within a couple of hours. If by any chance this book gets into the hands of the people in the postal delivery business, here's a word of advice: be more efficient.

Every day of waiting, I spent walking around town. I noticed whenever I'd communicate with others that they were very relaxed and open. A girl from the neighbourhood joined me in my walks and showed me the sights. The family that took me in offered me cooked meals every now and then, but I noticed that the pile of empty cans in my room was growing, as well. So, after a lot of effort and hassle that should not have been necessary in the first place, the mess started untangling. The planned five or six days turned into fifteen or sixteen. And what would have happened if I hadn't tried as hard as I did? Maybe today I'd be living in Astrakhan?!

The parts finally arrived at the service centre. I was relieved, because I could finally get going somewhere—anywhere. By the looks of the box, which was falling apart, this package had obviously been passed through more hands than a dollar bill. As soon as we opened the box, we started installing the parts. The guys at the service centre eagerly did the job. With the help of some primitive methods and "unavoidable damage," they mounted all the parts on the Tenere. Since they finished in the afternoon, I decided to get going the next morning. The engine fired up like gunpowder. I rode to my room, left my extra stuff, and went for a ride around the town, with which I was already pretty well acquainted.

The next morning, I put on my only glove. The wind in the Kazakh steppes was probably playing with the other one. Then I sat astride 'ol faithful Tenere, with its twisted handlebars. Since the handlebars were twisted, steering the bike demanded quite a bit of skill, especially at curves and circular intersections. But that didn't matter; I was back on my Tenere. So, from the Volga Delta, along the Volga Valley, I went towards—who'd have thought—Volgograd.

West of the Precaspian Depression, there is a somewhat lesser-known region: the Republic of Kalmykia. Kalmykians are descendants of the Golden Hordes, which are a part of the Mongolian population that once ruled over a great part of Russia. It's interesting how the Republic of Kalmykia is the only region in Europe where Buddhism is the dominant religion.

ASTRAKHAN–VOLGOGRAD

Though I was already used to staying in one place for a period of time (Astrakhan), as soon as I was back on the road, that love of movement and change returned. This road runs alongside the greatest river in Europe: the Volga. But since I still needed to get the hang of the "new" way of manoeuvreing this bike, I focused primarily on driving technique and couldn't enjoy the scenery much. To compensate, I stopped a few times by the side of the road to look around, and to rest, since getting used to this new driving technique was taking time.

After a few hours of riding in the same awkward position, my back was getting stiff and starting to ache. So, I stopped, did some exercise, and then got going again. When I reached Volgograd, I found accommodation

Two new motorcycles in Hungary.

through Couchsurfing. Ivan, my cheerful host, willingly took the time to help me get acquainted with this city and its interesting history.

Up until 1961, this exceptionally long city was known as Stalingrad, in honour of an "interesting" man with a moustache. During a conversation later on, I found out that this city is, in fact, about 70 km long. The city's name reminded me of history class back in high school. Though I did like geography and history, I spent hours just staring at the map that was tilted on the wall at the back of the classroom. I wish the lectures had been more interesting. Nevertheless, I did remember something about the Battle of Stalingrad.

One of the fiercest battles of World Chaos II occurred in the exact region I was in. And it hadn't happened that long ago. Only a bit more than fifty years had passed since then. At the moment, I was standing in front of the famous monument known in Russian as *Родина-мать зовёт* (*Rodina mat' Zovyot*, or, *The Motherland Calls!*)

One eighty-five-metre high statue with a few other smaller ones surrounding it symbolizes the Battle of Stalingrad, its victims, and, probably, hope for a better future. It's so huge that it's hard to describe it—in words or pictures. The statue is of a woman with her arm raised high holding a sword, and her mouth open, as if calling for victory. A lot of people lost their lives in this battle. It's hard to believe that human societies learn so little from history. Enjoying the view from the monument, I could see the city and one of the largest dams in Europe. There were a lot of people around, selling books, bullet shells and small statues. What impressed me more than anything else, however, was this one tree I could see; the only one that remained standing after the destruction. It still lives today.

In the evening, I ran into a group of dancers; entertainers who were catching the attention of passersby. Their act on the street was like a mini-manifestation: the music, street lights, and the dancers' synchronized moves intertwined.

Once again, I used Couchsurfing to find a place to stay. This time, my hosts did not have a garage, so I parked my motorcycle in a paid underground parking lot. When the employees at the garage saw the Croatian licence plate, they said cheerfully, "*Mi smo kao braća*," (which means, "We're like brothers!"). They were happy to see a Croat visiting Volgograd. I appreciated how the people here accepted me as if I were one of them, and felt assured that my bike was in good hands. I fell asleep on the floor in my room right after taking a shower, probably worn out from the day's events.

ROSTOV-ON-DON

In the morning, I woke with the thought that I needed to get a visa for Ukraine. The letter of invitation from the tourist agency was to appear in my inbox sometime during that same day. So the time came for me to head to Rostov-on-Don, where the Ukrainian embassy was. I sat astride the bike and cruised at an easy speed towards the southwest.

Great weather accompanied me all the way, and I enjoyed riding through the lowlands. A lot of freshwater fish from the Volga were being sold along the way. Nearer to Rostov, I noticed a lot of fish from the Don River, as well. After the Volga, the Don is one of Russia's most important rivers. Don Region, or Don Voisko Province, is the homeland of the Cossacks, who are known to be skilled horsemen, warriors and travellers. Once, they rode on horseback across Siberia to Alaska, then down to California, where they built a settlement.

Mikhail Sholokhov succeeded in producing the most faithful depiction of the life and mentality of this unique people in his book, *And Quiet Flows the Don*, published in 1934. This guy really put an effort into writing over 1 500 pages of text, and in the end got a Nobel Prize for this work. I tip my hat to him, because I'm having a tough time just writing these hundred or so pages. Actually, my primary goal with this book is to raise money in order to continue travelling. And what was his goal? I don't know. The story used to go that a Cossack pays as much as he pulls out of his pocket. And if the pocket is empty, then he doesn't pay. I believe times have changed since then.

I reached Rostov by dark, even though I had been convinced I'd arrive earlier. Since I hadn't put much effort into looking for a place to stay through Couchsurfing, I needed to rely on other sources. The main public square that I crossed was actually really big. That's how public squares

TOP LEFT: Village without a name.
TOP RIGHT: Volgograd.
ABOVE: Yalta.

TOP: Volgograd
ABOVE: On the road to Lvov.

should be, probably. As I went down the empty streets, I looked around, hoping to see some sort of hotel. None of the hotels "qualified." Finally, after the eleventh one, I found an acceptable place that was relatively close to the city's centre. In order to prepare for the next day's meeting with the Ukrainian consulate, I printed the letter of invitation at the hotel reception. Accustomed to Asian simplicity, I noticed more and more signs of the European way of life.

My Yamaha remained parked in the parking lot, and I took an "illegal" taxi to the embassy. In order to make sure I got the visa, I had called in advance to notify them that I was coming. When I showed up, of course I waited in line. Then, just as my turn was coming up, I realized I didn't have a pen. So I ran out of the building and burst into the first store I came across and asked if I could borrow a pen. The ladies at the counter stared at me as if I was someone they hadn't seen in ages. Maybe it was because of my torn jacket, dusty, unkempt look, and unusual accent. Or maybe I was already starting to behave like a Cossack. I repeated the question and they gave me a pen.

"I'll return it later," I said, while heading out the door. I returned to the embassy, and my turn was next. While talking with the consul, I mentioned the telephone conversation that we had had a few days earlier about processing my tourist visa, and asked whether it would be possible to stay about ten days in Ukraine, in case some part on the motorcycle kicked the bucket again as a result of the recent crash. They handed me some forms to fill out, and a bill that needed to be paid at a Kazakh bank. I took care of everything in a rush so that I wouldn't have to spend another day there. Moving onward was my goal, so, out of breath, I ran back to the embassy. Luckily, my turn came up right away.

"Everything is set. All the papers are here. You can come get your visa tomorrow," the consul said.

Great. I like it when the paperwork gets done easily. Relying on just my own two feet, I headed back to the hotel. Since I had the whole day ahead of me, I took the longer route. First, though, I returned the pen at the store. While strolling down the streets, the smell of pizza reminded me that I was hungry and that I needed to finally eat something with a higher calorie count. I followed the scent, and it led me to an over-crowded restaurant. Just by peeking through the window, I could see that I'd have to wait a long time, so I mumbled to myself to keep going, which was a test for my patience. I passed the test, because at the next restaurant I came to, there was no line.

After swallowing the last bite of food, I continued walking around town. I noticed a store with socks and underwear. The undergarments that I had taken with me from home were either lost or worn out, or had been thrown away because they were not wearable any more. So I bought three pairs of socks and some underwear. Right away, I put the new socks on. After just a few steps with my new socks on, I had a skip to my step. To save some money and avoid restaurants, I bought some groceries for dinner and went to my room. I wanted to take pictures of the city, but I didn't have my camera with me. "Ah, tomorrow I'll do that," I said to myself. "It's not like it's gonna rain."

But of course, the rain started falling during the night and continued throughout the entire next day, including when I went to pick up my passport, which was blessed with one more visa. Flipping through the pages, I found the one with the new visa. Great! Even the dates were right. Not wanting to lose any more time, I thought about how I might even be able to reach Ukraine the same day. I packed my stuff, put everything in its place as best I could and as quickly as possible, because of the rain. The Tenere started with a rumble, and I got going, weaving my way down the crowded streets of the city. With my wide load and the panniers, I had a hard time squeezing my way through. But at the right moment, I climbed onto the sidewalk and managed to pass a traffic jam. If I had waited for this chaos to clear up on the street, I'd still be there the next day.

For the next hundred kilometres, I rode with the rain pounding down on me as if it would never stop. Just to make sure everything didn't go perfectly, a police officer at a checkpoint about thirty kilometres ahead of the border had me pull over. Certain that he had stopped me only out of curiosity, I parked at the side of the road behind a truck. And I was right. But along with curiosity, he figured he could earn an extra buck. After combing through the contents of my panniers, he checked my papers.

Apparently, something was not right. The sign RUS was missing on my green card, which meant I did not have insurance for Russia.

No one had me about insurance until then. And now, as I was just exiting the country, these three letters on a green sheet of paper were more important than anything else in the world. I was angry, but helpless. Actually, I was angry *because* I was helpless. This officer blatantly wanted to take my money, and was pressuring me. I would have loved to "treat" him in a special way, but I knew that I'd just make things worse for myself. The border was just ahead, so, although I was almost down to my last penny, I offered him ten dollars. He wanted more.

"I don't have any more," I said.

Without saying a word, he just waved the paper in his hand.

"*Boljše ničevo!*" I said with a firm voice, while looking him in the eye and thinking, "You're not getting any more!"

We stood there staring each other some more. He probably read from my stance that I wasn't going to give in, and also knew that he could get into trouble for taking the bribe. So, with a shrug, he handed the paper back. I was relieved.

It's interesting how officials use the system to take advantage of their position and authority, instead of to help others. Had I more money, I probably would have given him more, just so he could quit bothering me. But, when will this come to an end? As long as we give, they take.

I passed the Sea of Azov and reached the border. It rained more heavily as I crossed the border. When I took my glove off, I could see that my fingers were purple once again. I went to get the necessary forms; the same forms that I filled out each time I crossed the Russian border. Once inside the office, I started looking for the forms. Water was dripping from me, and soon, a puddle formed around me. Knowing what to write by heart, I took a pen and filled out the forms. Handed them in. Stamped! Let's get going!

But, once again, the situation became complicated. While waiting in Astrakhan, my visa had expired. However, I had a trick up my sleeve: a voucher saying I could travel through Russia even if I didn't have a visa. When I reached the last phase of the process and handed over my visa to get the stamp that was necessary in order to leave the country, the official didn't try to hide his shock when he saw that my visa had expired. He showed me my expired visa and I showed him my voucher.

With a confused expression, the official asked, "What is that?"

"A voucher." I answered, "I was told I could leave the country, as if I had a visa," I said, after a moment of silence.

The official flipped through the pages of my passport a few times, from beginning to end. He slapped it on the table and then scratched his neck. Finally, he grabbed a phone and called someone. After a short conversation, he told me to step to the side. I did as I was told and went to a spot under a small shelter. I waited and waited. At one moment, I saw my passport "walking" from official to official. It went from booth to booth, along with officials who walked around in confusion, tripping over themselves at times, and climbing up and down stairs. I observed all of this, and even started to approach them at one moment. But then I returned to my spot, thinking, "So what if my visa expired, even if I had or didn't have a voucher. What can they do to me? I doubt they'd throw me in jail because of two numbers on my visa. Will these guys ask for money, too?" I could understand if they would not let me in the country, but to not let me leave? For the next three hours, I watched as the drama unfolded at the customs office. This must have been a trying test of patience for everyone. The passport was returned to the first official with whom I'd spoken, and he finally stamped the page, right next to my expired visa.

UKRAINE

Entering Ukraine was easier, but nevertheless, it did not come without surprises. After I filled out the immigration papers, which I was not allowed to lose while in Ukraine, my visa was checked. The dates in my visa were OK, but instead of a tourist visa, I had a transit visa. I hadn't even noticed that when I had picked it up.

"You're allowed five days in Ukraine," one of the officials said.

Hmm, obviously, I was going to have to speed through the country, which totally changed my plans. They checked my green card, and this time I had insurance for my stay in Ukraine.

I crossed the border and continued riding. Thoughts were running through my head: which route to take, and how to reach Hungary in just five days. I had been planning to spend twice as much time here. Right away, I could forget visiting Kiev, because I didn't want to miss walking along Yalta at the Crimean Peninsula. It would be good to spend the first day travelling as far as possible towards Yalta. But because of the precious time spent at the border, plus the rain and the fact that it was now night-time, I lay in a bed in Mariupol, along the shore of the Black Sea. My clothes were strung up all over the room to dry. By morning, everything was just partially dry.

I left the hostel and was first in line for the bank to open. I needed to change some money. The morning was cold, and all I had on was a short-sleeved shirt, but I didn't want to lose my spot in the line. Already, a lot of people had gathered, forming a long queue. So I just shivered and endured the cold. While waiting, I calculated how much money I'd need for all my expenses, so that I wouldn't have to change money again.

CRIMEA

I went to the market for some groceries. When I got back to the room, I stuffed the food down my throat and then rushed out. Hit the gas! The next stop: Yalta. This ride wasn't anything special, especially since I just sped through it to reach my goal. I don't like driving at night, but this night was an exception. When I reached Crimea, I noticed a lot of signs for private accommodation. I even thought about stopping to get a good rest, but in the end, I didn't. My determination kept me going. In Yalta, I realized this place is a popular summer resort. All over were hotels, res-taurants, and villas. I hadn't been expecting that. Everywhere I looked, the place was crowded. I could choose where I wanted to stay, so I chose a hotel and went inside. But as soon as I heard the price, I turned around and left. The price was "tops."

It really didn't matter where I slept, so I went to look for something more affordable. Exhausted, already thinking about putting up my tent behind some bushes, I came across the right hotel. It had a humble main entrance and "stunning interior décor," notable for mismatched furniture and a sweat-covered, worn-out check-in desk. That was what I needed! The price? Acceptable! While I was filling out the registration form, a group of construction workers kept entering and exiting the hotel. They passed by my motorcycle, which was parked in a dark spot, so I couldn't see what was going on. Since this all looked strange to me, I went down the stairs to the motorcycle, and waited for the guys to leave, then went back into the hotel. After paying for the room, I asked where I could park the bike so that it would be safe. With so many tourists around, there were surely some looking for a way to improve their budget.

The lady at the reception took me to a parking lot, where an older man kept watch. We made an agreement that he'd watch the motorcycle. But for some reason, I didn't have a good feeling about this. The parking lot was part of a stadium, where a lot of people kept passing by. And my hunch was that this guard was planning on snuggling up in his booth and falling asleep.

While removing all my gear from the bike, I noticed someone had stolen the fork. The crooked fork that I had kept as a souvenir. This got me angry. I wasn't sure about the motorcycle's safety anymore. So I went back to the hotel and asked for my money back. The receptionist refused, since they didn't have much business. I didn't care! I do have empathy for others, but people should have some empathy for me, too! Good thing just the fork was stolen, since it wasn't good for anything anymore except as a memento.

I took my money, hit the saddle, and went to look for another hotel. I rode in circles, hoping to see something more suitable. And just when I thought about heading out of Yalta, I came across a man sitting by a sign for private rooms. I asked him how much the parking cost. That was what I was looking for.

The motorcycle was safe in an enclosed patio. Finally, I could eat my second meal that day, and get to sleep. Early the next morning, I'd continue travelling. It would be good to reach Uman by crossing the Odessa Region. Ruckus from the drunken neighbours lasted all night long. As usual, I woke up before everyone else. I'm sure they didn't appreciate me honking at seven o'clock in the morning. But that was the only way I could get them to open the front gate so that I could leave. After about ten minutes, someone came downstairs with keys in his pocket. Judging by the way he looked, I could tell he had just woken up. He unlocked the gate. It squeaked as it was pulled opened, scratching along the cement, waking up all the other neighbours.

I got going down the streets of Yalta, following the same route as the previous day, which I had hardly managed to pass because of the crowds of people. Now, however, there was no one; the place was desolate, just some stray dogs and some bags being tossed around by the wind. I went across the city's centre and stopped at a kiosk to buy some fast unhealthy food. Then I went to a park and sat to eat.

The Crimean Peninsula is home to the Ukrainian Tatars. Tatars make up about six or seven per cent of the population. There used to be greater numbers of Tatars in this region. But then the aforementioned guy with a moustache, who liked playing with people's destinies, relocated them to the north. Though a great number of them have returned to the Crimean Peninsula, nowadays, most Tatars live in the Republic of Tatarstan, around their capital city, Kazan, in Russia.

After the aforementioned World Chaos II, three interesting indiviuals met in Yalta: a Brit, a Yankee, and that "popular" guy with the moustache. They got together to play around with the world map. While they were at it, they also mapped out the destinies of numerous nations. So, as would be expected, considering their limited abilities, since they hadn't learned the lesson from the war, they "gambled" away opportunities in order to build a lasting trust.

YALTA–ODESSA–LVIV

I studied the map of Ukraine, and the route I needed to take. With the sun shining and the warm weather, I'd surely make it. The only obstacles in my path were the frequent police checks along the side of the road. But, they didn't catch me.

One option was to return home by way of Romania. I studied the map, checking out the route from Odessa southward across Romania and Serbia. This way, I wouldn't have to rush so much and could even spend a day without riding. But in the end, I decided to go west to Lvov, and from there, ride along the border with Poland and Slovakia in order to reach Hungary.

When I reached the city of Odessa, I noticed a motorcycle like mine coming from the opposite direction. Actually, this motorcycle was the same kind I would use for my trip that coming winter across Latin America. The biker waved at me to stop. This middle-aged man was on his way to a biker gathering in Crimea. As usually happens, I was invited also, but I simply couldn't make it because of a piece of paper known as a visa. He even offered me accommodation in Odessa, but I had to take a rain check on that, too. Time to keep on moving.

The solidarity and hospitality among bikers that I experienced throughout this entire journey really is interesting. And I could add that, although bikers are often labelled as, hmm, tough guys and gals, their solidarity transcends all borders, nations, religions, and ages. And this can definitely serve as a positive example for all people's relations.

Yalta, Simferopol, Mikolayiv, Odessa. As I landed in the well-known Black Sea port of Odessa, I reflected on how this was one of those spots, along with Trieste and Peloponnese, that had been given the wrong name. This peninsula was named for the Balkan Mountains, in Bulgaria. Yet, this region is dominated by the massive Dinara and Carpathian Mountains, so if you ask me, it could have been named differently, had someone just looked at an atlas.

After a short tour of Odessa, I headed north towards Uman. The road, which had been patched up and repaired thousands of times, was enough to occupy all my time and effort, leaving me no time for boredom or anything else. In addition to the awful road conditions, the wind was pushing me about as if I had a sail mounted on the rear-end of my motorcycle. Of course, just like everywhere else, it was the beginning of October here. Convinced that I could ride all night long, at one moment, I suddenly found myself swallowed in pitch-black darkness. There were no street lights along the Ukrainian highway; not even near the gas stations. I rarely came across other vehicles, except for the few trucks that would huff and puff to climb hills, choking me with their exhaust fumes until I'd overtake them. There were some signs for rooms and beds along the way. Convinced I could ride some more, I passed them. But then came the phase where my eyes were starting to shut. I stopped at a gas station to tank up and rest a little. One Red Bull drink recharged my battery, at least for the moment. It worked, but it did not last long.

A light on the horizon looked like it could be shining from a hotel. My eyes opened wide and my body said, "Time for a break."

The light did turn out to be a hotel, and I was soon standing before it. But there was one problem: The hotel was on the other side of the highway, so, apparently, only accessible to travellers coming from the other direction. I was supposed to just continue riding. Eh, no way! I found a spot with access to cross, to the other side of the highway, and parked in front of the hotel. Driving any further would not have suited my weary eyes.

I entered the hotel at one o'clock in the morning. Whenever I'd enter a hotel, everyone at the front lobby would eye me from head to toe. Obviously, people here weren't used to handsome bikers with an accent wearing dusty motorcycle gear with Bigfoot-size Enduro boots. I got a room on the first floor, brushed my teeth, and then toppled over onto the bed. Then a thought woke me—I had forgotten to set the alarm. So I set it for half past five. I hadn't even shut my eyes yet, it seemed, and my alarm was already ringing. So I got up, washed up, packed my stuff, and went down to the lobby. The store by the hotel was open 24 hours. There wasn't much of a choice, but I wasn't looking for much anyhow. A chocolate bar would do the trick.

Just as the day before, I used the emergency passage to get to the other side of the highway. Invigorated, I continued riding. The morning was colder than I had expected. The only glove I had didn't help much to keep the cold out, but I kept riding, stopping every now and then to warm my hands in the smoke from the exhaust pipe. That would be enough for me to be able to move my fingers once again. I had no choice but to endure. At a gas station, I bought some handyman gloves, which helped. When I reached the roundabout in Uman, I turned left and headed west. Just 500 km to go, and I would be in Lvov. From there, I would head south.

Further north was Kiev, the seat of Ukrainian monarchy. Another hundred kilometres north, near the border with Belarus, was Chernobyl. After we had separated, my Canadian friends had visited this monument honouring human irresponsibility.

While riding towards Lvov, I was noticing names that reminded me of my native language: Vynyca, Staro Selo. By accident, I entered Lvov and lost some time getting out. But at least I used the opportunity to buy some motorcycle gloves. They were summer weight, but they were better than nothing. Night fell, but I continued towards Hungary.

CLOSING THE CIRCLE
(4/10–7/10/2009)
1 100 km

In the Carpathian Mountains, I endured the company of the rainfall and cold weather, and battled to keep my eyes open. An old story came to mind about the early migration of Slavic peoples, ancestors of modern Southern Slavs "from beyond the Carpathian Mountains . . ." Because of the burden of my luggage, my headlight continued to shine towards the sky more than the road.

Somewhere between Vorota and Mukachevo, I stopped at a hotel and treated myself to dinner. Some greasy salmon with potatoes would give me energy for the next day, maybe I wouldn't even have to eat breakfast in the morning. The alarm on my mobile phone woke me at six o'clock, just like the day before. I felt as if I had just gotten into bed. And, in fact, the salmon did keep me full. This was the day I'd reach Hungary. Crossing the border took much more time than I had expected. Since Hungary is now a part of the European Union, all vehicles are checked thoroughly. The sun was heating my black jacket, so I took it off and threw it over the motorcycle. I sat on the sidewalk and set the time on my watch back an hour. Returning to my time zone, I thought about how I was rushing towards the sunset and was "gaining" a day. I'd think about what to do with that day later.

I observed the whole procedure and realized that I should be filling out some forms. Since this was the first time I had seen such forms, I didn't fill them out, but rather, asked an official to fill them out for me. I pushed my motorcycle forward, opened the panniers, and showed them what I was "smuggling." They didn't pay much attention to my luggage. Who in their right mind would?

Just by the looks of the bike, it was obvious that it had circled the world. Dust from Mongolia was still holding firmly to the radiator. The layer of baked mud on the exhaust pipe was so thick, that not even later on, when I was home, did I succeed in removing it. The front fender was tied to my transport bags. The large dent on the right side of my bike was a keepsake from the crash. My panniers had been smashed and reshaped one hundred times, and wires hung down where my right turn signal should have been. The windshield was totally scratched; there were scratches all over . . .

I finally got the stamp that allowed me entrance into Hungary. The difference between Ukraine and Hungary was evident right from the start. "There's no joking around here." Trees lined the road, and the asphalt was in great shape. Just a few more borders to cross! While riding, I thought about how I'd soon see my friends and everyone who had followed my journey online.

A motorcycle just like mine, but new, parked beside me at a rest area. The man eyed me and then circled my bike. He knew that my bike was also new, but he was probably wondering what I had done with it. I couldn't explain anything, since I didn't know Hungarian. And it's not as if I was really trying. He said goodbye and left, still shaking his head in disbelief. I returned to my previous thoughts from before this incident. This weird feeling overcame me. I don't really have the ability to convey this feeling because I'm more of a traveller than a writer.

I wanted to see everyone who was expecting me home, but at the same time, I also wanted to continue travelling. If I had had the money, I probably would have done something like that. I'd go home, have a juice, and then hit the road. Head south to Africa. Winter was nearing, and the prices are cheaper there, so I'd get buy with lower costs. All sorts of ideas came to mind, and I got carried away while riding. My friend Pero would say, "He got carried away by the song."

I sped into Szeget in the evening and found a hostel. Soon I'd be in Vukovar, where members of MK Vukovar and a lot of others would be waiting for me. I thought about the Croatian emblems on my motorcycle. I hadn't been to Serbia yet. Everything was probably going to be OK.

The same comedy once again at the border! "Step to the side," a lady at the booth said, after she had thoroughly examined my crumpled passport,

ABOVE: Welcome in Vukovar.
LEFT: Welcome Home in Koprivnica.
BELOW: Cheers!

or actually, my picture. At first, they didn't want to let me pass. I hadn't had a haircut in five months. So because of my hair and tanned skin, the officials wanted to make sure that it was really me. They were expecting me to explain myself. Must I really get a haircut in order to look exactly like my passport picture? They called over someone with more expertise. The man held my passport by my face and began examining. I felt weird. With his expertise, he obviously found enough similarity between me and my picture. "Good luck," the man said and returned my passport.

When I stopped at a traffic light in Subotica, I noticed a man get out of his car and approach me.

"You've got a licence plate from Šibenik? How's it in Šibenik?"

"Probably good. I haven't been there in a while. Right now I'm on my way home from Mongolia!"

"Really?!" Surprised, he offered to shake my hand and congratulated me. The queue of cars behind us began honking!

"Have a good trip!"

I felt good! People were waving as I passed. I'm sure it was interesting to see a biker in worn-out gear riding such a harmoniously equipped motorcycle. Realizing I had taken a wrong turn, I stopped by the side of the road. Right away, a car stopped beside me.

A man came out and asked, "*Sprechen sie deutsch?* Do you speak English?" trying to figure out what language I spoke.

"*Može li na hrv . . . ?*" I didn't even finish asking if he knew Croatian.

"Oh, I didn't see that you're Croatian! Where are you going?"

"I should be going to Erdut. From there I'll be heading for Vukovar."

"You're off track. Here, I'll give you this paper with a list of villages that you need to pass. For starters, get back to Sombor."

"*Sretan put!* Have a good trip!"

"All right, thanks!"

I put the paper in my tank bag. When I returned to Sombor, I realized where I was supposed to have turned left, instead of going straight. A little further, and I'd be home. My friends, Mihajlo and Niven, were probably already in Vukovar.

Another border. This one was the last one. I won't write much about my homeland, Croatia; it's a place you need to see for yourself and experience yourself. At the Croatian border, the officials were surprised by the looks of me and my motorcycle. Everyone that worked at the border control came out and flooded me with questions. I replied with short answers, since I was in a hurry to see the crowd that was waiting for me in Vukovar.

The day was sunny; almost like the one five months ago when I set out on my journey. I stopped at an INA gas station, where I met with two friends from Koprivnica. It was hard to hide a smile after I hadn't seen them in five months. The loud greeting made everyone else turn to see what was going on. A huge Croatian flag was waving from the car they were driving. We went to the clubhouse of MK Vukovar. When we reached the city, I stopped at an OMV gas station, looked around, and then said:

"It was worth it!" I shifted into first gear and cruised slowly across the train tracks, then turned left. Just a dozen metres more, and I could see the crowd that had gathered. Quite a number! I honked and parked the bike. Within seconds, cheerful faces surrounded me. I was happy for everyone, and for myself. After the Croatian War of Independence, and all that the people of Vukovar had been through, this city—and other cities like it—are proof that the human spirit transcends the earthly confines of our limited human nature.

I excused myself from the crowd and went to give a short interview to some reporters. While talking to the reporters, I saw how people were examining my bike and commenting on the state it was in after five months of travel. The mayor of Vukovar arrived and congratulated me. After a while, I was able to talk with people in a more relaxed atmosphere about the trip. My friend Goran, the club's secretary, helped me transfer the motorcycle to the room where I'd be spending the night. Since this was a working day, and people had their own business to take care of, the crowd slowly dispersed.

My friends from Koprivnica had a lot to do the next day, so they also went home. Since the little celebration had ended, I went to hotel Lav. As a gift, the mayor had reserved the President's Suite for me. That was something I hadn't been expecting. I washed up and went to bed.

While in bed, I recalled most of the places I had seen: cities, mountains, swamps, undergrowth, deserts, taiga, the truck with vodka, the roads. And then, there I was lying in the President's Suite. Interesting!

In the morning, Goran and I were invited to join the mayor in laying wreaths at the memorial cemetery. There, I gave an interview for a television station from Vinkovci. After that, I went to the municipal building, where I received a gift from the city of Vukovar. I am grateful to the mayor and members of MK Vukovar for their hospitality, and for everything.

In the afternoon, I rode down the highway towards Koprivnica. Along the way, I met up with Mario. Mario is the guy who accompanied me to Vukovar just five months ago. We stopped by the side of the road to take some pictures. Then we got going, picking up speed as we headed towards Koprivnica. Just outside the city, we stopped at my friend Dominic's place, where members of MK Veterani, from Koprvnica, were waiting for me. It was good to see familiar faces after such a long time. From there, we proceeded slowly because of the bent steering, and soon reached Koprivnica.

When the crowd of bikers at the main public square saw me, they revved up their engines under the direction of the motorcycle and extreme sports legend, Mladen Rušak. I got goose bumps. I hadn't been expecting such a welcome! I even have goose bumps now while I'm writing this! People from Zagreb, Varaždin, Virovitica and all around, had gathered to welcome me and be a part of this journey. A lot of them from the online forum, Motori. hr, were there, as well. I noticed a large banner with "Welcome Home!" written across it.

I can't recall all the people who greeted and congratulated me, except, of course, my close friends and relatives. The mayor awaited me in front of the municipal building. I approached him, followed by a whole group of bikers. After a short speech by me and one by the mayor, we all sat on our bikes and rode in an honorary circle around Koprivnica, by which all the bikers present could become part of this journey. We rode around Koprivnica, and then returned to the main public square. The mayor treated everyone to a round of drinks at the city's pub. I spent some time with friends and guests. Thanks to everyone who came! Part of the crowd stayed in the pub while I sat astride my motorcycle, and went home.

And in the beginning was an idea.

Cheers!

WHERE ARE THEY NOW AND WHAT ARE THEIR PLANS?
(03/12/2010)

Tim–A few days after returning from his trip around the world, this successful Apple store manager quit his job and changed course in his life's journey. Now, he is travelling across the Americas with Cory.

Cory–After having financed his first journey by selling all his belongings, he continues travelling with Tim. The team TERRANOVA will most likely meet with the team OKO SVIJETA (Around the World) somewhere in the Andes in the spring of 2011.

Ralf–After his return home from North America, he underwent final preparations for the publication of his book. At the moment, he is in the process of opening his own printed T-shirt business.

Andrew–During the long Alaskan winter, he trained for the Antarctic Marathon, which he successfully ran in March of 2010. A few months later, he ran a 250 km marathon across the Gobi Desert in northwestern China. At the moment, he is preparing to ride his motorcycle from Siberia to Spain in the summer of 2012.

Lester–after his adventure in 2009, in the summer of 2010, he accomplished a five-week motorcycle journey from Southern California, across the Rocky Mountains, to Alaska. His next summer is reserved for his role in the educational system, since he is employed at a school in Dillingham, Alaska.

Pete–After his travels, he sold his motorcycle and bought a car to drive to North Dakota. There, he attended pilot school. He often thinks about the beauty of the regions in Canada and Alaska that he travelled across.

Melodie–Moved to a new apartment. There, she thinks about new journeys. At the moment, she is thinking about going to Iceland.

Doug–The famous biker-traveller. His life, and unique way of travelling astride a chopper motorcycle, deserves a book of its own. At the moment, he is getting his Harley ready for a journey across Central Asia and Mongolia, then from Russia to Magadan.

Fred–After he successfully reached Israel, where a new job was awaiting him, I recently received a message stating that he is now in Buenos Aires. He plans to head from there to Columbia in January, 2011.

Max–Still lives in Tinda, in Siberia, where he successfully sells Kamaz trucks.

Niven–Learned all there is to know about time zones. After finishing college in 2016, plans to successfully combine his career in the health sector with playing in a band.

Miška–Plans to wed happily in 2017, and towards the end of 2019 to become the Minister for Maritime Affairs and Transport.

Dominic–The guy that got me the used boots. He works at full speed and prepares for the sequel to the expedition, AROUND THE WORLD.

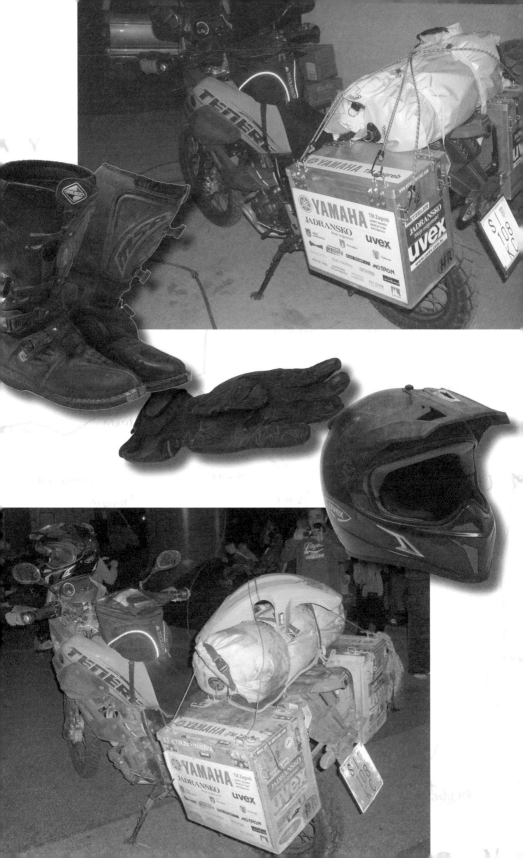

AND IN THE END, A NEW BEGINNING

"Hey, Dado!" I greeted my friend Dominic by his nickname.

"Hey, Peter!" Dado answered.

"I came to talk to you about something." I was warming up for the big question.

"All right, what's it about?" Dado asked, as he slumped on a couch.

"Wanna join me in the sequel to AROUND THE WORLD?" I asked, giving Dado enough time to think about it.

"Hmm, this is interesting." He smiled and nodded his head, a little to one side, and then to the other.

"I appreciate you asking me. I'm interested, of course. Hmm. I like the idea." Dado raised a brow, while imagining the new situation.

"How long do you think it would last?" He shifted about on the couch in the waiting room of his clinic.

"Ah, say, about three months." I halved the time, knowing that it was important to get things going first.

"Hmm, all right, all right, I like the idea. But where'd we go?" He was already interested.

"Probably Africa or South America," I answered.

"I really do like this idea, but I need to see if my brother will be able to take over my part of the business. I'll let you know for sure after I talk to him," he said.

He didn't take too long.

"When are we going?" he asked cheerfully on the cellphone.

"When we raise enough money," I answered, satisfied.

"Wise."

SO THAT WAS THE DEAL FOR THE BEGINNING OF A NEW EXPEDITION: PANAMERICANA 2011

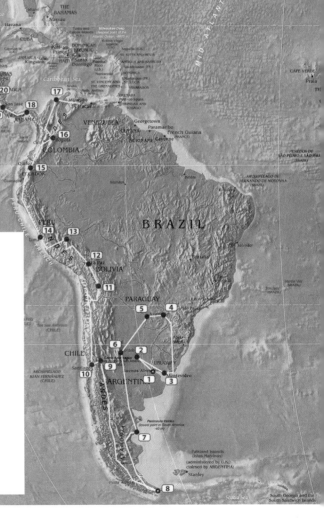

PANAMERICANA '11–56000 km+12000 km

1. Buenos Aires	18. Panama
2. Rosario	19. San Jose
3. Montevideo	20. Managua
4. Iguazu Falls	21. San Salvador
5. Asunsion	22. Guatemala
6. Cordoba	23. Merida
7. Comodoro Rivadavia	24. Mexiko
8. Ushuaia	25. Los Mochis
9. Mendoza	26. La Paz
10. Santiago	27. Los Angeles
11. Uyuni	28. Denver
12. La Paz	29. Tucson
13. Cusco	30. Salt Lake City
14. Lima	31. Calgary
15. Quito	32. Whitehorse
16. Bogota	33. Anchorage
17. Barranquilla	34. Prudhoe Bay